The Complete Idiot's Reference

## Lingo

**barndoor**   Losing balance and swinging away from the

**bell ringer**   Falling from a high anchor and swinging w

**beta**   Information

**bucket**   A big hold

**bomber**   A sturdy hold (the opposite of manky)

**comp**   An organized climbing competiti

**crag**   A small cliff

**crank**   Powerfully pulling through a

**crimper**   A tiny hold that can only be

**crux**   The hardest move of a route

**dyno**   Lunging for a faraway hold

**finger pocket**   A hold with a depressio... ...ge enough for one or two fingers

**flag**   When a climber holds one leg out to the side or below his body for balance

**flash**   Getting to the top of a route on the first attempt without falling

**free-climb**   To climb without assistance or protection (safety of gear)

**gripped**   Frozen from fear and unable to continue climbing

**hang dog**   Resting on the rope between attempts

**juga**   A large handhold

**manky**   An unstable hold (the opposite of bomber)

**match**   Grasping a hold with both hands

**mojo**   An inner-focus that enables climbers to get through extreme physical or psychological conditions

**pinch**   Grasping a hold by squeezing the sides of the rock rather than using a horizontal edge for purchase.

**pumped**   When a climber's arms are full of lactic acid

**pro**   Short for "protection"

**red point**   To climb a route from bottom to top without falling or resting on gear

**screamer**   A big fall

**send it**   To finish a route

**sewing-machine legs**   When climber's legs shake uncontrollably

**sloper**   A hold that slopes downward and is difficult to hang on to

**trad climbing**   Traditional climbing

**whipper**   A fall

**yo-yo**   The cycle of ascending to place protection, lowering to the ground, and going up again to place more protection

**zipper**   When protection rips out of the wall when the climber falls

alpha
books

## Pre-Climb Checklist for Top-Roping

➤ Check that both belayer's and climber's harness waistbelts are doubled back through the buckle.

➤ Check that the leader's tie-in knot (usually a retraced figure-8 or double bowline) has been tied correctly and is finished with a back-up knot. Also check that the knotted rope is correctly threaded through the waistbelt and leg loops of the leader's harness.

➤ Check that the lead rope is correctly threaded through the belay device and screwgate carabiner. Double-check that the belayer's screwgate carabiner is locked.

➤ Check that the rope is long enough get the leader back down from the anchors. It should be twice as long as the route.

➤ Check the number of bolts on the route. Clip at least this number of quickdraws plus two to your rack; you'll need the extra draws for clipping into the anchors at the top of the route.

➤ Check the route for suspicious and run-out (or dead-end) sections.

➤ Check that the belayer is in a good position. She should stand close to the wall, directly below the first piece of protection.

## Rock Climbing Rating Systems Worldwide

| UIAA | USA (YDS) | FRANCE | BRITAIN (technical) | BRITAIN (severity) | AUSTRALIA | GERMANY |
|---|---|---|---|---|---|---|
| I | 5.2 | 1 | | moderate | 9 | I |
| II | 5.3 | 2 | | difficult | 10 | II |
| III | 5.4 | 3 | | very difficult | 11 | III |
| IV | 5.5 | 4 | 4a | severe | 12 | IV |
| V- | 13 | V | | | | |
| V | 5.6 | 4b | | very severe | 14 | VI |
| V+ | 5.7 | 5 | 4c | | 15 | VIIa |
| VI- | 5.8 | 5a | | hard very severe | 16/17 | VIIb |
| VI | 5.9 | 6a | | E1* | 18 | |
| VI+ | 5.10a/b | 6a+ | 5b | | 19 | VIIc |
| VII- | 5.10c/d | 6b | | E2 | 20 | VIIIa |
| VII | 5.11a | 6b+ | 5c | | 21 | VIIIb |
| VII+ | 5.11b | 6c | | E3 | 22 | VIIIc |
| VIII- | 5.11c | 6c+ | 6a | | 23 | IXa |
| VIII | 5.11d | 7a/7a+ | | E4 | 25 | IXb |
| VIII+ | 5.12a/b | 7b | 6b | | 26 | IXc |
| IX- | 5.12c | 7b+/7c | | E5 | 27 | Xa |
| IX | 5.12d | 7c+ | | | 28 | Xb |
| IX+ | 5.13a | 8a | 6c | | 29 | Xc |
| X- | 5.13b | | | E6 | 30 | |
| X | 5.13c/d | 8b | 7a | | 31 | |
| X+ | 5.14a | 8b+ | | E7 | 32 | |
| XI- | 5.14b | 8c | 7b | | 33 | |
| XI | 5.14c | 8c+ | 7c | E8/9 | 34 | |

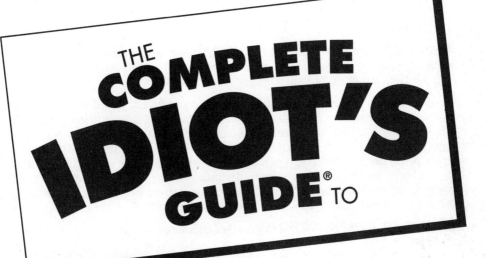

# THE COMPLETE IDIOT'S GUIDE® TO

# Rock Climbing

*by Stefani Jackenthal*
*with Joe Glickman*

**alpha books**

Macmillan USA, Inc.
201 West 103rd Street
Indianapolis, IN 46290

A Pearson Education Company

*To the adventurer in each of us.*

## Copyright © 2000 by Stefani Jackenthal

Grateful acknowledgment is made to Michael Amaditz, for permission to use his knot drawings in Chapter 8, and to Nels Akerlund, Mark Eller, and Jay Farbman for permission to use their photographs throughout the book.

THE COMPLETE IDIOT'S GUIDE TO and Design are registered trademarks of Macmillan USA, Inc.

International Standard Book Number: 0-02-863114-5
Library of Congress Catalog Card Number: 99-65419

03   02   01   00       4   3   2   1

Interpretation of the printing code: the rightmost number of the first series of numbers is the year of the book's printing; the rightmost number of the second series of numbers is the number of the book's printing. For example, a printing code of 00-1 shows that the first printing occurred in 2000.

*Printed in the United States of America*

**Note:** This publication contains the opinions and ideas of its author. It is intended to provide helpful and informative material on the subject matter covered. It is sold with the understanding that the author and publisher are not engaged in rendering professional services in the book. If the reader requires personal assistance or advice, a competent professional should be consulted.

# Alpha Development Team

### Publisher
*Marie Butler-Knight*

### Editorial Director
*Gary M. Krebs*

### Associate Managing Editor
*Cari Shaw Fischer*

### Acquisitions Editors
*Randy Ladenheim-Gil*
*Amy Gordon*

### Development Editors
*Phil Kitchel*
*Amy Zavatto*

### Assistant Editor
*Georgette Blau*

# Production Team

### Development Editor
*Chris Marquardt*

### Production Editor
*Mark Enochs*

### Technical Editor
*Mark Eller*

### Copy Editor
*John Sleeva*

### Cover Designer
*Mike Freeland*

### Photo Editor
*Richard H. Fox*

### Illustrator
*Brian Mac Moyer*

### Book Designers
*Scott Cook and Amy Adams of DesignLab*

### Indexer
*(to come)*

### Layout/Proofreading
*Angela Calvert*
*Mary Hunt*

# Contents at a Glance

# Contents

## Appendices

# Foreword

Nearly a quarter of a century ago, when my friends and I learned to climb, we had only trial and error as instructors. Sure, for inspiration we could read the great mountaineering classics—Heckmaier's *My Life as a Mountaineer*, Herzog's *Annapurna*, Terray's *Conquistadors of the Useless*, and Patey's *One Man's Mountains*—but they taught us more about *acting* like climbers than *being* climbers. We learned that climbers should remain stoical under pressure, maintain a keen sense of humor and humility about their craft, and, above all, have utmost respect for the sanctity of partnership.

The aforementioned texts also provided role models and templates on proper mountaineering etiquette and behavior. From these books we could conduct ourselves properly while on the way to the cliffs—and while celebrating in the bars after completing great feats of bravery and glory. But the books left out something very important. What they *didn't* tell us was how to climb.

Later, Yosemite-legend Royal Robbins wrote *Basic Rockcraft* and *Advanced Rockcraft*, which offered savvy advice on rope work, setting protection, and the all-important technique. John Long's *How to Rock Climb* took instruction one step further, providing information on everything from training to applying technique to different tangents of the sport. Eventually, the profession of guiding developed so that beginners had an alternative to risking their necks while learning the ropes.

In the past quarter decade, the sport has developed at a surprising rate. Not only has the number of climbers in the United States increased from several hundred to hundreds of thousands, but climbing itself has become as multi-faceted as the Hope Diamond. In the early 1970s, we merely climbed, whether it be to the top of a mountain or the top of a rock wall. Since then, myriad specialties have developed, including bouldering, aid climbing, ice climbing, sport climbing, indoor climbing, traditional climbing, alpine climbing, and mixed climbing. Not only does keeping up with the disparate splinters of the sport take Herculean effort, but understanding the jargon is more difficult than translating at a United Nations conference.

The strength of *The Complete Idiot's Guide to Rock Climbing* is that it offers a comprehensive survey of the state of the sport. The *Guide* provides a road map for the beginning climber, from answering often-asked questions on equipment to providing a solid basis for understanding safety and technique.

While a book can never replace actual experience on the rock, ice, or mountain, *The Complete Idiot's Guide to Rock Climbing* does an admirable job of providing sufficient background information to get started in the sport. I suspect that this book will soon become the standard text for climbing courses and guided trips. As climbers know, the more knowledge one has before attempting a route, the better one's chances for fun and safety.

With the *Guide* in hand, climbers can rest assured that they've done their homework.

—Nancy Prichard, Ph.D.

**Nancy Prichard, Ph.D.**, began climbing in the early 1970s. She has appeared in a number of climbing programs, including National Geographic's *The New Ice Age*. She has successfully competed in both national and international climbing competitions, including ice climbing in the ESPN X-Games. She is a former editor of *Rock & Ice* magazine and now writes for *Sports Afield, Outside*, and *Men's Journal*, as well as a weekly "Backcountry" column for *Denver.Sidewalk* online. She is the author of *"I Hate to Train" Performance Guide for Climbers* and is currently working on a book titled *Every Woman's Guide to Outdoor Sports*.

# Introduction

So you want to climb rocks? Good decision. Climbing demands skill, strength, stamina, fortitude, and a chess player's mind. The act of scaling a sheer wall of rock is like nothing you've experienced before, except maybe in your dreams.

This book will teach you the basic rock-climbing skills you need to get started. Develop a passion for climbing and you will follow a path that can take you to a variety of places—from your local rock gym to some of the most beautiful and secluded places in the world. (Bhutan, anyone?) Whether it becomes a life-long journey or a momentary diversion, dealing with the physical and mental challenges that climbing presents is an experience you won't forget. In vertical places, the term "peak experience" truly applies.

## What You'll Find in This Book

Before you finish reading this book, we hope you're climbing the walls to start climbing some walls. We introduce basic concepts, skills, and the gear needed to get started. We discuss the nuances of the climbing culture, safety procedures, technique to get up and down, lingo (not all dudes are created equal) and whatever else falls between the cracks.

The book is divided into five user-friendly parts. We start with basic climbing principles, move on to advanced tips, and end with fabulous places to play and training tips that will enable you to play harder (or at least better). As we say in the book, climbing is an apprenticeship. Do not tempt fate by rushing through the basics. Human error and hubris are the biggest killers in the mountains. For this reason (and others), we strongly recommend that you hire a knowledgeable guide before grappling with gravity.

Here's the book in a nutshell:

**Part 1, "What's Up?"** provides a basic overview of the sport. It discusses climbing's history, what to expect, jargon, types of climbing, and basic gear. Learning to talk the talk is just the beginning if you're going to walk the walk.

**Part 2, "Tech Talk,"** goes beyond fashion advice as we address finding the perfect shoes, harness, helmet, and rope needed to get started. You'll learn to safely belay your partner and properly handle the rope. By the end you'll care as much for your rope as a parent does for a child.

**Part 3, "Base Camp,"** delves into the technical side of climbing. The chapters give you the tools to build a solid foundation for your climbing career. We illustrate how to tie secure knots and get the skinny on top-roping and belay techniques. Finally, you'll get the low-down on trying it out on an indoor wall.

**Part 4, "Take It to the Mountain,"** is about the pleasures and complexities of climbing outdoors. We discuss the importance of paying attention to detail, provide a few tips about crack climbing, and show you how to pick a partner and lead a climb. We also highlight something climbers spend a lot of time talking about—Mother Nature's nasty tricks—and offer advice on how to save yourself in an emergency.

**Part 5, "The View from the Top,"** gets into the variety of rating systems used to evaluate climbs around the world; and there's a fair bit about all the amazing climbing areas in the United States and across the globe. There's a bit about life on the big mountains like Rainier, McKinley, and Everest, and a few chilly tales about ice climbing. Finally, we show you how to enhance your climbing pleasure by keeping appropriately fit.

Regardless how big you dream, remember to take it slow and steady. Becoming a proficient climber is like earning a black belt in karate: It takes time, dedication, and intelligence. Be patient and humble. Above all, remember: *safety first.*

Climb on!

# Extras

Check out the sidebars throughout the book. They're packed full of fun and informative facts.

**Finger Tips**

Nifty tips to make your climbing life a little easier.

**Nuts and Bolts**

Definitions of terms germane to the sport.

**Hold On**

Read these boxes carefully. They warn you of the sometimes life-threatening dangers of rock climbing and show you how to stay out of harm's way.

## Cliff Notes

Random climbing tales and useful cocktail party information.

# Acknowledgments

Writing a book is a bit like scaling a mountain: You always imagine it will be a cruise; however, at some point the journey becomes a test of endurance with unseen obstacles, unexpected joys, and a lot of grunt work in between. Inevitably, one is forced to ask, "Why am I doing this?" The answer is always personal and often complex, because any large task requires time, diligence, and sacrifice. In the end you're almost always glad you ventured into new territory, because, as all wise climbers come to realize, the triumph is in the doing, not at the summit.

The same can be said of trying to take a subject as broad and complex as rock climbing and distilling it into a readable, useful guide for newcomers. While writing this book wasn't easy, we hope it offers inspiration and insights into a sport that has limitless possibilities. Regardless of our success, we both learned a lot.

Without the help of a bunch of people, this book would not have been possible. In no particular order, we'd like to thank the following people:

➤ Our literary agent Giles Anderson at Scott Waxman Agency. He got us the gig and prodded us to keep cranking out the text.

➤ Our selfless editor Chris Marquardt, for coordinating the whole production, even while on vacation.

➤ Ivan Greene, the head climbing honcho at Chelsea Piers in Manhattan, who has no body fat and naturally curly hair.

➤ Mark Eller, another first-rate climber who saved our cookies countless times with his technical expertise. Many of his fine photos grace this text.

➤ Photographer Nels Akerlund, for sharing his captured beauty in the pages of this book.

➤ Illustrator Mike Amaditz. May his knots always stay tight.

➤ Photographer Jay Farbman, for giving us a glimpse of the intensity and absurdity of the Raid Gauloises.

—Stefani Jackenthal & Joe Glickman
New York City, 1999

*Stefani adds:*

Special thanks to Mom, Dad, Cathy, Mike (Jr.), Ron, Jen, Sammy (Spike), Grandpa, Florence, and my dear friends. I cherish your constant strength and support. You're always with me. To my partner Joe—el escritor de noche—may your life be awash in adventure. Live. Love. Learn.

*Joe adds:*

Special thanks to Steve Ilg—climber, writer, coach—who taught me the physical and spiritual value of training hard and soft. (The Ilgster's book *The Winter Athlete* is an invaluable training guide for any outdoor athlete.) Thanks also to Beth Umland, my wife, best friend, and mother of our young social climber, Willa. Beth is a terrific writer who graciously edits my turgid prose no matter the time of day or night. Finally, thanks to my "multi-tasking" partner, Stefani Jackenthal. May all your projects lead to higher ground.

# Part 1
# What's Up?

*Learning to rock climb is one of those good news/bad news deals. The good news is that this often misunderstood sport is a lot easier than you might think. Under the watchful eye of a good instructor or knowledgeable friend (you won't want to figure out this unforgiving sport on your own), you will experience the thrill of negotiating a vertical wall of rock.*

*The bad news is that you're almost assured of being scared. Don't worry. Fear is natural and healthy when you're not used to standing on a narrow ledge of rock.*

*Part 1 will talk about our desire to ascend and the inherent fear that goes along with it. I'll give you some insight into how to know if you're ready to climb—my guess is you are if you're reading this book—and how to prepare your body and mind. I'll highlight the different styles of climbing you can pursue and clue you into a lot of the cool climbing hardware that will help you realize your vertical dreams.*

# Because It's There

I fell for Spiderman at age five and never looked back. Every so often, when I'm hanging out on a narrow ledge hundreds of feet above terra firma, I wonder: Had I loved Superman, would I be into hang gliding instead of rock climbing? Or, had I bonded with the Incredible Hulk, would I be writing *The Complete Idiot's Guide to Body Building*?

No matter. I was a Spiderman fan, even though actual spiders sent me scurrying for cover. I loved the way this fearless foe of evil would fire webs from his wrists and scamper up twenty-story buildings as effortlessly as I could cruise up a flight of stairs.

In the persona of Spiderwoman, I'd climb up the inside of my bedroom doorway. This move never failed to tick off my mom (something about footprints on the wall), and a promising career as a TV action hero was nipped in the bud. But years later, when I got into adventure racing (team multi-sport racing, including things like kayaking, mountain biking, and rock climbing), I discovered the sport of rock climbing and the spider in me reemerged.

And I'm not alone. Although the sport was once reserved for mad dogs and Englishmen, today respectable citizens of all ages, shapes, and sizes are taking to the rocks—to which I say: Climb on, Spiderdudes!

# Why Humans Climb

It's virtually impossible to write about what draws people to vertical places without quoting mountaineer George Mallory. Asked why he wanted to be the first man to stand on the earth's highest summit, he said: "Because it is there"—a classic bit of British understatement that says everything and nothing at the same time.

This explanation generally doesn't cut it with non-climbers, including my mother. To her, rock climbing seems about as sensible and appealing as swimming in shark-infested waters.

## The Jungle Gym in Our Genes

Sorry, Mom, but there is ample evidence to suggest that climbing is as natural as crawling. A two-year-old on the loose indoors will scramble up everything in sight: chairs, shelves, toilets, you name it. I've seen kids who could barely walk get up onto a couch by kicking up a leg and pressing down with their arms—what rock climbers call a *mantle move*.

### Nuts and Bolts

A **mantle move** is an advanced down-pressure technique that allows you to get your feet onto the same hold your hands are on. Think of getting out of the deep end of a swimming pool without a ladder and you've got the move down.

Take that same curious tike outside and he or she will gravitate toward staircases, walls, and rocks. It's no coincidence that the most popular apparatus in the playground when I was a kid was the monkey bars. And it's not unusual to hear a triumphant tot atop a jungle gym mimic a chimp and shout, "I'm a monkey! I'm a monkey!"

Some anthropologists suggest that this desire to ascend is innate. We are genetically programmed, they say, to swing from the treetops in search of food or to flee from predators. When I was firmly entrenched in my Spiderman phase, my brother and I would pick a tree and challenge each other to see who could climb the highest. And the one time I ran away from home, at the age of nine, I climbed the highest pine tree in my backyard. (I stayed there for 45 minutes, got bored, climbed down, and then slunk home.)

Conversely, studies show that the fear of heights is nearly as universal as our desire to climb. Psychologists have put babies just hours old onto a glass table and noticed how they recoiled from the perceived drop. (Interesting stuff, but one wonders about parents volunteering to scare the diapers off their newborns.)

This contradiction is part of what makes climbing so captivating. We are pulled upward toward risk and the unknown and, at the same time, drawn downward to safety and certainty. Go figure.

*Climbing vertical rock face. (Photo courtesy of Mark Eller.)*

One note of caution: While this man-as-ape theory makes perfect sense to me, be careful when expounding this concept. If you tell people that you climb in order to get in touch with your simian side, you're likely to raise some eyebrows. You'd probably be better off telling folks you're rediscovering your inner child. On second thought, why not just go with "Because it's there." It worked for Mallory.

## *The Mountain Top Ten*

Here, in no particular order, are my top 10 reasons why humans climb:

1. Dogs may be man's best friend, but the ape is his kissing cousin.

2. High places are magnets to the escapist, forcing one's attention away from humdrum responsibilities like earning a living and toward the stark reality of gravity.

**Nuts and Bolts**

A **route** is a path up a rock that can follow a pre-mapped direction or cover new and unknown territory.

3. In rock climbing there is no one to compete against and no rigid set of rules (other than essential safety procedures). You can still measure your progress over time, however, since climbing has a structured rating system to judge a *route's* degree of difficulty. (To learn more about rating systems, see Chapter 19.)

4.  As a social sport, climbing is tiptop. Not only is there a lot of down time to schmooze, but there's something powerful about the bonding that occurs between rope-mates working together to do something rigorous, risky, and rewarding.

5.  Parents and kids both get to play.

6.  No sport makes a beer taste better. Since the earliest days of British climbing, a day on the rocks has been followed by a night in the pub.

7.  Climbing can help get you in great shape. Superb climbers are built like boxers and have the flexibility of gymnasts. Climb regularly and your strength, endurance, and balance will improve. My friend Ivan Greene, head instructor at Chelsea Piers indoor gym in Manhattan and one of the best sport climbers in the United States, literally looks like he's been chiseled out of stone. (See Chapter 3 for more on sport climbing.)

8.  It's a terrific cross-training opportunity. Many of the coolest crags require long hikes to reach. You can hang out, camp, and make it a weekend—the backpacking is arduous by itself—or for you multi-sport types (like me), ride your mountain bike to the site, do the climb, and ride home.

9.  There are routes for every ability level. Anyone who can lift a coil of rope and slip on a pair of climbing shoes can have fun.

10. You can do it indoors or out—and if you do it outside, it's almost always in beautiful places.

### Cliff Notes

When other areas are suffering from crazy weather, Joshua Tree is the place to be. October through December, March, and April are the best times to visit this mountainous southern California area.

# Spiderman Rules!

Because I'd always loved to climb, the first time I actually put my feet on vertical rock—in the Shawungunks (a.k.a. the "Gunks"), roughly 100 miles north of New York City—I expected to take to it like a baby to a bottle. I was with a friend who had climbed extensively in the Gunks as well as out west in Wyoming and California.

He loaned me a *harness* and helmet, and I joined the ranks of the 900,000 rock-climbing enthusiasts in the United States. My buddy set up a top rope and basically said, "Climb away, dude!" (See Chapters 3 and 9 for more on top roping.) Six feet off the ground, wearing clumsy hiking boots, I felt like a cat running on ice. Twenty feet higher, I clung to a fissure listening to my heart pound like a bass drum. I looked down and tried not to act as if I'd seen a ghost.

At the end of the day I was sore, stiff, and grateful to be alive, even though I had been safer on that rock under my friend's watchful eye than I would have been on any street in Manhattan.

### Nuts and Bolts

A typical **harness** is made of wide nylon webbing and fastens around the waist with a metal buckle. Straps made of webbing wrap around the thighs. The harness secures the climber to the rope and distributes the force of the fall.

## Let's Try That Again

"When do you want to go again?" my friend asked. I almost answered "Maybe in 10 years!" But pride prevailed. "How about next weekend?" I said.

This time I came equipped with tight-fitting, grippy climbing shoes, which not only made it easier to climb but also made me feel more like a climber. I was still scared (and you will be too, it's only natural) but I was no longer hoping to be airlifted off the rock by aliens. But truth be told, by the end of the day I still couldn't say that I actually enjoyed climbing.

## The Breakthrough

Then came my breakthrough. While visiting Santa Monica, California, I took part in a group climbing lesson on a cliff overlooking the ocean. Instead of just cracking my knuckles and grunting up the rock as I had in the Gunks, I first listened as my instructor went over some basic techniques, including safety procedures. "Your climbing safety depends on your judgment as well as the judgment of your partner," he said. "Remember, there are bold climbers and old climbers, but no old, bold climbers."

With an instructor walking me through the basics, I felt much more at ease. Instead of clinging to the rock like a koala to its mother, I leaned away from the wall and used my legs (my secret weapon from my days as a pro cyclist). The higher I climbed, the less frightened I felt. And instead of being gripped by fatigue, I felt energized.

### Finger Tips

Find an instructor who has solid credentials and a good sense of humor. Remember: This isn't your career; it's a sport for you to enjoy.

I was even relaxed enough to take in the killer view beneath my feet. The sky was a sublime powder blue, and the sun glistened off the ocean. Two whales dove and resurfaced in the distance

### Finger Tips

Stay focused on the task at hand. Gaze at the scenery after you are safely perched on a ledge.

### Nuts and Bolts

By using a rope and a friction device, **belaying** is the system used to stop a climber if he or she falls. The climber is "on belay" when the belay partner is ready to apply the brake to the rope in the event of a fall.

### Hold On

Climbing can be dangerous, so establish good habits and don't take shortcuts.

and seals frolicked in the surf. "Stay focused!" came the cry from below, and I resumed my delicate dance up the single crack that wandered up the cool granite slab.

"So this is climbing," I thought. Instead of fighting the rock I started to feel the balance. Gradually, my *belay* partner and I began to work as one. And I was totally absorbed in the task of getting my butt up a slab of vertical rock that cared little if I went up or fell down. An experienced climber would have traipsed up the route I was on with barely a deep breath, but for me getting to the top was a puzzle to be solved with strength, creativity, and willpower.

Afterward, as I looked out at the ocean, I felt a bit bolder and a bit more humble. And unlike the last time I climbed, I couldn't wait to go again. That endorphin rush that often fills my body after a good workout was there, only stronger, especially in my head.

The high that I felt—a combination of fear and elation—is the closest I get to the state of being that Rimbaud called "supernaturally sober." It's why humans find climbing so addicting. At least, it's why I climb.

# Rock of Ages

Had ESPN2 been around during the Neanderthal period, we'd probably have been privy to some awesome displays of climbing. Getting chased by a saber-toothed tiger, even if you are barefoot and carrying a spear, will inspire even the most lead-footed soul to climb high fast.

And while we have no visual proof of the climbing prowess of the cliff-dwelling Native Americans in the southwest, one has only to head to places like Mesa Verde National Park in Colorado to imagine what some of these hotshots were capable of. Clearly, this was a culture comfortable on vertical rock.

## *Mountains, Mystics, and Mayhem*

Of course, mountains and mysticism have figured prominently in history. A great Jewish mountaineer named Moses led his people up Mt. Sinai. In the second century A.D., Emperor Hadrian climbed Mount Etna to view the sunrise. And no doubt there were some nimble rock jocks on Mt. Olympus, home of the Greek gods.

*Rocks are for all ages. (Photo courtesy of Mark Eller.)*

Given man's reverence for lofty heights, it's probably no coincidence that some of the most spiritual cultures in the world are found among the highest mountains. For example, the Himayalan peaks of Kangchenjunga (26,167 feet), Machapuchare (22,944 feet), and Kailas (21,982 feet and considered the Throne of Shiva and the center of Hindu and Buddhist worship) are still believed to be sacred, with the actual summits being off limits to devout believers.

In the seventeenth century, man was more preoccupied with the plague, invading armies, and famine than with climbing. Still, at least once during the century climbing played a famous role in putting food on the table. In 1690, the Bishop of Geneva set out on a "journey of mortal peril" to exorcise the glaciers of Chamonix. Local farmers believed the Devil was living there and wreaking havoc on their crops.

## Mountaineering Is Born

In the eighteenth century, the climbing scene started to heat up in the European Alps. In 1786, two Frenchmen—a scientist and a crystal hunter—summitted the 15,771-foot Mont Blanc, the highest peak in the Alps. The event is considered to be the birth of true mountaineering. Thirty-five years later, the Jungfrau in Switzerland, a mountain many thought impossible to climb, was scaled.

## Cliff Notes

The western world generally considers the birth of true mountaineering to be the ascent of Mont Blanc in 1786 by local Chamonix climbers Michel Paccard, a scientist, and Jacques Balmat, a crystal hunter.

In 1857, the first mountaineering club—appropriately named the Alpine Club—was formed. Eight years later, a disaster on the 14,692-foot Matterhorn—one of the most sought-after summits in the Alps—made headlines. A British team had beaten a French party to the summit. On the way down, however, three members of the triumphant team slipped and fell to their death—the first major tragedy in the history of the sport. By then, more than 200 of the great peaks of Europe had been climbed (mostly by Brits led by local guides), and the so-called "Golden Age of Mountaineering" was in full swing.

Of course, climbing has come a long way from those days when these manly men (and a few tough women) used hemp ropes, hobnailed boots, and wooden staffs to get to the top of a mountain any way possible. As technology improved, climbers began pushing the envelope. Instead of choosing the "easiest" route they could find to get to the top, climbers deliberately tackled a peak's sheerest face.

## Notable Firsts

Here's a survey of some of the noteworthy achievements in climbing history:

➤ **1889:** First ascent of Africa's Mt. Kenya (17,058 feet) in Kenya.

➤ **1889:** First ascent of Kilimanjaro (19,341 feet) in Tanzania, the highest mountain in Africa.

➤ **1897:** First ascent of the 22,832-foot Aconcagua in Argentina, the highest point in South America.

➤ **1913:** First ascent of Alaska's Mt. McKinley (20,322 feet), the highest mountain in North America.

➤ **1925:** First ascent of British Columbia's Mt. Logan (19,850 feet), the highest point in Canada.

➤ **1950:** First ascent of Annapurna (26,504 feet) in Nepal.

➤ **1953:** Sir Edmund Hillary and Sherpa Tenzing Norgay make the first ascent of the Mother Goddess of all mountains, Mt. Everest (29,028 feet).

➤ **1954:** First ascent of K2 in Pakistan, the second highest mountain on earth at 28,252 feet.

➤ **1958:** First ascent of El Capitan, America's most famous rock face in Yosemite National Park. The climb took a total of 47 days over a period of 17 months. (The record for the same route today is 4 hours and 22 minutes.)

➤ **1978:** Reinhold Messner becomes the first man to scale all 14 8,000-meter (26,000-foot) peaks on earth, and he and Peter Habeler are the first to ascend Mt. Everest without bottled oxygen.

➤ **1993:** Lynn Hill's free ascent on the Nose Route on El Capitan in Yosemite draws the attention of the climbing world. Climbing such an exposed route at such a high standard made Hill's climb one of the great ascents in the annals of rock climbing.

# Climbing Culture

To the casual observer, the world of climbing can look like a foreign country with its own language, manners, and dress code. But once you learn the ropes (forgive the pun), you'll see that this fast-growing sport is more about safety than risk, and more about humility than bravado. Serious climbers tend to be intelligent, eco-friendly sorts who respect the outdoors. Think of them as hikers who enjoy stepping off the trail and onto sheer faces of rock.

## Rock Jocks

You see, the biggest misconception about rock climbers is that they're either funky youngsters with blood-and-guts tattoos and too much testosterone or adrenaline junkies looking for their next fix. Not so. It's true that hardcore climbers enjoy the challenge and risk that comes with doing something difficult—and more than a few have tattoos—but those who push the envelope too hard or disregard basic safety procedures get seriously hurt or die. With few exceptions, the climbers I know are some of the most rational, safety-conscious folks you'll ever meet. They have to be; their lives depend on it.

Modern climbing was shaped by a handful of innovators like Royal Robbins, Yvon Chouinard, and Fritz Wiessner. During the 1950s and 1960s, Chouinard, an itinerant blacksmith, spent a lot of time in Yosemite and made his own *pitons* out of the back of his battered truck. He invented a host of ingenious devices and went on to form a little company called Patagonia. He also contributed a spirit of single-minded dedication to the sport: Legend has it that climbing kept him in such a constant state of poverty that he often ate cat food. (The next time you complain about a stale Powerbar, think of dining on Liver & Salmon Bits.)

**Nuts and Bolts**

**Pitons** are steel wedges or blades hammered into cracks to anchor climbers to the rock.

*Hanging out on the rock.*
*(Photo courtesy of Nels*
*Akerlund.)*

Although I've never met these legendary rock jocks, I've read enough about them to feel like I have. And when I'm climbing in the Gunks or Adirondacks and hear that one of the grand men of climbing pioneered a route that I've climbed, I feel a connection to the past—like I'm part of a grand tradition.

### Cliff Notes

At the ripe old age of 14, Katie Brown, an 85-pound lass from Paris, Kentucky, won the Junior National Championship and the Youth World Championship in sport climbing. Afterward her coach predicted she would be the next Robyn Erbersfield, winner of the 1995 ESPN X-Games Sports Climbing Women's Difficulty competition. Sure enough, the next year Brown claimed Erbersfield's title.

And the tradition continues in ways these pioneers probably could not have envisioned. Today, teenage sensations like Chris Sharma and Katie Brown perform outrageous feats of gymnastics in the increasingly popular arena of competition climbing. (For more on competition climbing, see Chapter 3.) The competitions featured on ESPN's *X-Games* are an outgrowth of the indoor climbing boom—a temperature-controlled environment far removed from the tattered tents and dank caves Chouinard and his cronies slept in after putting up new routes in Yosemite and other legendary places out west.

## Asking Questions

Here's the other cool thing about climbing: You don't have to be afraid to ask questions. The general misconception that beginners bring to the rock is that asking experienced climbers about technique or safety means you're a goof. Wrong. By and large, those in the know are happy to help. What savvy climbers don't like are posers—people who clearly don't know what they're doing but pretend they do.

## Looking for Help

Climbing is a gear-intensive, technique-oriented sport. In other words, you need to know what you're doing before you can get off the ground (or at least before you can get back down). Although experience is the best teacher, there is a wealth of information out there to guide you. Instructional books like the *Complete Idiot's Guide* are a great first step. Then there is the climber's Bible, *Mountaineering: Freedom of the Hills*, a comprehensive A-to-Z book on all aspects of mountaineering. It's a bit on the dry side, but it's got what you need to know to get going.

Magazines like *Climbing* and *Rock and Ice* are helpful as well, offering tips on technique, neat places to climb, and, most of all, inspiration. Instructional videos like *Basic Rock Climbing* (Vertical Adventure Productions) cover most of the same stuff but have the advantage of showing you the right way to do what you're doing wrong. (Don't forget to use the rewind button.) To learn more about what's available out there, check out Appendixes B through F at the end of this book.

# Screen Heroics

Movies like *The Eiger Sanction* with Clint Eastwood and *Cliffhanger* with Sly Stallone or ESPN's *X-Games'* coverage of Sports Climbing are fun to watch on a rainy day when you can't get to the real thing. Remember, however, not to try any of their psycho stunts unless you're on the ground or tired of living. Of course, if you want inspiration and knowledge at the same time, check out *Masters of Stone I-IV; Big UP!* and *Free Hueco!* (distributed by *Rock & Ice* magazine); and *The Real Thing*.

## Cliff Notes

The opening scene of Sylvester Stallone's movie *Cliffhanger* shows a broken buckle that leads to a gnarly fall. This outraged many athletes and manufacturers in the climbing community since the odds of it happening are slim to none.

# Rules of the Rock

There are a few rules you'll need to follow to fit in. It goes without saying that you should respect the rock and the land around it. Remember: If you pack it in, pack it out. ("It" is anything you bring with you that isn't biodegradable.)

Also, be considerate to those climbing above and below you. If you do dislodge a chunk of real estate, be sure to yell "ROCK!" If another party wants to pass you, let them pass at a safe spot, such as a wide ledge. If you overtake a party, make sure you have the chops to stay ahead.

Finally, rock jocks have their own language. Talk to climbers to learn the lingo, but don't become a linguistic hipster before you've earned your stripes. "Dude"-ing everyone in sight or using the word *rad* (short for *radical*) or *awesome* more than a hyper Valley Girl will earn you the contempt of all but the most tolerant.

## The Least You Need to Know

➤ Climbing is one of the fastest-growing sports in America.

➤ We all climbed as kids; learning to climb is mostly a matter of rediscovering something we already know.

➤ Mountains have been home to the gods and places where bold men (and women) go for a taste of immortality.

➤ Knowing the roots and ethics of the sport will help you appreciate this thrilling activity.

➤ Although vertical rocks are intimidating, if you learn the proper techniques from the pros, you'll be less scared and have more fun.

# Chapter 2

# Are You Ready to Rock?

---

**In This Chapter**

➤ The key elements of successful climbing

➤ What happens when you fall

➤ Staying out of harm's way

➤ Staying happy by getting fit

➤ Finding a guide

➤ Respecting the rock

---

The thought of climbing is often scarier than the act. Typically, when you're grappling with gravity you're too consumed by what you're doing to panic. Some people who are genuinely afraid of heights try climbing, see how controlled it is, and learn to love it. Conversely, I've seen risk-and-adventure types who climb once and have no desire to do the vertical dance again. So the question remains: How do you know if you're ready to go?

Try this test: Go to Yosemite National Park—the Mecca of big-wall climbing in the United States—and stand at the base of El Capitan, a 3,000-foot wall of rock that dazzles the eyes and boggles the mind. Take some high-powered binoculars with you and train them on the minuscule specks of humanity inching up the sheer face. If within the first 10 minutes you say, "I'd rather be pecked to death by ducks," then you're probably not ready to climb. If, however, you start evaluating what it would take to scale this seductive monster; if you start imagining what it would be like to peer down at the valley like a soaring eagle; or if you simply can't take your eyes off this stunning outdoor cathedral, well, my guess is you're ready to climb.

# The Key Ingredients

*Climbing* is a broad term that encompasses various different styles that will take you to many locales:

➤ There's **traditional rock climbing**, where the climber uses removable *protection*. This adventurous, self-reliant style is what most people think of when they picture rock jocks scaling vertical walls of rock.

➤ **Climbing indoors in a gym** provides fitness benefits and convenience, albeit without the aesthetic thrill of a pristine wilderness setting.

➤ **Bouldering**, which often requires difficult, even gymnastic, moves, is done without a rope, rarely more than 10 feet off the ground.

➤ **Alpine climbing**, which combines hiking with rock or ice climbing, is for those who love humping huge packs into the mountains for days or weeks at a time.

➤ **Sport climbing** is done on pre-bolted routes usually on vertical to overhanging rock. This style emphasizes safe, often difficult climbing.

➤ **Aid climbing** is the most gear-intensive style of rock climbing. In aid climbing, the protection is used to help the climbers move up the wall. (In other styles, protection is called upon only when a climber falls.)

### Nuts and Bolts

**Protection** (or **pro**) for climbing comes in two forms: removable anchors and permanent anchors. The best known example of a permanent anchor is the *piton*, a metal spike that can be pounded into a crack in the rock. These are no longer popular because the hammering often breaks off pieces of rock. These days bolts can be quickly drilled into a wall, which offer a climber a great deal of security, especially for the style called sport climbing. Removable pro, which is wedged into the rock and used in traditional climbing, is easy to retrieve.

Whether you're inside wearing lycra tights and a tank top or outside toting thick plastic boots and a 50-pound pack, you'll need many of the same basic skills and techniques. The common denominator is desire, and you have at least a little of that already or you wouldn't be reading this guide. From my experience, the best way to nurture that desire is to climb in a safe setting—indoors or out—on routes that are hard enough to keep you motivated but easy enough to build confidence. Nothing turns off beginners faster than the good old-fashioned whuppin' you get when trying to climb an overly challenging route.

Here's another basic truth: Confidence and conditioning go hand in hand. If you have the physical chops, you'll be able to push past the initial uncertainty that's *de rigeur* for novices. Of course, just being fit won't get you up the rock if your brain says, "No way, Jose!"

The other key ingredients to a successful climbing career are knowing your limits and paying close attention to safety procedures. (We'll talk more about safety throughout this guide, and especially in Chapter 14.) Sounds obvious, right? Unfortunately, many climbers suffer from a dangerous condition known as "summit fever." When they're in the grip of the fever, the goal of getting to the top comes first, while safety comes second. As journalist and world-class climber Greg Childs writes: "This state of mind is what is both fantastic and reckless about the game."

Stated simply, you'd better know what lies on the other side of risk and luck. Remember the cardinal rule: Be safe and live to climb again another day.

## Will I Fall?

You will fall. But the important thing to remember is that you won't fall to the ground. You'll be in a harness, which will be attached to a rope, which will be attached to something solid, like a tree or a rock.

So perhaps the more germane question is: Will the rope hold? This is asked with particular urgency by beefy beginners. Take heart. Nearly 500 years ago, Galileo demonstrated that gravity increased the velocities of falling objects at the same rate no matter what they weighed. In other words, a ballerina and an NFL lineman will plummet at the same speed—roughly 70 mph (assuming, of course, they fell in a vacuum).

I'd rather belay the ballerina, but in either case, the anchor bolts you're using for protection have been tested to be able to hold prodigious amounts of weight, and the rope can withstand nearly three tons of static weight. So unless you weigh more than the average circus elephant, you should be fine.

The more important ingredient isn't the equipment, it's the way climbers uses it. Modern climbing gear—properly used—will withstand thousands of normal falls. You should be more concerned about using the gear correctly than you are about it not working. The number of incidents where climbing gear fails is nearly zilch.

Regardless, the first time you accidentally peel off the rock, your stomach does cartwheels and your brain screams "Waaaaaaa!" You're not likely to ever get used to it, but remember that anyone who climbs regularly falls. In fact, taking intelligent risks, which often lead to falls, is the only way you get better. Once you see first-hand how redundant your protection is, the thought of a fall will be much less intimidating.

### Hold On

Never take your safety on granite for granted. Double-check every safety system and be on guard for the unexpected.

### Finger Tips

Falling is inevitable, so don't panic the first time you lose your footing and grip. Stay relaxed, let the harness take the load, and always keep your feet out in front of you to protect yourself from crashing against the wall.

There is a bit of tricky climbing terminology you'll need to know. The standard call when you're falling is: "FALLING!" You may be tempted to use slightly more colorful language; though not as accurate, it's just as effective when said loudly enough.

To help ease pre-fall jitters, some instructors have their students climb a short distance and then step off the rock in order to feel how foolproof their protection actually is—provided it's set up correctly.

### Nuts and Bolts

**Belaying** is the system for, or act of, managing the rope to protect the climber. In this case the rope is called the *belay,* and the places at which the rope is attached to the rock are called the *belay points.*

*Belaying,* the system of setting up the rope to hold a climber when he falls, is the be-all and end-all of climbing safety. A *belay* consists of a rope that runs from a climber to his partner, the belayer, who is ready to break a fall by putting sudden friction on the rope. While it's relatively simple to learn, it must be done correctly. (Chapter 6 discusses belaying in detail.)

As is often the case, dealing with this natural fear of falling takes time and experience. Climbing in the Gunks one day, I found myself stuck on a ledge as wide as a silver dollar. I knew what I needed to do to advance, but I couldn't seem to muster the courage to leave my precarious perch. I yelled down to my partner to watch me carefully. "Gotcha!" he said. Even though I trusted him implicitly, I stuck there like a spooked squirrel. My partner shouted that old climbing line up at me: "Don't worry about falling. It's not the fall that gets you, it's the sudden stop." The gallows humor was what I needed. I sprang for the hold, stuck like a fly, and giggled most of the way to the top.

Will you fall? Well, yeah, but if you trust your equipment, know your partner, and climb on routes that you can handle, all should be peachy in paradise.

## Will It Hurt?

Like any sport, rock climbing demands specific muscles that your body needs to fine-tune. Typing on the computer may give you quick and nimble fingers, but holding your body weight with your paws is a very different story. Even after the body (especially the fingers) has had a few weeks to adjust, it is still advisable that novices stay off of climbs they can't complete in less than 2 to 3 falls, for example, climbs that are far beyond their ability.

As any good climbing instructor will tell you, the most important advice for novices is to start off by emphasizing good technique over "thrashing" away at routes that are too hard. Just as a cycling coach would have riders "spin" for the first few weeks of training, emphasizing form over speed, the beginning climber should strive to move beautifully and efficiently before attempting to push their physical limits. Observation is key here: Watch more experienced climbers at the cliff or in the gym and note how smoothly they move.

**18**

*Learn proper technique before you push your limits. (Photo of courtesy Mark Eller.)*

## Sore Muscles

When I started climbing I assumed that after a regular regime of swimming and kayaking my upper body would be up to the task. When I woke up the morning after my first two-hour session, however, I could barely brush my teeth. My arms, shoulders, stomach, and back were as stiff as a climbing shoe. Even laughing hurt. The lesson I learned was to start slow and build climbing strength from the ground up.

In other words, you might have moose-like biceps and be able to do pushups like Jack LaLanne, but unless you're used to hanging from your fingers, standing on your toes, and twisting like a corkscrew, you'll probably feel like you were mugged if you climb too hard or too long. Do it once and you'll be stiff, sore, or, worse, you'll pull a muscle. Do it chronically, and you run the risk of being shelved with tendonitis.

### Finger Tips

Take your time building climbing-specific muscles. Don't overdo it; you can always go back to the crag or wall tomorrow. It's better to leave eager for more than to be a played-out mess.

While you're likely to learn the the hard way, remember that because muscles develop faster than tendons, you'll need to start slowly to develop the sport-specific strength necessary in your hands, elbows, arms, and shoulders—the body parts that bear the brunt of the grunt work during the climbing season. Unless you're being pursued by an American Gladiator or fleeing from an avalanche, pace yourself and save some strength for another day.

### Hold On

Be patient if you can't climb a route the first time out. It's better to come back eager to try again than to be forced to the sidelines by stubbornly trying until you're hurt.

The best way to build climbing strength is to climb. However, especially during the off-season, serious climbers often do pull-ups from a chin-up bar or "hangboard," a device with specifically built handholds. If you can't do a pull-up, don't despair; simply hang from the bar and pull yourself up as far as you can, or get someone to hold your legs and help you up. Any way you do them, pull-ups are a good way to improve upper body strength and ward off those nagging pulls and sprains that plague rock jocks.

## Fingers, Bloody Fingers

News flash: Rock is hard, fingers are soft. Nicks, cuts, abrasions, scrapes—whatever the word or severity of the wound, you'll find it an unavoidable part of climbing. Look at pictures of someone who's just done a multi-day climb; their cracked and taped digits look like the mitts of a lobster fisherman.

Here's what your manicurist probably never told you: You want to climb enough to get your hands tough but not enough to rip 'em to shreds. A good way to avoid cuts is to tape your fingers and wrap the backs of your hands with athletic tape.

### Finger Tips

Because chronic tension is perhaps the biggest cause of climbing injuries, warming up is essential. A great way to ease your hands into a climb is to squeeze a tennis ball before you go vertical.

## Hands Up

Muscular stress is an even bigger enemy to your hands. The great climbers contort their hands in a variety of ways that you probably won't. Let pain and common sense be your guide. Seasoned hands can endure stress in reasonable doses. Do it too often, though, and you might have to switch from the violin to the harmonica.

Here's some more common knowledge: Warming up is key to injury prevention. En route to the rock you can squeeze an old tennis ball, handgrips, or pliable putty. (I often do this when I'm talking on the phone to build strength.) And try to begin your day with a few easy routes that will help get your whole body going.

When you climb, try to keep your hands as relaxed as possible. Chronic tension is perhaps the biggest cause of injuries in climbing and in all sports. In other words, if you're standing on a ledge thinking about your next move and clutching the rock like an eagle clawing a rabbit, your hands are much more susceptible to injury.

To quote the old master from *Kung Fu*, one of my all-time favorite TV shows: "Go light, Grasshopper." Use an *open grip* whenever possible, and save the iron claw grip for when it's absolutely necessary. If a particular move continues to stymie you, be patient and come back when you're rested. Odds are the rock isn't going anywhere. Battering your body to complete a route will be a temporary victory in a losing battle.

**Nuts and Bolts**

The **open grip** is the easiest on your finger's tendons since the bones in your hand absorb most of the stress. The key to the open grip is that the fingers are left unclenched, with the knuckles as low as possible. When the knuckles raise up, above the hold, the grip is called a **crimp**.

## Elbow Macaroni

Elbow injuries have shelved some of the best climbers and even ended more than a few climbing careers. Probably the most stressful move on an elbow comes when you try to pull yourself over an overhanging ledge. Whenever possible, use your legs to lighten the load on your upper body. As always, let common sense be your guide: If it feels weird, don't do it unless you have to.

## Shredded Shoulders

Shoulder problems seem to come in two varieties:

1. Hanging from a straight arm with a fully extended (non-flexed) shoulder puts a lot of strain on the joint. If your arm is slightly flexed, the muscle absorbs much of the pressure on the joint.

2. Your shoulders are used to do pull-up movements. Reaching out to the side, however, can put the big hurt on your shoulders.

A good way to strengthen your shoulders is to do pulling exercises. Pull-ups and lat pull-downs, an pulling exercise you'll find at your local gym, are good, but remember to work the *antagonistic muscles*, too, by doing pushups and military presses.

**Nuts and Bolts**

An **antagonistic muscle** is the muscle that opposes the action of the muscle with which it is paired, for example, triceps to the biceps.

## Listen and Learn

"Body awareness" is as simple as it sounds, but it's something that many driven athletes are good at ignoring. Basically, when I feel hot flashes of searing pain in a particular part of my body, I back off. It's the intermediate pain—pain that I can ignore—that I often have problems with.

Here are a few tips to avoid injuries:

➤ **Work within your established range of motion.** Some climbers can hyper-extend their joints like toddlers. If you can do it naturally, great; if not, don't force it.

➤ **Warm up with a few easy climbs and, once you're revved up, do some gentle stretching.** Stretching cold often does more harm than good.

➤ **Drink, drink, drink—water, that is.** Wilting on the wall from dehydration like a neglected plant can turn a beautiful day ugly.

➤ **Know when to stop.** Being sore after a long day of climbing is one of the great feelings in sports; being too sore to touch your nose is one of the worst.

➤ **Don't just run off after your workout.** Take a few minutes to cool down properly. Just like a muscle needs time to warm up, it needs sufficient time to cool down. This is the ideal to time to stretch warm muscles gently, keeping them long and limber for your next workout.

➤ **If you pull or strain something while climbing, apply ice ASAP.** A cold can of beer (or soda, if you're underage) works well, but you'll need to save the bubbles for later.

### Hold On

Beware! A 150-pound person needs at least 2 $\frac{1}{2}$ quarts of water a day for basic health maintenance; athletes who lose water through perspiration should double that. This doesn't mean you need to carry massive amounts of water up the wall on a day climb. Simply hydrate like a madman before and after. Remember to drink before you're thirsty and keep hydrating until your urine is clear.

# Will I Die?

Learning proper technique, training in the gym, and managing your body on the rock are all essential skills to a safe and long climbing career; however, there persists for beginners the nagging question: Will I die?

According to the American Alpine Club, 1,100 climbers have died in mountaineering accidents in North America since 1947. Improved equipment and climbing techniques have made life in the hills easier, but they haven't eliminated human error or the capricious power of Mother Nature. Either one can still wreak havoc. Knowing what can go wrong is one way to prevent it from happening to you.

Modern gear rarely fails, unless it is used improperly. Improper use or faulty placement of protection is the bigger risk. One well-known example of this involved Marty Hoey, a former guide on Mt. Rainier. While descending Mt. Everest in the 1980s, this incredibly fit and skilled climber neglected to secure the buckle on her climbing harness. When she leaned back on a sheer slope, she plunged thousands of feet to her death.

Always climb with experienced people and never climb above your ability. The best way to learn is from a reputable guide or guiding organization.

The majority of accidents involve a fall, a slip on rock or ice, or falling rock. The most common contributing causes are as follows:

➤ Climbing unroped

➤ Attempting a climb that exceeds one's ability

➤ Being improperly equipped for the conditions

### Cliff Notes

The danger of climbing unroped on steep ice hit home in May 1998 when Chris Hooyman, a seasoned climber and guide, was descending Alaska's Mt. McKinley during a storm. At 17,000 feet, one of the members of his party slipped and seemed unable to get to his feet. Chris, who had summitted McKinley three times, unclipped from his rope to help. In the blink of an eye, he slipped and tumbled to his death.

Some experts think that the majority of fatalities in the climbing world involve beginners and experts. Beginners are done in by inexperience, they say, and the experts fall prey to carelessness, overconfidence, and choosing extreme routes.

# Go for a Guide

As I mentioned in Chapter 1, the first few times I went climbing I was shepherded by a friend who was a great guy and fine climber but not a particularly refined teacher. Only when I went with an accredited guide did I realize what I was missing.

### Hold On

Good judgment is a climber's best friend. Beginners need to watch and ask questions, and the experts must use intuition and intelligence to judge the difference between recklessness and calculated risk.

The American Mountain Guides Association (AMGA) has tried to establish standard practices for the profession. Contact them at www.amga.com to locate an individual guide or climbing school in your area. While there are some fine guide services that refuse to belong to any organization, it's probably a good bet to go with an accredited school or individual. See Appendix D for more information on guides.

# Learning the Ropes

Books like this provide a map to get you off the couch, onto the road, and into the hills. Clearly, however, learning the subtleties of safety procedures, equipment, and route-finding requires a period of apprenticeship. As my grandmother likes to say, "A body makes her own luck, good or bad."

*Risk is part of the game. (Photo courtesy of Nels Akerlund.)*

The journey from beginner to expert is long, winding, and different for everyone. And yet there seems to be a predictable learning curve. Initially, new climbers are safety freaks, checking every knot, anchor, and piece of hardware like a mother hen. As time passes, some climbers get a bit cocky, ease up on safety procedures, and continue on until they nearly get zapped, read about an accident that strikes close to home, or, one hopes, wise up. Whatever flips the switch, this more vigilant attitude acknowledges that risk is part of the game and that one must be as careful in the mountains as a motorist driving down a crowded highway.

Learn to climb skillfully and safely, and respect the venue and the tradition in which you tread. The rewards are endless. John Muir, one of America's great naturalists and a superb climber in his own right, said it about as well as it can be said: "Climb the mountains, and get their good tiding. Nature's peace will flow into you as sunshine flows into trees. The winds will blow their own freshness into you and the storms their energy, while cares will drop off like autumn leaves."

---

## The Least You Need to Know

➤ If you think you want to climb, act on it. Check out some cool venues and see for yourself.

➤ Climbing safely requires proper instruction, proper fitness, and a sense of commitment.

➤ Learn the proper belaying techniques, and that slip will make for a good story and not an accident report.

➤ If you climb wisely, know your body's limitations, and do sport-specific exercises, you'll minimize your risk of injury.

➤ Because most fatalities result from human error, good judgment is a climber's most valuable ally.

---

# Chapter 3

# From Molehills to Mountains

## In This Chapter

➤ Bouldering in your backyard

➤ Going topside with a top-rope

➤ Getting a bead on traditional lead climbing

➤ Why "sport climbing" isn't redundant

➤ Competing for fun and profit

➤ Warming up to winter climbing

Saying "I want to climb" is a little like expressing the desire to travel; it's such a broad term that all it really means is that you want to go up. So what are your options? Let's see. You can climb rock or ice or, indoors, on textured fiberglass. You can practice top-roping, bouldering, or lead climbing. There are "sport," "trad," and "competitive" forms of climbing. There's even something called "buildering"—an esoteric niche for urban climbers hell-bent on scaling buildings without using the stairwell or elevator.

It can all get a bit confusing. The good news is that there's something for everyone, depending on your desired challenge and rock climbing experience. As long as you have basic physical fitness you should take to the rock like a potato to a couch (or something like that). So whether you're game to try your hand on Suicide Rock or content to just romp on a boulder in your back yard, it's good to know the options available to you.

**Nuts and Bolts**

**Bouldering** is the most basic form of rock climbing. It's usually done close to the ground and does not require the use of anchors, ropes, and harnesses.

**Bolts** are small rods of metal that are secured into pre-drilled holes in the rock.

# Getting High Real Low

*Bouldering* is climbing without rope, anchor bolts, or harnesses, often no more than six feet off the ground. It's becoming popular both on rocks and in climbing gyms, thanks to its accessibility, uncomplicated format, and instant intensity.

In an essay on mathematician and boulder climber extraordinaire John Gill, Jon Krakauer wrote that bouldering can "distill the cumulative challenges of an entire mountain into a compact chunk of granite or sandstone the size of a garbage truck or modest suburban house." Huh?

For some, bouldering is all the climbing they need. For others, it's a relatively safe way to practice intricate moves in preparation for multi-day climbs on towering walls of 1,000 feet or more.

*Your basic bouldering. (Photo courtesy of Mark Eller.)*

## *Live the Rock, Be the Rock*

Witness Yuki, a Japanese bouldering devotee and the unofficial custodian of Rat Rock at the south end of Manhattan's Central Park. When I first showed up at this massive granite slab of rock, I saw a man with the body of Bruce Lee and the face of a Zen master working on a series of strenuous moves on the rock's wrinkled face. His focus, grace, and serenity made it look easy. But it wasn't. Only when I tried in vain to replicate the first in a series of intricate moves he flawlessly executed—or "dialed in," to use his phrase—did I realize how ridiculously hard they were.

The next time I saw Yuki, I asked where he climbed outside of the park. "Only here," he said in his accented English. When I asked why, he replied, "Because there are an infinite number of things I can do here."

**Hold On**

Because even a short fall can be serious, it's best to have a partner on the ground "spot" the climber by bracing him if he falls. Using a crash pad, a portable foam mattress, is also a good way to protect landings in short falls.

**Cliff Notes**

Since 1983, Bobbi Bensman has won 12 Phoenix Bouldering Contests at Camelback Mountain in Scottsdale, Arizona. During her two decades of climbing, Bensman has racked up over 100 5.13 ascents and has won 20 national climbing competitions. This ardent spokesperson for women climbers travels throughout the United States giving workshops and seminars.

## Solving the Puzzle

Such pinpoint focus á la Yuki is a bit beyond my ken since climbing in new locales is one of the things I like best about the sport. For many, however, bouldering is the be-all and end-all in climbing. Why?

Bouldering is pure, no-frills climbing. It's just you, your shoes, some chalk, and the rock. Whether you're practicing difficult moves that you'd be hesitant to try five stories high or just traversing the base of a wall, bouldering will improve your strength, endurance, balance, and technique.

**Finger Tips**

When you're bouldering, it's a good idea to bring along a chalk bag for your hands and a mat to keep the soles of your shoes clean. Even if you climb with a partner, a crash pad is advisable. A company called Metolius makes the best pads on the market, starting at about $100.

Climbing aces like Ivan Greene, author of *Bouldering in the Shawungunks*, see a seemingly unclimbable rock face as a puzzle to be solved piece by piece; in the lexicon, boulder climbs are known as "problems." Many of Greene's solutions involve a series of insanely difficult moves requiring copious amounts of strength, flexibility, concentration, and moxie. Whereas Greene works on complicated moves on what I'd call the black diamond area, you'll be starting on the bunny-slope rocks where you can take your first fun steps. Moves you found awkward and intimidating will become second nature as you spend time on the rock; you'll gain balance and strength, increase your problem-solving ability, and be moving like an action hero.

Greene is one of those climbers who enjoys bouldering more than roped climbing. "It's the quickest way to improve your skills," he says. According to him, true bouldering problems require strong hands and fingers, excellent footwork, and balance. And because you can swiftly practice the same sequence of moves until you master them—without the fear of falling—you'll improve faster than if you'd spent the same amount of time doing roped climbs.

One of the best things about bouldering is that you don't need any gear other than a pair of good climbing shoes. Basic bouldering can be done on most rocks. Just traversing a route for 20 to 30 minutes a few times a week will reap significant improvement.

Before you start bouldering, here are a few common-sense tips:

➤ **Be aware of what's under you should you fall.** Rocks, glass, shrubs, and even your egg salad sandwich are poor landing zones.

➤ **Work on *downclimbing* rather than jumping off the rock.** You'll save your legs as well as get to practice a valuable (and difficult) skill.

➤ **Use a *crash pad* when you climb high enough to risk injury should you fall.** A crash pad is a large square of foam that will soften the landing. More broken bones result from bouldering than from roped climbing. And whether you have a pad or not, it's always a good idea to have a *spotter*.

**Nuts and Bolts**

**Downclimbing** is a way to retreat from a difficult route or to lower yourself off the rock.

A **crash pad** is a large square of foam you should use when climbing more than a few feet off the ground—just in case.

Your **spotter** is an invaluable partner who is on the ground following you along your bouldering route poised to assist you or control your landing if you should fall.

**Nuts and Bolts**

**Buildering**—bouldering on buildings—is a prime example of someone literally climbing the wall.

## Buildering

A funky alternative to bouldering is *buildering*, which is doing the Spiderman thing on the outside of buildings. Rough-hewn brick walls are best. My college roommate routinely scrambled up the outside of the Administration Building to the roof—a locale she considered the best place on campus for nude sunbathing. While a successful climb may earn you a great tan (sans lines), you are almost always breaking the law and run the risk of climbing the inside of a jail cell.

## Top-Rope Talk

Virtually all beginners who learn to climb with an instructor start by top-roping—and with good reason. It allows you to experience the sport in a controlled, safe way with far less stress than a multi-*pitch* climb that takes you hundreds of feet off the ground.

It's called "top-roping" because the belay comes from above the climber—as when a belayer brings up the second climber on a multi-pitch route. A "re-directed," or "slingshot," belay—the setup most beginners learn on—is where the rope system resembles a pulley. No mechanical advantage is gained, however. Typically, in a slingshot belay, your guide or seasoned partner will hike up a trail to the top or scramble up an easy route and rig the top-rope through a secure anchor—such as a tree, boulder, bolt, or gear placement—using *webbing runners*.

### Nuts and Bolts

A **pitch** is the section of a climb between progressive belay positions, restricted by the length of the rope—usually 60 meters (190 feet)—and typically kept within shouting distance for effective communication.

An **anchor** is the point at which a rope is fixed to a rock. Trees and rock outcroppings are natural anchors; nuts and bolts are artificial anchors.

**Webbing runners**, also called **slings**, typically are used for securing anchors, because the one-inch tubular nylon "webbing" from which they are made holds about 4,000 pounds.

*Top-roping. (Photo courtesy of Mark Eller.)*

# Climb On, Dude!

Because most folks start with top-rope climbing, it's a good idea to understand the basics even though you won't be rigging the setup yourself until you understand every facet of it. If any aspect of the top-rope setup is rigged improperly, disaster awaits you! As they say: The laws of gravity are strictly enforced—indoors and out.

What follows is an overview. For more detail on this vital skill, check out Chapter 9.

Once the rope is anchored above, you're nearly ready to rock. One end of the rope is for the climber; the other end is for the belayer, who is anchored to the ground—again, to a tree, rock, or some artificial form of protection that you devise.

When the climber is ready to climb, there's a fairly basic standard set of commands that climbers use. Here's the standard chain of commands that begins a climb (whether top-roped or leading):

> **Climber:** Am I on the belay?
>
> **Belayer:** Belay is on.
>
> **Climber:** Ready to climb.
>
> **Belayer:** Climb on (dude).
>
> **Climber:** (after a fall or reaching the top) Lower me!
>
> **Belayer:** Lowering!
>
> **Climber:** (reaches terra firma) Off belay.
>
> **Belayer:** Belay is off.

A word to the wise: To an experienced climber, top-roping feels extremely safe. For the beginner, however, the first few times are likely to be filled with anxiety. Fret not! This is natural. Unless you were a falcon or Anastasia Indian in a past life, standing on a minuscule ledge of rock 50 feet above the ground should feel as profoundly uncomfortable as it is exhilarating.

**Finger Tips**

Climbers tend to have muddy calves from wiping clean the bottoms of their shoes on the opposite lower leg. Why? Dirty shoes are slippery on rock.

## Slacking Off

When you learn to belay, you need to concentrate on giving a slight bit of slack to the climber. Too much and you run the risk of scaring the crap out of your friend if he falls; too little and the climber will feel as if he is being rushed up the route. Seasoned climbers, however, generally prefer a fair bit of slack in the rope when they go the top-rope route since they don't want their movement restricted. Assuming they trust their belay partner—and they'd be nuts to climb if they didn't—they know that if they fall they'll travel further but otherwise will be fine.

Anxious beginners (like I was) will feel more comfortable if the rope is pulled tighter. In fact, the first few times I climbed I yelled "tension!" so often that my belay partner considered legally changing his name.

## The Bottom Line

Most top-rope setups range from 40 to 80 feet. In the Verdon Gorge in France, however, climbers top-rope the enormous limestone cliffs on ropes that are nearly 200 feet long. Fall on one of those suckers and it will feel like bungee jumping.

The bottom line with top-roping is that it is a simple and safe way to climb without a lot of the time-consuming procedures required in lead climbing (which we'll talk about next). However, once you understand the mechanics of setting up the rope, you must check (and double-check) each of your anchors and knots. Done correctly, top-roping a joyous way to climb. We'll talk more about it in Chapter 9.

# A Leading Tradition

The consensus among serious climbers is that the real climbing doesn't begin until you take the lead. When you lead, you chose your own route, place your own "pro" (short for "protection"), and set your own anchors. That's why leading is called "taking up the sharp end of the rope." Making these important—and often life-threatening—decisions adds a powerful new dimension to a profound physical challenge: problem-solving. Do it well and you're likely to get hooked. Do it prematurely and you might not be able to do it again.

How does lead climbing differ from top-roping? The lead climber starts with no set anchor above. As the leader starts out ("Climbing!"), the belayer ("Climb away!") gives out the appropriate amount of slack. As the lead climber moves up the wall, he places protection that he carries either on his harness or on a *rack*—a piece of webbing worn bandoleer-style. How often he places the pro depends on the difficulty of the route, his skill level, and his sense of safety. If the leader falls, he will fall to that piece of pro, plus the same distance past the anchor until the rope tightens—assuming the belayer does his job.

### Hold On

Beware! Lead climbing should be done by experienced climbers only. Books like this can help you understand the principles of leading, but before you try it out, have an expert climber or professional guide review your skills.

### Nuts and Bolts

A **rack** is the whole selection of gear you carry on a climb. It's made up of carabiners and anchors that are clipped to standard runners or padded gear sling worn around shoulder.

If the climb is a single pitch, both climbers will rappel to the ground. If it's a multi-pitch effort, once the leader reaches the top of a solid ledge on the first pitch en route to the top, he anchors himself and belays his partner from above. The second climber then removes the pro as he follows the leader to his safe perch.

### Nuts and Bolts

In **traditional**, or **trad**, **climbing**, climbers place their own gear and protection.

A **crag** is a small outcropping of rock, usually with routes of one or two pitches.

### Hold On

Learn to lead from an expert. Plenty of things can go wrong, even for experienced leaders. Rock climbing is not like learning to play golf; you can die up there.

Lead climbing can take several different forms. Traditional leaders place gear in the rock as they go, whereas sport leaders rely on protection—such as bolts—that is already in place. Traditional, or "trad," climbing tests the leaders ability to find gear placements—and trust them—while moving up the route. In sport climbing, the protection is basically trouble-free; the real challenge comes from doing the moves that will get you to the top.

It goes without saying that you better know which end is up if you decide to lead. Not until you've mastered the basics—placing pro, rigging and equalizing anchors, and more—should you assume the risk.

Leading should be a natural progression in your climbing career. Just as you'd never enter a car race after receiving your learner's permit, you'd never take the sharp end of the rope until you've logged major rock time.

Put another way: Lead climbing is complicated stuff, involving far more risk than top-roping. Start by having an experienced leader show you the basics. A season or two later you might be ready to tie in on the sharp end. Be sure that the person you are learning from really knows what he's doing. A lot of leaders get by on luck and guts—at least for a while. If you have the money to hire an accredited guide, do so; you can expect to learn the right way a lot faster than if you just try to pick up leading skills from watching your buddy.

## The Sporty Cousin

If climbing is a sport, what the heck is "sport climbing?"

*Sport climbing* is climbing on routes protected exclusively by pre-drilled *bolts* instead of by a leader who places removable pro in the rock as he moves along. (There are also "mixed" routes, which require both.)

Because the emphasis in sport climbing is on gymnastic movement, it's a bit like the high end of bouldering. (Another similarity is that the emphasis is on shorter, extremely difficult moves.) Because the anchors are pre-set steel bolts (read: basically bomb proof), experienced climbers are able, with a minimal amount of risk, to push the limits of what was previously thought possible.

Technology has played a significant role in this increasingly visible side of climbing. Since the advent of battery-powered drills, it's been easier than ever to bolt a route. Looking a bit like a cable-TV installer, a climber can ascend and bolt a desirable climbing route, *rappel* down, and then try to climb it in one fell swoop.

As you might have guessed, bolting is a controversial subject among environmentalists and traditional climbers who feel it degrades the rock. No matter which side of the argument you're on, there's no debate that sport climbing has raised the standard in climbing. The fitness and refined, ultra-athletic skills sport climbers nurture have been transferred onto longer alpine as well as traditional routes.

One example of how sport climbing has inspired its traditional cousin is Lynn Hill's inspiring and historic climb on the Nose route on El Capitan in Yosemite. While Hill utilized her traditional climbing background and placed her own gear on the entire route, she used pre-placed protection on the hardest pitches—a style she learned from sport climbing. Hill's blending of sport and traditional climbing made for an inspiring and historic ascent that's still talked about with awe today.

**Nuts and Bolts**

**Rappelling** is when a climber lowers herself on a stationary rope, using one of many available friction methods to control the speed of the descent.

## Compete with Your Hands and Feet

Take two guys paid to count toothpicks for a week and they'll eventually start a contest to see who can count the fastest. The roots of climbing lie in the concept of man harmonizing with nature, working with the rock or mountain rather than against other climbers. With man being the competitive beast that he is, however, competition climbing has become a very visible part of the vertical scene.

**Cliff Notes**

Most of the early competitions took place on actual outdoor cliffs. This was soon abandoned, however, in favor of artificial climbing walls. Today, all sanctioned international competitions take place on man-made walls with extreme overhanging sections (five or six meters out from vertical) and routes designed to push the envelope of what's possible. The first World Cup competition held in the United States was in Snowbird, Utah, in 1989.

Competition climbing grew out of sport climbing, which evolved from traditional climbing. In short, one led to the other. And though they're all different, they're all very much the same. Now that we have that out of the way, know this:

➤ Traditionally, rules and climbing have been like oil and water. Not until the 1980s did national climbing federations start to organize competitions with established rules and regulations.

➤ The first major event recognized by the powers that be took place on the shores of Lake Garda, Italy, in 1985. The hosts set a route on the steep outdoor rock faces below an ancient citadel. Bolting the rock caused major agitation in the climbing community, and subsequent competitions around the world took place indoors or on unaltered crags.

While the bolting issue created controversy in the climbing community, that's no longer the case in Italy. Some areas are now equipped as sport areas and others are left for traditional climbing. At the time of the first Arco competition, bolting was less popular, and especially the thought of bolting a crag just for one competition offended many climbers. Today bolting is the norm in that same region.

➤ ESPN's *X-Games* have done a lot to popularize this blitzkrieg style of climbing. Men and women compete in three categories: difficulty, speed, and bouldering. Difficulty is the most popular and prestigious class. Time is not a consideration in this category time; the winner is the climber who gets to the highest hold on the route.

While many traditional climbers look at sport and competition climbers as wimpy prima donnas who retreat at the first sign of a raindrop, both the latter disciplines have made climbing more popular and, therefore, more accessible to the general public. Once you've tried climbing, you will marvel at what these ripped climbing machines are able to do. The training necessary to compete in a contest at your local indoor gym will improve your fitness and make you a better all-around climber.

### Cliff Notes

Height doesn't mean might: David Pothier of South Africa, at 6'2", was the tallest climbing competitor in the 1995 ESPN *Extreme Games;* Mari Guillet of France was the shortest, at 4'11".

*Competition climber, Katie Brown on an indoor wall. (Photo courtesy of Mark Eller.)*

## Chills in the Hills

Many rock climbers once looked at winter as the no-fun season when they'd have to shelve their vertical desires until spring. Now the same folks break out their ice-climbing gear, take to the chilly hills, and rejoice.

What's made winter climbing safer, more comfortable, and chic is the advent of lighter, warmer, water-resistant clothing (thank you, Gore-Tex); improved (and cool-looking) hardware, such as tubular ice screws and lightweight ice axes; and telecasts on ESPN's *Winter X Games*. As a result, it's never been more popular to climb frozen waterfalls and often-fragile curtains of ice that result from winter run-off.

### Nuts and Bolts

Used for climbing or trekking on ice, **crampons** are metal-framed devices that attach to the bottom of boots. They usually have 12 "points," two pointing forward and ten pointing down.

**Hold On**

Don't attempt ice climbing on your own; learn from a reputable guide or guiding service. Many top guiding services are accredited by the American Mountain Guides Association and provide quality ice climbing gear to rent or buy.

To get started, go to a guide service, rent some gear, learn from an expert, and check it out. You'll need lined, plastic mountaineering boots, *crampons*, a harness, a helmet, and ice axes—or "tools," as they're commonly called.

Know this: Ice climbing with a top-rope is dangerous enough because you'll be swinging sharp steel picks like a frenzied blacksmith and kicking into the ice with spiky footwear that could shred the tires of an 18-wheeler. A multi-pitch climb without the proper safety procedures, however, is suicidal.

That said, ice climbing, done properly, is much safer than most people imagine. Ed Palen, the head of a guide service in the Adirondacks called Rock & River, says that "climbing ice becomes dangerous when the route is too hard or if someone doesn't know what they're doing. The deadliest thing in the mountains is the male ego."

### The Least You Need to Know

➤ Bouldering is the simplest way to practice your rock climbing technique.

➤ Most beginners learn to climb by using a top-rope.

➤ Lead climbing is the next part of a natural learning curve.

➤ Sport climbing tends to be the province of advanced rock jocks.

➤ As seen on ESPN's *X-Games*, competition climbing is a spectacular new development.

➤ Improved clothing and gear has made ice climbing more accessible, and more popular, than ever.

# Gearhead 101

Some women adore cashmere; others, jewelry; still others have a weakness for fur. Me, I'm a gearhead. I love the high-tech look and feel of a good rack stocked with all sorts of cool, shiny climbing hardware. But I'm getting ahead of myself.

Before you run out and buy the whole enchilada—harness, helmet, carabiners, a belay/rappel device, shoes, gear sling, chalk bag, chalk—make sure you're ready to take the plunge. (Sorry, bad choice of words.) Make sure you're committed to climbing, because the whole package can run you anywhere from $1,500 to $3,000, depending on where you plan to climb and how deep your pockets are.

Beware when it comes to buying or borrowing second-hand gear—unless you know where it comes from and how much wear and tear it's endured. If you're borrowing shoes or a harness from your 105-pound friend who's used it for a season, fine. But if you don't know your gear's history, you're compromising your safety. In a sport that depends so heavily on sound equipment, it's only sensible to buy the best gear you can afford; it's worth it when your live literally depends on it.

This chapter provides an overview of the various types of gear you'll need. We'll examine them in greater detail in Part 2.

# Carabiner Classics

They're *carabiners*, but everyone calls them *"biners,"* and they've come to symbolize climbing. In fact, biners have replaced the bottle-opener as the key chain of choice.

**Nuts and Bolts**

A **carabiner** (or **biner**) is a metal device that opens on one side (the *gate*). **Locking carabiners**—they feature a screwgate that requires you to twist a sleeve to lock the gate—ensure a higher level of safety than non-locking carabiners.

(Just for the record: I use a biner to clip my keys to my clunker commuter bike, Fireball.) To start, you'll need just two *locking carabiners* to use with your belay device. As you progress in the sport, however, you'll acquire these indispensable devices the way Amelda Marcos acquired shoes.

Biners come in many shapes, but the two essentials are the oval and the D." The oval is the all-purpose, heavy-duty momma. Expect to pay about $5 or $6 for an average biner and a few dollars more for some of the fancier models. If you're checking out biners at a climbing shop for the first time, you'll notice models with oddly shaped bent gates. These are designed for sport climbers where clipping into the rope quickly is at a premium.

The "D's" are stronger than the ovals because more of the load is transferred away from the gate (the typical point of failure) and along the shaft. When it comes to biners, getting "shafted" is a good thing.

In addition to size, there's another way to distinguish between types of biners; they're either locking or non-locking. The locking variety, the heavier of the two, has a small sleeve that screws over the gate to stop it from opening when you don't want it to. This is your workhorse; you'll use it when belaying and rappelling. A locking biner looks stronger than the non-locking variety, but it's not. It just stays closed better—assuming you remember to lock it!

How strong is strong? Made from aluminum alloy, biners have a minimum breaking point of roughly 4,000–5,000 pounds along the long arm (or axis) and about 500 pounds along the minor axis. The numbers vary according to the manufacturer and the particular biner. The strength of a biner is usually marked somewhere on the gate, generally in kilo Newtons (kN). (No relation to the fig variety.) One kN is equal to a heavyweight boxer: roughly 220 pounds. Said simply: They're bleepin' brawny. However, don't store them in your freezer, don't use ones that you drop out of an airplane, and shy away from abandoned biners that you find at the bottom on the cliff—unless, of course, you plan to turn them into key chains.

Given the consequences of a biner popping open when you don't want it to, you might be wondering, "Why not use locking carabiners all the time?" As I said, for top-roping and rappelling, absolutely! For lead climbing, however, where you will climb hundreds (sometimes thousands) of feet up a big wall, weight becomes an issue. More importantly, because clipping in and out of the biner must be done quickly, under great strain, with one hand, and often with gloves, the locking variety are dangerous.

That's the basic biner skinny. Here are a few helpful do's and don'ts:

### Finger Tips

Carabiner gates should be cleaned regularly. Apply a solvent or lubricant (such as oil, kerosene, or white gas) to the to the hinge and work the hinge open and shut until it operates smoothly. Then dip the carabiner into boiling water for 20 seconds to remove the cleaning agent.

➤ Check your biners like a mother hen would her chicks. Even locking gates can open from vibrations or rubbing against the rock.

➤ Make sure that the gate (the little arm that clicks open and shut) doesn't receive the brunt of the load. This is important for both locking and non-locking biners.

➤ The gates should open with a minimum of pressure. If they don't, the hinge might be jammed with grit. Any solvent should fix this problem. To get rid of the excess solvent, dip it in boiling water. Truly devoted climbers drink the water afterwards. (I'm kidding!)

➤ Make sure the gate has good side-to-side integrity when open. If not, toss it.

➤ Always retire a carabiner that has fallen more than 15 or 20 feet onto a hard surface; its structure may be weakened. Beginners tend to resist this advice and continue to use dropped biners. Don't! Spending money on climbing gear can (and will) save your life.

➤ Oh yeah: Biners sold as key chains are intended for this use only. Never use one for climbing unless you're prepared to drive down the side of a cliff.

# Cinderella's Slippers

The first time you try on a pair of climbing shoes, they're so snug you'll feel like one of Cinderella's stepsisters, cramming your foot into a shoe meant for someone else. Once you try climbing with them, however, you'll realize that the discomfort is well worth it. (See Chapter 5 for more on shoe selection and fit.)

Most rock shoes are low cut and worn sans socks. The uppers are soft and flexible on the top; the soles are made of smooth, stiff (yet pliable) rubber and are s-n-u-g as a ballet slipper. Today's shoes are made with stickier soles than in the past, which help climbers push the proverbial envelope. (I wear "Diamonds," a model of shoe made by a company called Five Ten; the shoes are cut narrow and are specially designed for women. Before I found these I had to cinch my shoes so tight that the material on top would overlap.)

These grippy shoes are a far cry from the old ankle-high, rubber-soled boots wore by mountaineers in the '40s and '50s. Those leather boots were fine on hard snow and for hopping across boulders, and they kept toes warm in cold weather. The soles were cleated, however, which reduced the surface area in contact with the rock.

### Cliff Notes

When Spanish rubber arrived in the United States in the early 1980s, the revolution in climbing shoes began. Fires (*FEE-rays*) were the new shoes on the block, sporting super-sticky soles. Friction moves that had been impossible soon became the norm. Today, all top-quality shoes have sticky rubber soles.

It seems counterintuitive, but the smooth sole is what makes the shoes so effective. Cleats can't bite into rock, no matter how hard they are. But rock digs into rubber. So the more contact, the better the grip.

As you'll see once you start climbing, your shoes will be called on to do different things depending on the rock and the steepness of the wall you're on:

➤ On low-angled smooth granite, the shoes must be flexible enough to maximize rubber-on-rock contact.

➤ On steep sandstone or sharp granite, the shoes need to be stiff enough to stand on tiny footholds.

➤ On limestone, a soft stone with a lot of pockets, the shoes need to be thin enough so that you can actually feel for holds with your toes, much like a monkey climbing a tree. Sometimes you'll have to jam your toes into cracks to gain a foothold when there are no others. This is a rather miserable feeling that will have you hunting for your floppiest slippers when you get home.

Although there is considerable debate over which shoe is best, some contend that it's the climber, not the footwear, that makes the difference. While training in the Gunks in upstate New York for the Raid Gauloises, a 10-day multi-sport race I did in Ecuador in 1998, I was talking to my climbing partner about which pair of climbing shoes I should bring.

A wiry guy standing next to me said, in so many words, that it didn't matter what shoes I brought, since nothing I would climb there would be technically difficult. I said there might be stuff as challenging as what we were standing under—a route that I was working hard to ascend. He walked up to the wall in his battered tennis shoes and scampered to the top.

After a moment of stunned silence, I called up to him, "Do those come in a women's size 7 1/2?"

# The Rope Is Your Friend

A rope is a climber's best friend: his lifeline, security blanket, guide-wire, and safety net all wrapped in one. Your dependence on the rope is obvious: If the section of rock you're climbing exceeds your skill; if the ledge you're on or handhold you grab breaks away; or if a falling rock knocks you off the wall, you'll instinctively pray to the Rope God to catch your airborne butt.

At the same time, a climber's reliance on the rope is psychological. The first time you tie this coil of braided nylon onto your harness, you'll check and re-check your *figure-8 knot* so often that you'll embarrass even yourself. The first time you rappel off the rock, you'll have a hard time letting go of the rope.

When I was rappelling for the first time off a 300-foot cliff during my first multi-day adventure race in Xichang, China, my teammates continually had to remind me "to lean back and let go of the rope." When I touched the ground, I kissed the rope and my guiding teammate—though my affection for the rope was far more profound.

This experience of psychological dependency on the rope (and your mate belaying you), coupled with its practical necessity, is why the rope, more than any other piece of equipment, symbolizes climbing and a climber's relationship with his or her partner.

## *From Hemp to Kernmantle*

In the early no-guts, no-glory days of climbing, ropes were made of natural fibers such as manila, sisal, and hemp. These ropes were not reliable, however, especially when a climber took a severe fall. With virtually no elasticity, they couldn't stretch and often snapped.

The advent of nylon ropes during World War II changed the sport. Before you could say "General

### Nuts and Bolts

**Figure-8 knots** are easy to tie, strong, and won't freeze up under a heavy load. They are used where an overhand knot would work and are the choice method for tying into a harness, using a retraced figure-8 knot. (See Chapter 8 for more on knots.)

### Nuts and Bolts

**UIAA** stands for the *Union Internationale des Associations D'Alpinisme*, the internationally recognized authority for setting standards for climbing equipment. All gear sporting the UIAA label meets with strict safety standards. Look for the little UIAA tag on harnesses, helmets, ropes, and various brands of carabiners.

MacArthur," climbers had lightweight ropes capable of bearing more than two tons. And, more important, instead of bringing a falling climber to an abrupt halt, nylon ropes stretched to reduce a lot of the impact. Having endured a few short plunges myself, I can only imagine how intense climbing was in the hemp rope days when you knew that a fall probably would be fatal. Give me elasticity or give me death!

Eventually, nylon ropes were replaced by an improved version called kernmantle, which consists of a core of braided nylon filaments inside a smooth, woven sheath of nylon. Kernmantle ropes have the same properties as regular nylon rope, only they're better. Today, kernmantle ropes are the only ones approved by the *UIAA*, the international authority in setting standards for climbing equipment.

The UIAA tests are thorough. To be approved, a rope must withstand five UIAA test drops. Some manufacturers make ropes that are supposedly able to withstand 12 or more. Suffice it to say, the UIAA simulated fall is far more intense than any fall you'll subject the rope to. As expert climber John Long said of the UIAA test, "...It's about like tying off a dairy cow and marching her off the cliff's edge for a 300-footer."

## The Dope on Rope

Here are a few linear facts on the climber's lifeline. The following information concerns a single rope. For the record: Ropes are also sold to be used in tandem. Double (or twin) ropes have a UIAA label of "2" on the end; single ropes are marked with a "1".

➤ Ropes come in a range of lengths, thicknesses, and colors. The heavier the rope, the more falls it will usually be rated for. The new lightweight lines don't last as long.

➤ Typically, climbers use a 50-meter (164-foot) rope, though there's been a recent trend toward longer (60-meter or 196-foot) and slightly thinner ropes.

➤ If you use a rope shorter than 50 meters, you may run out of line before the next anchor. This realization often inspires a high-decibel string of expletives acknowledging that a severe tactical error has been made.

**Finger Tips**

Use a 50-meter or longer rope; most established climbing routes assume the climber is using a rope of at least that length.

➤ The term "working elongation" refers to the amount of stretch a rope provides in a typical fall. A lot of stretch makes for "soft" catches but increases the risk of banging into something you might not want to bang into.

➤ Water-resistant ropes also are available. These "dry" ropes absorb far less water than non-water-resistant ropes and are favored by ice climbers, who often must contend with melting snow and ice and extreme temperature swings. These dry ropes are expensive but can save you wear and tear on your body, since a wet rope is a heavy rope. If the water-resistant coating gets frayed, however, it will take on $H_2O$ just like an uncoated one.

➤ You'll spend between $120 and $200 for a 50-meter rope, depending on the brand. Don't buy a second-hand rope unless you're using it to walk your dog.

# Hip Harnesses

Long before climbing became trendy and harnesses became fashion statements (well, in some circles), climbers wrapped the climbing rope around their waists a few times and tied in with a funky knot we'll discuss later called a bowline-on-a-coil. They don't anymore. Long falls with that system are likely to fracture your back and ribs or restrict your diaphragm so severely as to reduce your IQ to double digits.

Although you can construct a safe and fairly comfortable harness out of webbing, it's best to buy one of the many commercial models out there. They're comfortable, lightweight, safe, and strong.

Made of wide nylon webbing and padded in strategic areas, harnesses are really just waist belts with leg loops. The waist belt, fastened by a metal buckle, holds you when you fall. The leg loops are designed to distribute the force of a fall over a larger percentage of your body (read: butt) and ensure that you won't look like an hour glass if and when you find yourself dangling over a crevasse.

**Cliff Notes**

Sylvester Stallone's movie *Cliffhanger* opens with a gnarly fall that occurs as a result of a buckle breaking. Since this is next to impossible, it outraged many climbers and manufacturers.

While there are separate designs for men, women, and children, the two basic harness types are the diaper and the leg-loop. The differences are too tedious to explain; suffice it to say that the diaper style has adjustable leg loops that enable you to drop the loops and, thus, your pants, without unbuckling the harness—a key feature for women who cannot avail themselves of a fly.

Regardless of the style, the harness must fit snugly around your waist just above your hipbones. The waist belt must be long enough for you to double it back through the buckle.

**Finger Tips**

When using a leg-loop style harness, tie the climbing rope directly though both the waistband and the leg loops—*not* through the belay loop.

**Hold On**

The harness's waist belt is what actually holds you in, so make sure it fits very snugly around your waist at the top of hipbones. Remember: Double back your buckle. If you don't, you will get hurt or killed.

Doubling back the harness buckle is essential! I repeat: Failure to do so may result in death. Most harnesses have a red stripe on the buckle that remains visible if you don't double it back. Remember the old adage "see red and you're dead," and you're likely to enjoy many more opportunities to drop your drawers out of doors.

# Chalk It Up

Like gymnasts, most climbers use chalk when climbing, especially when it's hot. Chalk (a.k.a. magnesium carbonate) helps to keep your hands and fingers dry and improves your grip on the rock. A block of chalk costs around a buck; the bag, which hangs from a cord or belt worn around your waist, goes for around $15.

*Climbing instructor, Ivan Greene, on an indoor wall at Chelsea Piers Sports Center. Note the chalkbag hanging from his waist. (Photo courtesy of Mark Eller.)*

No big deal, right? Well, sort of.

In the southwest or in southern California, where it rarely rains, the liberal use of chalk is frowned upon since it leaves white splash marks and mars the aesthetics of the rock—making it look like a kitchen where two-year-olds were making bread.

Another objection is that these splotches make the handholds as obvious as the color-coded ones you find on indoor walls. This, in turn, takes away some of the challenge of discovering the best line—a subtle and important skill climbers learn as they progress in the sport.

When I started I loved chalk marks for this reason. And I really don't mind these "tic marks" now, especially since I live and climb in the East, where Mother Nature regularly washes the evidence from "the scene of the crime." Regardless, cagey climbers use tic marks like Hansel and Gretel used breadcrumbs, because they often lead to hard-to-find footholds or hidden handholds. Big tic marks are ugly, of course, so feel free to practice good housekeeping and brush them off the rock.

### Cliff Notes

Some climbers carry a small toothbrush with them to clean not only chalk on frequently used routes but also holds that have been left slimy from sweat. They're not known, however, to bring toothpaste and floss—unless they plan to spend consecutive days on the rock

There are colored chalks available that blend in with the rock, as well as a product called Grrrip, which absorbs perspiration without leaving a visible mark. The bottom line is to check with locals to learn what flies in that particular locale. When in Rome, climb as the Romans do. Even if it's considered kosher to chalk up, however, do so judiciously.

Finally, when buying a chalk bag, make sure your hand slips easily in and out of the little sucker. It would be embarrassing to fall because your hand got stuck. Don't laugh; it's happened.

# Always Use Protection

Climbers use a host of artificial anchoring devices collectively called "protection," or "pro." When you start out, of course, you won't be placing pro in the rock, so you won't need to know how a chock differs from a cam. You're likely to feel a lot better, however, if you know how these gizmos work and why they're a standard part of a climber's arsenal.

## Chock-Full of Nuts

A *nut*, or *chock*, is a tapered metal wedge designed to be placed in a crack. Placed correctly, these small wedges, strung with a cord or wire cable, are perfect pieces of protection should a climber take leave of the rock. They might look flimsy, but they're not.

### Nuts and Bolts

A **nut**, or **chock**, is a metal wedging device designed to be slotted into a crack as an anchor. Unlike pitons, which often damages the rock, nuts are placed into narrow cracks—with solid surface contact—and easily removed.

*Chock-type gear. (Photo courtesy of Mark Eller.)*

Here's a bit of chock history:

In the beginning, British climbers used naturally wedge-shaped stones (chockstones) that they stuck into cracks and wrapped with cord. Some of these cheeky chaps fell far and hard on such half-assed protection, but it was better than nothing when they logged airtime.

**Nuts and Bolts**

The **Hex**, which is short for the Hexentric, is a six-sided chock that comes in at least 10 different sizes. This relatively inexpensive barrel-shaped device is wedged between cracks and has been called "the strongest nut in town."

How did nuts enter the equation? In England, inventive climbers used machine nuts that they found along the railroad tracks leading to their climbs. By looping a cord through the center hole, they manufactured a sturdy metal chock that could be used as a removable wedge. Hence, "chocks" took on the additional name "nuts."

The next big leap in technology was the *Hexentric*, designed by that brilliant climber and one-time blacksmith, Yvon Chouinard. Known as the "*Hex*," this six-sided, barrel-shaped chock resembles the original machine-nut shape.

Whether you hear the term *chock* or *nut*, *taper* or *stopper*, *Hex* or *Hexentrics*, all you need to know right now is that these artificial metal anchors come in different sizes and shapes and are designed to fit different-sized cracks in the rock.

## The Cam Is Your Friend, Too

In the late 1970s a funky-looking piece of pro made a big splash in the climbing world. Unlike the chock, which is simple in form and function, this "active," or *spring-loaded, camming device* looked like a kitchen device on the Starship Enterprise. Invented in 1978 by Ray Jardine, it was called the "Friend." Simply put, this ingenious protection device revolutionized free climbing.

Suddenly, climbers didn't need a bottleneck crack to place their pro in. For the first time, parallel cracks were no problem, since the harder you pulled, the more the cams were forced outward and the better they held. They were easy to insert and almost always easy to remove. These clever, adaptable gadgets became testament to the expression, "A friend in need is a friend indeed."

### Nuts and Bolts

A spring-loaded camming device (SLCD), or *cam*, widens as it rotates. Unlike a nut, which needs to fit snugly in a crack, the beauty of the SLCD is that the crack doesn't need to constrict to afford a solid placement. When pulled from below, it expands into its hold in the rock.

## Everything in Its Place

Placing pro is not for beginners. Climbing with an experienced rock jock is the only way to learn this subtle skill. Right now, feel content to gaze with admiration at these nifty devices. If you're feeling cocky, you might want to greet a climber carrying a loaded rack with an admiring "Cool nuts, man!" (On second thought, save it for your friends.)

### The Least You Need to Know

➤ Climbers get to play with all sorts of fun and inventive hardware—especially if they play it safe.

➤ Carabiners, or "biners," have come to symbolize climbing.

➤ You won't wear climbing shoes one second longer than you have to, but you'll wear them.

➤ The kernmantle rope is the most indispensable part of a climber's arsenal.

➤ Today's harnesses are designed for men, women, and children.

➤ Chalk improves your grip on the rock, but try not to leave it lying around.

➤ Chocks, Nuts, Hexes and Friends might sound like a law firm, but they're actually the hardware lead climbers carry up and down the rock.

# Part 2
# Tech Talk

*Unless you're climbing indoors, the farther you venture from the parking lot, the more gear you'll need to take along. In fact, Himalayan expeditions require enough gear to feed and clothe an army. While few of us will ever climb Mt. Everest, the fact remains that climbing is a gear-intensive sport. Not only must you protect yourself from the elements, but you also need ample equipment for the actual climb, including proper shoes, a harness, hardware, a helmet, and a rope.*

*In Part 2, I'll give you the low-down on what you need and what to think about when you buying it. While climbing gear isn't cheap, the fun part is that it's really cool stuff. And if you're a gearhead like me, you'll enjoy perusing the shelves for what suits you best.*

*I'll also talk about the mechanics of belaying (belay who?) and the X's and O's of caring for your vital lifeline—the rope. Figuring out what makes this risky sport far safer than you may think is a big part of learning the ropes.*

# Chapter 5

# Mind, Body, and Sole

## In This Chapter

➤ Finding the right shoes

➤ Shoe care and wear

➤ Harnessing your climbing desire

➤ Harness do's and don'ts

➤ Helmets are warm, but are they cool?

The first time I went climbing I was too cautious (read: cheap) to buy dedicated rock climbing shoes. Since I wasn't sure whether this far-out sport was for me, I couldn't see shelling out $100 or more for a pair of specialty shoes—even if I do have a major shoe fetish. (Luckily, I don't have a harness or helmet obsession...but more on those key pieces of equipment later in the chapter.)

That first day of climbing in my hiking boots was comical—though not for me. While my friends were scampering up the rock in stiff-soled climbing shoes like squirrels up a tree, I was spinning like a poodle on ice—scrapping, sliding, and unable to find solid purchase with my bulky clodhoppers.

The next time I hit the crag, I wised up, stopped into the local climbing store, and dropped $169 on a pair of tight, grippy shoes. The difference was shocking. As my grandmother once told me: "You can use a shoe to hammer a nail, but a hammer works better." Wise woman, my grandma.

## Shoes Your Weapon

You don't need an excellent pair of climbing shoes to start out with, but if you try to climb in hiking boots or running shoes, you're likely to regret it. Years ago, there weren't that many styles of climbing shoes. Today, however, there are as many as there are breakfast cereals in a supermarket, including all-purpose models that do well on a variety of rocks, as well as specialized shoes made for specific types of climbing.

*There are many kinds of shoes to choose from. (Photo courtesy of Mark Eller.)*

While the selection can be dizzying, they're basically variations on a theme, since all of them have sticky, stiff rubber soles. The most important things to keep in mind when choosing a pair are (1) fit and (2) the amount of flexibility in the sole.

## The Rule of Toe

With climbing shoes, of course, "fit" is a relative term. Unlike hiking boots, running shoes, or just about any other footwear you'll ever slip into, climbing shoes should be snug—real snug. Actually, they often fit as tightly as the designer jeans many women (like me) were nuts enough to wear in the early '80s. (You know, the paint-them-on-so-tight kind that forced you to ask a stranger for help if you dropped anything on the ground. I'd like to see Lynn Hill, one of the greatest female climbers, get up El Capitan in a pair of those.)

Typically, you'll wear them without socks and squeeze into a pair that are a size or size-and-a-half smaller than your street shoes. Experts, who often use their feet like a second pair of hands, often wear shoes that are two sizes too small—a claustrophobic fit that actually crunches the toes together like commuters on a rush hour subway. For first-timers, a better benchmark than size, however, is to find a pair where the toes push against the end of the shoe. Within that decidedly uncomfortable feel, find the pair that feels the "best."

Author Don Mellor, a first-rate rock and ice climber in the Adirondacks, has a good rule of thumb that I call the "try-it-on-and-see-if-you-faint theory." He suggests you slip on a pair of shoes and browse the store for about 15 minutes. If you contemplate strangling the shoe salesman (or wish someone would strangle you), the shoes are a tad too tight. If it seems as though you could walk a half-mile without losing a toe, then you're close. But if you can imagine walking two miles comfortably, well, the shoes are too big. This is a similar, if slightly more bizarre, version of what top running shoe stores like the Super Runner in New York City do when they insist you run up and down the sidewalk for a few minutes to make sure your shoes feel fine.

**Finger Tips**

Keep in mind that shoes with fabric linings don't stretch very much. Unlined shoes, meanwhile, have just a single layer of leather that, with use, will stretch at least one full size and conform to your foot.

**Hold On**

You want your shoes to feel like they've been buried in sand. The fabric should not have any gaps when you tighten the shoe, and your foot should not have any breathing room. This doesn't mean you need be in pain; think snug, not suffocating.

In essence, the perfect fit will feel as though you've immersed your bare feet into wet cement. The perfect fit will be as if the shoe were molded to your foot. Think of yourself as Cinderella without the high heel.

Here's all you'll ever need to know about buying your first pair of climbing shoes:

1. Sizes vary for different manufacturers—even year to year within the same company. Try several sizes and types for the best fit.

2. All shoes stretch. Lined shoes stretch less and hence feel tighter longer than unlined shoes. Conversely, unlined shoes, which initially are more comfortable, stretch several sizes with use.

3. Don't buy climbing shoes through a mail-order company unless you've actually tried on the model.

# That Much?

Unless you find a terrific sale, you can expect to spend around $90–$110 for your first pair of shoes. And unless you rent or borrow the first few times, once you decide to buy a pair, it's probably not worth it to get the super deluxe model with bells and whistles. The top-end models run from $130-170.

### Nuts and Bolts

A **boardie** shoe has a very stiff sole. It supports your foot when standing on a hold and is good for beginners who need to slowly develop foot strength.

The rationale behind not going wild on your first pair of shoes is that beginner's usually sport sloppy footwork, which is rough on shoes—especially outdoors on sharp rock. (Indoor gyms are much more forgiving.) Essentially, you'll want a decent, good-fitting pair that you can beat on and not fret over when you see how fast they get chewed up. Unless you've been climbing indoors on rental shoes a lot, think of your first pair of rock shoes as a cross between training wheels and a sacrificial lamb.

## Board Stiff

*Boardies*—the general term for "the stiffest of the stiff shoes"—are better suited for sustained, steep climbs, where you need to stand on the edge of your sole on small, sharp rock features. Conversely, really stiff shoes are a liability on lower-angled climbs, where you want to maximize the amount of contact between rubber and rock. In other words: Stiff shoes are for seasoned climbers. Some of these specialized shoes are so tight that they do sinister things to your feet in a matter of hours. To me, these restrictive shoes are also important for another reason: They're the closest thing men will ever know to what it's like wearing high heels all day.

### Finger Tips

Stiffer soles make it easier to stand on small surfaces, but softer, more flexible shoes grab surfaces better. Beginners should seek out a moderately stiff, all-purpose model.

## The Happy Medium

The best route to take early on is to get a moderately stiff, all-purpose model. Ask other climbers and knowledgeable store clerks what they prefer and, again, try a lot of different kinds.

Here are a few things you should know about a good, all-purpose shoe:

1. It's stiff enough to let you *edge* yet flexible enough to allow you to *friction*. In other words, you can use the outside of the shoe to stand on a nub of rock and plaster it on a low-angled rock face to stick like glue.

2. Just because it claims to be an all-purpose shoe doesn't mean it's sub-par. Actually, a good quality shoe that can "do it all" is often referred to as a "long-route" shoe—meaning it can waltz its way up a variety of rock surfaces and remain comfortable all day.

3. It comes in low or high top—98 percent of the shoes on the market are low tops. Your choice is really a matter of style, although if you're climbing in an area with a lot of cracks (long, vertical fissures in the rock), you may want high tops for better ankle protection.

## The Friction Option

In the good old days of climbing, before there were a dozen different styles of shoes for as many kinds of rock, some of the more difficult overhanging routes were done barefoot, because that was the only way climbers could grab the precarious holds. (Essentially, they turned their feet into hands.) If tackling funky boulder problems is your cup of tea, or if you plan to climb primarily indoors where overhanging features are popular, go with friction shoes—even if you're a beginner. Remember, however, that at first your feet and toes will lack the strength necessary to try these moves. Be patient, and in no time you'll be picking up loose change with your toes.

### Nuts and Bolts

**Edging** is the using the side of a climbing shoe or boot to stand on a thin ledge.

**Friction climbing,** or **frictioning,** typically is done on low-angled rock where the climber tries to get the optimum amount of shoe rubber onto the rock for adhesion.

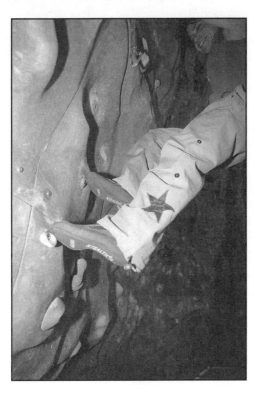

*Some climbing shoes in action. (Photo courtesy of Mark Eller.)*

# Gripper Slippers

*Slippers*, climbing shoes sans laces, are the skimpiest of climbing footwear. Because they're so thin and offer far less protection than traditional shoes, they force your foot to work much harder. Conventional wisdom suggests that unless you are a superb climber or a TV action hero, you won't need to own a pair. The wafer-thin soles give the feel of climbing barefoot without the agony of skin-on-rock. Having said that, I know a first-rate guide who often recommends slippers to novices since they're cheap, climb well in a gym, and will get the job done for the first outdoor foray as well.

Yet, as one of my climbing friends says, "Wearing slippers requires mondo foot strength." And if you don't know what "mondo" means, don't think about wearing them.

### Nuts and Bolts

**Slippers** are climbing shoes that you "slip" on. They have no laces and feature a very flexible sole, requiring superior foot strength to support your body weight.

# Sole Food

If you take care of your shoes, you should be able to use them for two or three years. If you climb once or twice a summer, of course, they should last you 40 or 50 years. The bottom line is that all shoes, no matter how pampered, get stretched out. Once the correct fit is compromised, performance drops.

Clearly, you need to make sure the laces aren't frayed and about to snap—not a good move halfway up a route. Moreover, pay attention to the wear on the soles and the *rand*—the thin rubber strip that wraps around the side of the shoe.

### Nuts and Bolts

The **rand** is the thin rubber strip that wraps around the side of the shoe.

When I buy a new pair of running shoes, I know they have only a certain number of miles in them; I wear them only when I run or work out. Similarly, you should don your climbing shoes only when you climb. En route to the climb or cliff, wear an old, comfortable pair of running shoes or something similar. I wear Fila trail-running shoes when I climb up in the Gunks. They're sturdier than running shoes, easy to pack, and really comfortable. On more aggressive approaches, I wear my Hi-Tec light hiking shoes, which offer more support with no less comfort.

Again, no matter how well you care for your shoes, they're going to break down. A well-made pair, however, can be resoled a few times. (It usually costs around $40.) It's time to resole when the rubber bottom has nearly worn through to the rand. It is possible to replace the rand, but it's far better to stop the bleeding before the shoes get to that point. A word to the wise: Don't ask your local shoe cobbler to work on your climbing shoes. Instead, look in climbing magazines or ask local climbing experts about repair shops.

It's quite instructive to note the wear pattern on your shoes; it says a lot about your technique. If the toe is worn to the bone, you're probably not being creative enough with your foot placement. If the toe is getting thread bare where the sole meets the upper rubber, it's likely that you're dragging your foot lazily as you head upward. If you spread the brunt of the work around, your shoes and your manicurist will thank you.

## Shoe Review

In general, better climbers pamper their shoes. Here's how to prolong your shoe's life and your image:

1. If you're not climbing, don't wear your climbing shoes. Often climbers take them off while they're belaying.

2. When you must wear them away from the rock, be mindful of oily surfaces. Quicksand is also a no-no.

3. Before you start climbing, brush off the bottom of the shoe with your hand to make sure the rubber is free of dirt.

4. A light brushing with a brass suede brush can roughen up the bottom and restore stickiness to the sole.

5. If your shoes need to be revamped, let an experienced rock-shoe repair shop do the handiwork.

6. Carry spare laces with you. Break one mid-climb and you'll find out why.

7. If your rock shoes get wet, stuffing them with newspaper helps them dry out faster.

### Hold On

Don't have your local shoemaker work on your climbing shoes. It's safer to search the back of climbing magazines or ask the friendly climbing store about local repair shops or mail-order climbing cobblers.

### Finger Tips

To keep the soles of their rock shoes pristine while they're belaying their partner on the ground, some climbers have been known to wear large socks over their climbing shoes.

## If the Shoe Fits...

It seems the deeper you get into climbing, the more shoes you acquire. Actually, it can get a bit embarrassing. When my friends look in my closet, they usually scream in mock horror: "What are you, the Imelda Marcos of outdoor footwear?" Let me just say that while there is overlap out there, it's a good feeling to have the right tool for the right job.

**Nuts and Bolts**

An **adventure race** is a multi-sport team event that includes kayaking, mountain biking, rock climbing, hiking, and more.

**Finger Tips**

Remember that one pound of weight on your feet is equal to five pounds on your back. You should wear lightweight and flexible trail shoes for hikes to the crag, for stream crossings, and when you're hanging out.

It has little to do with rock climbing, but just for the record here's a vertical-shoe sampler of what I carried when I did a 10-day *adventure race* in Ecuador.

1. Lightweight, flexible trail shoes for hiking on the easier trails.

2. Rigid, ankle-high boots suitable for fitting with 12-point crampons for glacier travel and ice climbing. I wear Salomon Super Mountain 9 boots and love them.

3. Lightweight nylon-mesh socks for wearing around camp or for crossing streams. They dry quickly and have waffled soles for traction. Note: They provide no support.

4. Down booties for lounging around camp and for added warmth in the sleeping bag. (I hate cold feet.) If it's warm, sport sandals such as Tevas are a fine addition to any pack.

Okay, I admit it: I have a shoe problem.

## Let Your Fingers Do the Walking

A myriad of companies make fine footwear these days. You can check them out on the Internet or dial them directly for a catalog. Refer to Appendix F for a list of vendors that we endorse.

# Your Derriere in a Sling

Choosing a harness, especially for a beginner, is far simpler than picking a solid pair of shoes. Although there are hundreds to chose from, virtually any UIAA-approved harness will get the job done.

Your selection will depend on the type of climbing you intend to do and the season in which you'll be doing it. Sport and competition climbers—speed demons who begrudge every extra ounce—typically wear lightweight harnesses. (For the record: The lighter the harness, the more it costs.)

Climbers who climb outdoors in a variety of conditions prefer padded and adjustable models. The pads make belaying markedly more comfortable, and the adjustable leg loops are essential when you're ice climbing or climbing in cold weather and wearing bulky clothing.

## Keeping It Snug

To misquote one of our founding fathers, "All harnesses are not created equal." Different models fit differently. Some harnesses, as I've already noted, have adjustable leg loops—an excellent feature when you need to add a layer or two of clothing. In addition, on some harnesses the *rise*—the distance between the waistbelt and the leg loops—is adjustable.

## For Women, Too

Women's models differ from men's in the length of the *rise* and size of the leg loops. Thank goodness! When I climbed with a borrowed man's model, I felt like I had a permanent wedgie.

In fact, the only possible evidence I can think of that God is a man is the ease with which males can relieve themselves while climbing (while driving, too, but that's the topic of another book). A man's plumbing allows him rather effortlessly to take care of that excess coffee that can cause even world class climbers to lose their concentration.

For women, the harness story was not a happy one…until the advent of special harnesses where the leg loops can drop out while the waistbelt stays fastened—to which I say that maybe God is a woman after all!

## What's with These Other Loops?

Like leg loops, gear-racking loops are standard on all harnesses and are designed to hold anchor devices and other climbing doodads. This is particularly important to the lead climber and shouldn't worry the beginner too much. In general, avoid harnesses that look like tool belts and have superfluous bells and whistles.

Though it may be obvious, it must be said: Never clip into these stiff loops as a means of protection. They are designed to carry gear, not to hold people—especially inexperienced boneheads.

### Hold On

The nylon that harnesses are made of loses its resilience and strength after about five years. This time period varies according to use; a frequently used harness should be retired early. Be wise and retire your harness before it retires you.

### Nuts and Bolts

The **rise** is the distance between the waistbelt and the leg loops on a harness.

### Finger Tips

The Petzl Bonnie is a woman's best friend. Built for women, it offers an adjustable belay loop and belt height for comfortable fit, a plastic ring to clip your chalk bag to, and four gear loops. The detachable leg loops are a woman's best friend.

### Hold On

Closely examine your harness for nicks and tears before donning it for a day of climbing. Be especially aware of damaged and abraded stitching. When in doubt, don't use it.

### Nuts and Bolts

In **aid climbing**, the climber uses gear (protection), on routes devoid of features, to manage an ascent. It's the polar opposite of free climbing.

A **hanging belay** is when the second climber belays the leader, on a multi-pitch route, while dangling from the rope and her harness.

### Hold On

Check that the waistbelt on your harness is doubled back before you begin climbing. Then check your partner's harness. And check periodically throughout the day. Failure to do so may prove to be fatal.

## Nice Pad, Man!

Some harnesses have more padding than others. If you're going to spend a lot of time hanging in the harness for *aid climbing* or doing *hanging belays*, you'll want some extra cushioning in the waist and legs—a big help if you want blood to flow to your feet. There are some light-weight, comfortable harnesses out there with enough padding to inspire you to leave them on after you climb. Unfortunately, the added price might make you wince every time you strap them on.

## Body Harnesses

I've never climbed with a body harness, but I mention them because they're out there. These "full-figured" models have both a chest and a seat harness, as well as a higher tie-in point. This is excellent for kids and, in theory, for alpine-style climbers who do a lot of vertical work with a heavy pack. The bottom line, however, is that you shouldn't concern yourself with these harnesses; they're going the way of the dodo bird.

## Try It On

Just as you would try on a new pair of climbing shoes, try on several harnesses before you make a decision. Ask to hang in it before you lay down some cash; many stores allow you to do this. Most of the load should be transferred to your butt and upper thighs, and the waistbelt shouldn't be up around your ribs. Remember that the waistbelt should be large enough to fit over extra layers, if needed, and yet small enough to fit snugly when you're wearing nothing more than lycra shorts.

## It's a Cinch

To state the obvious, fastening your harness's waistbelt properly is of the utmost importance! You should have at least three inches of extra webbing after fastening the buckle and threading it back through to secure it. Most harnesses aren't considered safe until the waistbelt has been threaded through the buckle, doubled back on itself, and then passed through the buckle. Some metal buckles have a red strip to remind you to thread it back through. The phrase "See red and you're dead" is a fine way to remember this simple but crucial task.

And don't be like a rapper, gunslinger, or shredding snowboarder and wear the thing halfway down your butt. (Since when did the plumber look become cool after all?) The waistbelt should fit snugly above your hipbones so that in the dreaded circumstance that you do flip upside down, you don't slide out of the harness. Sadly, such accidents have happened.

### Cliff Notes

Just because you know how to fasten your harness doesn't mean it's ready for action. A few years ago I was in an adventure race in China called the Mild Seven Outdoor Quest. One frigid morning I emerged from my tent and struggled into my harness as we attempted to race out of camp. Although I fastened the harness correctly, my hands were so numb from the cold that it remained comically loose. Unable to wrestle the thick webbing any tighter, I eventually asked a teammate, who happened to be built like a linebacker, to help me. In the blink of an eye, he yanked on the belt so hard that both my feet left the ground. Needless to say, the harness stayed buckled the rest of the day.

## Velcro Harnesses

Harnesses with velcro fittings are designed so that the harness stays snug while you cinch the buckle. Good in theory, bad in practice. Why? The potential for disaster is too great. The temptation is to use the velcro to close the harness and wait until you need to cinch it tight. If you forget, you may be reminded in a very rude way.

# Hard Hats

Woody Allen once said that his brain was his second favorite organ. As a climber, you should have it at the top of your list.

When I was a professional bike racer, the rules required me to wear a helmet to compete, which was fine with me. Speeding along in a crowded pack at 28 mph, your front wheel inches from the wheel in front of you, was scary enough even with a helmet. Nevertheless, I knew countless riders who hated wearing them and donned one only when they had to.

### Hold On

Bike helmets are *not* a safe substitute for climbing helmets. Make sure your climbing helmet has a UIAA-approved, micro-hard (certified plastic shell) covering.

Here are five solid reasons for wearing a brain bucket:

1. Morons above you drop gear, rock, cans of beer, and so forth. Such projectiles can kill you.

2. Random rocks fall. Such projectiles will kill you.

3. Even if you're being properly belayed, falling can result in your head meeting stone. Such a fall can kill you.

4. Gear pulls out in a fall, hits you in the noggin,' and kills you.

5. A helmet is a good place to put a sponsor's logo. If you don't have a sponsor, post a notice that paid advertisements are welcome.

## Don't Look Up

If you climb with a guide service, chances are you'll be required to wear a helmet. Otherwise, depending on what kind of climbing you do and where you do it, helmets are optional. In areas like the Gunks in upstate New York, where falling rock isn't common, more climbers do their thing without a helmet than with one. And helmets aren't often worn on sport routes, in top-roping, or in photo shoots.

Most climbers, however, recognize the importance of helmets on longer routes, where conditions vary, or on big mountains, where falling rock or ice is common. While the above list is a bit on the glib side, many fine climbers who weren't wearing a helmet have been killed by falling objects.

Indeed, falling rock is a climber's nemesis. Holds can break off anytime, even on the most solid rock face. Sometimes rock is dislodged by a hiker at the top of the cliff, another climber above you, the rope, or just the random nature of Mother Nature. Such capricious acts of nature are part of what makes climbing so intense.

### Cliff Notes

When my co-writer Joe Glickman climbed Boundary Peak in Nevada without a helmet, a rock the size of a softball went whizzing by his head. He heeded the cosmic warning and wore a helmet when he later climbed Granite Peak in Montana. No rocks came close to his head, but while downclimbing he was so focused on his footwork that he whacked his head on the rock several times. The moral of the story? Wearing a helmet will improve the quality of your climbing life.

Now that more people are climbing than ever, the danger of getting brained by a piece of dropped gear is much greater. A carabiner that drops 100 feet and nails you on the head can cause serious damage. And if you fall and bang your head on the way down, a helmet can save your life. Considering the objective risk, wearing a helmet is the only prudent way to travel.

## Image Isn't Everything

Flip through the photos in climbing magazines or books and you won't see many climbers wearing a hard lid (except for ice climbers, for whom helmets are the norm.) Rock jocks list many reasons for eschewing these protective devices:

1. "They're too hot." Although this argument has some merit, the newer plastic and fiberglass models, which range from 11 to 20 pounds, are better ventilated and lighter than the older models.

2. "They restrict my vision." This is a poor argument unless the helmet is way too big or you refuse to buckle it. Today's lightweight models are quite unobtrusive.

3. "They cramp my style and limit my freedom." This is a plausible but largely bogus argument. Hockey players and motor-cyclist said (and say) the same thing when helmets became mandatory. Climbers who resist wearing them feel restricted when in fact it's a state of mind.

4. "They aren't cool." Wearing a helmet makes you neither a nerd nor a safety freak. Only if you wear one while climbing indoors will you be considered a goof. A cool climber is someone who climbs well and with integrity. A climber who shuns a helmet in an area where the rock quality is shaky is young, foolish—or both. The beautiful people in the magazines don't look as glamorous with bloody gashes on their heads.

### Finger Tips

Don't clip your helmet to your harness when down-climbing, and don't set down your helmet upside-down; it will most likely will roll away. You don't want to be chasing a stray helmet, and your partner doesn't want it to be raining helmets.

## Hat Tricks

Here are a few final helmet tips:

➤ Make sure your helmet fits properly and is fastened securely. You shouldn't be able to move it back and forth or from side to side. The front should rest just over your eyebrows.

➤ Wear it not only when you're climbing but also when you are belaying or any time you are near the base of the cliff.

➤ Wear a helmet approved by the UIAA. Their test dummy (wired with sophisticated sensors) has taken a brutal beating for your safety.

---

### The Least You Need to Know

➤ The type of shoes and harness you get depends on your level of experience and the kind of climbing you expect to do.

➤ The beginner's best option is to get a moderately stiff all-purpose shoe.

➤ Care for your shoes as a dog cares for a bone.

➤ Make sure you fasten your harness correctly and check it throughout the climb.

➤ Ignore the hip magazine photos; protect your head from falling rock—and worse—with a proper climbing helmet.

---

# Chapter 6

# Belaying Basics

## In This Chapter

➤ How do you spell safety? B-e-l-a-y

➤ Direct and indirect belays

➤ Making those anchors bombproof

➤ The body belay: An oldie is still a goody

➤ The wide world of belay devices

➤ Can't find your belay device? It's "Munter Time"

Not long ago I was belaying a friend who was climbing for the first time. To put it mildly, she was a panicky mess. "I'm going to fall and die," she whined, convinced that one slip would spell the end. "Don't worry," I said, poised to stop the rope the moment she took leave of the rock. "You couldn't kill yourself if you tried."

I wasn't kidding. Had she decided to end it all and jump, I could have easily applied friction to the rope and stopped her fall before she'd gone much more than a few feet.

Unless you're a train conductor, a brain surgeon, or pack parachutes for a living, you will never feel so directly liable for the life of another person as when you're belaying. When you inform your rope mate that she is "on belay," you—and only you—are able to stop her should she peel away from the rock. This combination of trust and personal responsibility is part of what makes the bond between rope mates so profound. In *Deborah: A Wilderness Narrative*, David Roberts talks about the "synchronization" he felt with a preferred climbing partner. "We had begun to feel the instinctive awareness of each other's movements, even when out of sight, and the confidence in each other that can make roped climbing one of the most sensitive means of communication."

# The Whole World in His Hands

*Belaying*—managing the rope to save your partner's cookies in the event of a fall—is as fundamental to climbing safety as a net is to a trapeze artist. Belaying isn't difficult. If the climber falls, the belayer *locks off* the rope, usually with a *belay device*, and often lowers the climber back to terra firma at the end of the climb. Anyone who can talk, listen, stand, and chew gum at the same time can do it. Like any skill, however, belaying requires practice. Have a good teacher show you the proper techniques and you're on your way to a safe climbing career.

Three essential components must be in place to make the system work:

1. A knowledgeable, conscientious belayer who knows when and how to apply friction to the rope.

2. A solid belay station (usually a wide ledge) and a solid anchor—a tree or rock spike, for example—for the belayer to tie into to absorb the pull of a fall.

3. A way to intensify the friction at the belayer's disposal.

## Nuts and Bolts

**Belaying** means to manage the rope for the climber, who is said to be "on belay." A climber can be belayed from above or below. If the climber falls, you can stop him or her from hitting the ground by **locking off** the rope—that is, using one hand to bend the rope across a metal **belay device**, which helps create friction on the rope. That hand is called the *brake hand*.

*Setting up to belay a partner indoors. (Photo courtesy of Mark Eller.)*

The beginner must first learn the mechanics of the belay: how much slack to allow, how to stop a fall, and so forth. A belayer's responsibilities extend far beyond that, however. A good belayer acts as a traffic cop and crossing guard all in one, checking that the leader's harness waistbelt is doubled back, that the anchor is solid, and more. Once the leader is climbing, it's very important for the belayer to focus on his mate. Simply put: A belayer holds his partner's life in his hands.

## *Unbelayvable*

In the early days of climbing, belaying involved little more than the top climber getting to a safe stopping point and reeling the rope in, hand over hand, for the next person to follow. This evolved to the *waist belay* and, eventually, to the neat little gadgets that are used today.

Typically, beginning climbers are so consumed with getting up and down the rock in one piece that they often don't pay attention to the safety systems set up around them. Because belaying appears easy—and it really is if you're paying attention—climbers occasionally space out. Beware! Lose your concentration and you may pay a steep price. Forty percent of all climbing fatalities in Yosemite National Park result from failures in the belay chain.

Here's a classic miscalculation that happens far too often: The belayer should tie in to the end of the rope if there is a possibility that the team could run out of line. Why? It's not uncommon that a leader goes to the anchor, clips in the rope, and then lowers for the ground. If the anchor is more than half a rope's length, the end of the line may run right through the belayer's hand during the lower-off. This miscue has led to many deadly accidents.

Here are the basics of belaying:

1. When there are two climbers, each is tied into an end of the rope. As one climbs, the other belays.

### Nuts and Bolts

The **waist belay**, or body belay, is the predecessor of modern belaying devices, such as the Gri Gri. A basic technique that involved wrapping the rope around your body, the body belay considered an archaic friction method of controlling the force of a fall.

### Hold On

The belayer's brake hand should always be firmly on the rope! He should be poised to immediately move his braking hand across the belay devices.

### Finger Tips

Gloves aren't necessary to prevent rope burns if your mate falls. Why? The belay device bears the brunt of the friction.

2. When belaying from below, the belayer pays out rope as the climber moves up the rock. The belayer passes the rope through a belay device (more on these later) and clips it into a locking biner that attaches to his harness. He stands ready to stop the rope cold in case the climber above falls. When the climber reaches the top (or a safe resting spot on a multiple-pitch climb), she becomes the belayer for the person below and reels in the rope as the other climber climbs.

3. The belayer's hand should never leave the rope! Lack of concentration by the belayer can result in death.

4. In a top-rope setup, the belayer takes up slack through a pulley system he's set up. As a result, the climber will rarely fall more than a few feet—assuming the belayer is doing his job. In a top-rope setup, the belayer (who is standing the ground) usually doesn't need to tie into an anchor. If the belayer has a good stance and the climber above is not too beefy, there is little advantage to doing so.

5. In lead climbing—moving up the cliff in stages—the climber assumes greater risk, since the point of protection is actually below. When the belayer is standing (or sitting) on a ledge, tying into a solid anchor (like a rock or tree) is essential.

*Two climbers in Italy, one belaying the other. (Photo courtesy of Mark Eller.)*

When we say that the point of protection is below, we mean that the leader is placing pieces of protection as he ascends, climbing above each one before placing the next.

## The Indirect Belay

In an *indirect belay*, the less common of the two methods, the belayer is "outside the system," meaning the rope is not tied directly to the harness but rather to the anchor. With an indirect belay, the anchor holds the fall, and the belayer just has to brake the rope. Therefore, the fall does not pull on the belayer at all—just the anchor. If I rig my belay device to a tree and just hold on to the brake side of the rope when my partner falls, I have an indirect belay. One of the benefits of this set up is that makes it easy for the belayer to get clear of the system and go for help if the needs arises. Setting up an indirect belay is the province of an expert, but it's good to know why climbers use it.

Here's a key point: The belayer should be tied securely to the anchor. If there is significant slack between the two, a long fall can pluck the belayer off the ground as easily as one would pull a toothpick from a sandwich. The ramifications of this are rarely good: The belayer is yanked violently until the slack is out of the rope. This often causes the rope to be ripped from his hands, ending in certain disaster.

## The Direct Belay

A *direct belay* is when the load of the fall is transferred to the belayer's harness. If his partner logs air time, the impact of the fall on the rope is transferred through the belayer to the anchor, thereby lessening the impact on the anchor.

The downside of a direct belay is that the anchor points need to be elephant-proof—although it would take a very nimble pachyderm to get too far off the ground. If the anchor isn't sound, the climber who falls is likely to end up very dead.

**Nuts and Bolts**

The **indirect belay** is when the belayer is "outside the system." The belayer always should be tied in to the line; however, the belay device is not on the belayer's harness but directly connected to the anchor. The anchor holds the fall, and the belayer brakes the rope.

**Nuts and Bolts**

A **direct belay** is when the load of the fall is transferred to the belayer's harness rather than the anchor. The anchor will, in turn, hold the belayer.

**Hold On**

A solid anchor is essential in direct belaying. Your life depends on it. Triple-check its structure. Then check it again. It is essential that all belay anchors—whether indirect or direct systems are used—be beyond reproach.

71

# At the Root of It All: The Anchor

The *anchor* is the guts of the safety chain in lead climbing. And just like the hatch on a submarine, it must be secure. An anchor must be able to hold the full weight of both climbers many times over. Remember to never trust your life to a single piece of gear. This rule is considered sacrosanct in climbing circles. A bolt or tree is insufficient, but both, connected together, would be acceptable. This is true for single pitch or multi-pitch routes. Many beginners make the mistake of overestimating how grounded a large rock actually is. Don't tie into the first anchor that looks good, because often times a large rock can be on a slope and unable to withstand the force generated by a long fall.

By the way, how do you tie in to an anchor? The best way to learn is to have an expert show you!

**Nuts and Bolts**

The **anchor** is what the belayer ties his end of the rope to. In top-roping it can be anything secure at the top of the route—a tree, a boulder, or a reliable bolt. The same applies on a multi-pitch route, although climbers often use several nuts to create a solid anchor.

# The Body as Anchor: The Body Belay

Before mechanical belay devices were part of every climber's arsenal, the *body belay* (or *hip belay*) was the way to go. These days, the body belay isn't used that often, but it's valuable to know if you drop your belay gadget halfway up a wall, if the rope gets caked with ice and is unable to pass through the belay device, or if you're moving quickly over relatively easy terrain and want to save time.

You need to have an experienced teacher show you the mechanics of this old-fashioned technique, but the body belay is done pretty much the way you'd expect it to be. The belayer assumes a braced stance against the mountain (back and feet braced forward like the last person in a game of tug-of-war). He reinforces his position by tying the climbing rope to a solid anchor. He then wraps the rope around his waist or under his butt to establish enough friction to stop a fall, and handles the rope just as he would with a mechanical belay device. The only difference is that your body substitutes for the device.

**Nuts and Bolts**

The **body belay** (or **hip belay**) is the traditional (old-timer) method that preceded mechanical belay devices. It is used—only for top-roping—as a last resort if you lose your belay device. The belayer wraps the rope around her waist or under her bottom, thereby creating friction to halt a climber's fall. Body belays are rather uncomfortable and hard to control.

Rigged correctly, this no-frills technique works well; a petite woman can catch a big old climbing Clydesdale effectively—although I certainly wouldn't try it with one of those old hemp ropes.

# Belay Doohickeys

Although climbers sit around a campfire and debate the advantages of the Sticht Plate versus the Lowe Tuber, beginners will find such talk about as exciting as watching rope dry. However, it's helpful to know a few facts about some of the most popular belay devices. (See Appendix F for a guide to manufacturers.)

A variety of belay devices are on the market. Although they have different wrinkles, they all work on the same principle of creating friction on the rope so that the belayer can hold his fallen comrade. These belay gadgets are clipped to the front of the harness with a carabiner. Some climbers think that these devices offer an automatic clamping effect when a climber falls. Generally speaking, this isn't so. The belayer stops the fall by pulling back on the rope to create a 90-degree bend against a post on the so-called "belay doohickey."

The cool thing about these devices is that it takes a minimum of strength to stop a fall; they are basically bombproof if the setup is rigged correctly. Of even more concern is that the belayer maintains good form; that is, a brakehand on the rope at all times.

### Hold On

Look at many anchoring options before picking your ideal anchor setup. Take your time and check out the different shapes and "rootedness" of nearby boulders and trees before making a decision. The bottom line is that deciding on an acceptable anchor for a lead belay is the province of experts.

### Nuts and Bolts

The original belay device, the **Sticht Plate** slows down or locks off the climber's rope by means of friction. It is known generically as a *belay plate* because of its design, and can also be used for rappelling. Here's a circular climbing fact: All Sticht Plates are belay plates, but not all belay plates are Sticht Plates.

### Cliff Notes

John Long, author of *How to Rock Climb!*, fell countless times during the years he climbed with female phenom Lynn Hill. Thanks to correct belaying techniques and the proper hardware, she caught him easily even though he outweighed her by more than 100 pounds.

### Finger Tips

Tube-style belay and rappel devices are the lightest gadgets available. This is important because you never want to haul more weight up the mountain than is necessary.

### Nuts and Bolts

The **Gri Gri** is one of the newest belay devices on the block. It's favored in many gyms around the country due to its automatic lock-off feature.

### Hold On

The *Gri Gri* will not hold a falling climber if the unit is improperly loaded, held on the incorrect side during lowering, or if the belayer panics and holds the release lever open.

## *Sticht and Stones*

A German engineer invented the *Sticht Plate* in the early 1970s. This four-ounce aluminum disk (with either one or two holes) was the first belay device. Its simplicity is part of its effectiveness; a bend of rope passes through the plate and clips into a locking carabiner, which is then clipped to the belayer's harness.

## *Go Figure*

Not to be confused with the figure-8 knot (the standard knot for tying into your harness), figure-8 belay devices were originally designed just for rappelling, not for belaying. These days, some figure-8 belay devices are suitable for both. To state the obvious: Make sure the one you use is capable of handling both belaying and rappelling before you use it as an all-purpose workhorse. It's important to note that you rig the rope differently in the figure-8 when you use it to belay. Instead of rappel style—around the big and little end—the rope is pushed through the small eye and used like a belay plate.

## *Totally Tubular Tubes*

Tubular belay devices are currently more in vogue than figure-8 and flat-plate devices, because they are lighter, feed the rope a little more smoothly, and are equally as good for rappelling and belaying. They are shaped like a cone or pyramid and have cool names such as Black Diamond's Air Traffic Controller (ATC) and Trango's Pyramid. During a fall, the tube, like the Sticht Plate, locks off the rope at the biner.

## *I Dream of Gri Gri*

Designed by the French company Petzl, the *Gri Gri* is the exception to the non-locking norm. It works a bit like a car's automatic seatbelt setup. When the climber is on the way up, the rope moves easily through the cam. When it is pulled tight—as in "FALLING!"—the cam locks, and the rope stops even if the belayer is asleep at the wheel. As a result, the Gri Gri has become popular in top-rope setups in indoor gyms and with sport climbers, who may spend a lot of time hanging on the rope to perfect a move.

There is a big *caveat emptor* with this cool gadget: The Gri Gri is far from idiot proof, as evidenced by the lengthy instructions that you need to follow to become proficient at using it. Set up improperly and it's like having no belay at all. Furthermore, climbers who use a Gri Gri exclusively may develop poor belay habits when forced to use more traditional devices. The bottom line is that you need to sharpen your belay skills with whatever device you choose—the simple Sticht Plate or one with gizmos like the Gri Gri.

# The Munter Hitch

Introduced in Europe in the 1970s by Swiss climber Werner Munter as the *halbmastwurf sicherung* (half clove-hitch belay), the *Munter hitch* has also been called the *friction hitch*, half-ring bend, carabiner hitch, running R, and half-mast belay. Most of the climbers I know, however, call it the Munter hitch. It's a useful belay technique to know since it requires only a single, large, pear-shaped locking carabiner clipped to your harness (assuming you know how to tie the knot).

This isn't the place to show you the simple knot that wraps cleverly around the biner; that should be left to an instructor. Suffice it to say that the knot can be a life-saver if you lose your belay device.

The downside of the Munter hitch is that the rope usually gets twisted and worn faster. And since it puts constant pressure on the biner and can open the locking gate, you'll need to make sure the gate is secure.

**Nuts and Bolts**

The **Munter hitch**, also known as the **friction hitch**, is a simple hitch in the rope that puts friction on the line (for belaying) when clipped into a pear-shaped locking carabiner.

**Hold On**

The Munter hitch isn't good for rappelling because it twists the rope and frays it fuzzy with regular use.

## The Least You Need to Know

➤ Belaying is essential to safe climbing. Fortunately, anyone who can walk and whistle can do it.

➤ Practice and alertness are the tickets to safe belaying.

➤ The anchor is the foundation of your belaying system.

➤ The body belay frequently is used when you're climbing quickly on less technical routes.

➤ Many belay devices are available. Choose one type and learn to use it well.

➤ The simple but practical Munter hitch is a good knot in a pinch.

# Chapter 7

# Respect the Rope

> **In This Chapter**
>
> ➤ How strong is that sucker?
>
> ➤ How much? How long? How wide?
>
> ➤ Do I use fabric conditioner or send it to the dry cleaner?
>
> ➤ Packing and unpacking
>
> ➤ When enough is enough

I once read the following in a climbing guide: "The rope absorbs energy by elongating, and the amount and speed of this is determined by a complex interaction between the macromolecular structure and the braiding pattern."

"Well, yeah," I thought, "and the rope catches your macromolecular butt when there's nothing between you and the ground but thin air."

Put another way, the rope is your best friend, the most essential piece of equipment in your arsenal. In fact, there isn't a hardcore climber out there who hasn't been caught many times by his or her trusty rope. Unless you are bouldering (climbing low to the ground) or free-soloing (climbing way up high with no protection), the common bond in all styles of climbing is the rope. (Just for the record: Bouldering is a terrific way to improve your technique; free soloing, for all but a select few, is a great way to court death.)

## Link to Life

The first time I was saved by the rope, I felt such gratitude to that multi-colored lifeline that I considered taking it out for a four-course meal. (Yes, the conversation would have been stilted, but a debt is a debt.) Since then the long, thin, flexible nylon *cord* has caught me many times, and my bond with it has grown more intense.

**Nuts and Bolts**

**Cord** is climber lingo for a rope or line of any diameter or function.

Obviously, the rope doesn't save you just because you take it along to vertical venues. Rather, it's one (very important) link in the safety chain that includes your harness, webbing, carabiners, and more. However, since it literally connects climbers and plays such a pivotal role—when you fall or rappel—the rope plays both a physical and psychological part in climbing.

Take the time I climbed Cotopaxi, the highest active volcano in the world at 19,400 feet, during the Raid Gauloises, a 10-day adventure race in Ecuador. After an anxious and mostly sleepless night at 14,500 feet, my two male teammates and I headed out at 2 A.M. into the inky blackness for the summit. An hour and a half later, after a grueling hike up scree-strewn switchbacks we clipped into our rope. Soon after we headed out, two other climbers joined us. Because we were moving at night through an area with a lot of crevasses, they clipped into our rope. I knew they were competent athletes—they had to be to have survived this long in such a brutal race—but I knew nothing about their climbing skills and found it unnerving to be tied to strangers. As it turns out, they were solid climbers, and, by the time we trudged to the top of Ecuador, we had bonded in that non-verbal way rope mates often do.

**Cliff Notes**

When my co-author Joe Glickman was climbing Granite Peak, the highest mountain in Montana, he slipped while crossing a steep snow bridge that was pitched like the top of an A-frame roof. Had the rope not caught him, he would have fallen at least 1,000 feet. Instead, he traveled less than five feet. Said Joe: "Even a minor incident like that will quickly change the way climbers feel about their rope."

# The March of Technology

As I mentioned in Chapter 4, climbing ropes have come a long way since the days when the Carthaginians used horsehair cords or when, centuries later, European climbers used those funky hemp ropes.

The advances from horsehair to hemp to today's ultra-strong, elastic ropes mirror the impact technology has played in the vertical world. Here are some random rope facts you can use at your next cocktail party:

➤ The natural-fiber ropes used by early European mountaineers were eschewed by lead climbers; instead, they were used primarily to help struggling climbers up difficult sections and to assist on the descent. Why? Hemp and sisal ropes would not survive a long lead fall.

➤ World War II ushered in a new era in the manufacture of rope with DuPont's miracle material, nylon. Now climbers could push their limits and know that their ropes would endure a hard fall.

➤ The early nylon models were built much like their hemp forebears: bundled and twisted. Although these ropes were strong, they stretched as much as 40 percent—which made a fall seem too much like bungee jumping for the stricken climber.

➤ In the 1950s, kernmantle ("jacketed-core") ropes entered the picture. These ropes absorbed a fall without stretching as much. And because kernmantle ropes have a woven nylon sheath, the wear and tear that takes place on the outside doesn't compromise the strength inside the braided core.

# Dynamic and Static Ropes

There are two basic types of ropes: dynamic and static. *Dynamic* ropes are the standard, energy-absorbing climbing ropes. Typically, they have white cores and a colored (dyed) outer sheath for easy identification.

*Static* ropes have little stretch and are used primarily for rappelling, caving, and ascending. Many static ropes are white and are identified with colored strips. Don't assume, however, that you can judge whether a rope is dynamic or static simply by the color of its sheath. Some companies do not dye their dynamic ropes at all, claiming the dyes degrade the rope's integrity. Mistaking a static rope for a dynamic rope can have devastating results. A two-meter fall on a static line can break a climber's back or worse. The bottom line is to thoroughly research ropes before making a selection.

**Nuts and Bolts**

A **static rope** is rigid and has little elasticity. It's used mostly for specialized areas like aid and big-wall climbing. A static rope should not be used for belaying.

A **dynamic rope** stretches under a load and absorbs much of the force of a falling climber. It reduces the impact on the climber, belayer, and belay device.

# How Does Your Rope Rate?

Ropes that are approved by the UIAA are checked, poked, and prodded more carefully than astronauts heading into space. In fact, no modern climbing rope has ever snapped from a hard lead fall—proof of all the overkill built into this crucial piece of equipment.

The next time you doubt the strength of your UIAA-tested rope, know that they tie a 176-pound iron block to the end of a nine-foot piece of rope, feed it through a carabiner, and then attach the other end to a fixed point. The rope is raised as high as it can go and dropped at least five times. Experts agree that this test is far more intense than any fall you'd ever take; in fact, some think it's the rough equivalent of a cow taking a plunge off a 300-foot cliff. (Perhaps one of these plummeting farm animals coined the expression "Holy Cow!")

### Hold On

Because static ropes don't absorb shock, they are not safe for leading or even serious top-roping, where falls of two feet or more are common.

### Finger Tips

Treat your rope as you would a silk top. Avoid laying it over sharp edges, don't throw it in the dirt, and never step on it. Stepping on a rope grinds pebbles, slivers of sand, and other unidentified particles into the sheath, and will weaken its structure.

Even these super-strong ropes are vulnerable to abrasion, however, and occasionally are severed by sharp rock edges and crampons. So remember: Beware of all objects that can slice and dice your rope. While it's unheard of for a rope to break from a fall, dozens of climbers have died from sliced ropes.

# A Coil of Your Own

After all the tests and analysis, all the graphs and formulas, and all the fancy terminology that manufacturers throw at you about the various qualities of a kernmantle rope, there are only a few specs that you really need to worry about:

➤ Make sure the rope has been approved by the UIAA. The UIAA performs extensive drop tests to determine the rope's characteristics and durability under extreme conditions. The UIAA fall-rate tests determine the number of "worst-case" falls the rope model held during the procedure. The higher number, the more durable the rope.

➤ How far a rope stretches during a fall is called *working elongation*. Know this: A stretchy rope means longer, but softer, falls than a less elastic model.

➤ It's important to know if a rope has been treated with a waterproofing compound.

Because all UIAA-approved ropes are strong enough to pull a locomotive, most climbers—especially the pack rat bums I hang out with—tend to buy the cheapest model they can find. Ropes range in price from $99 to $200. Once you've owned a coil or two, you'll become more discerning.

In general, proper care for your precious lifeline is more important than the rope you choose—as long as the rope is new and considered kosher by the UIAA.

## *Size Does Matter*

Typically, ropes come in four lengths: 45, 50, 60, and 70 meters (150, 165, 190, and 220 feet, respectively). They range between 10 and 11 millimeters in diameter. There are narrower ropes, called "half ropes," which means you need two of these slim lines to have a safe system. Half ropes are more commonly used in Europe, especially in England. While managing a single 10–11 millimeter rope is easier, the advantages of two come into play when your route wanders all over the cliff. Using two different-colored half ropes enables you to avoid the drastic jags that you'd have to contend with using a single rope.

In the good old days, the 150-foot rope was standard. Today, few climbers carry ropes that short. Why? Because most established routes are designed for at least 165-foot rope. The newest climbing standard is 190 feet, and some new-wave routes require 220 feet. A "designed" route demands that a specific-length rope be used in respect to the placement of the belay anchors. If the belay anchor on a bolted route is 35 meters off the deck, you need a rope of at least 70 meters. A shorter rope can lead to deadly results.

**Hold On**

Many novice climbers have been killed or seriously injured in climbing accidents due to poor rope selection. Make sure your rope is long enough for the selected routes.

## Can You Handle It?

In *How to Rock Climb!*, John Long writes that "the ideal rope would stretch little when weighted, would have a low impact force, would handle like a mink's pelt, would weigh one pound, would fit in your back pocket, and would cost around five dollars. But no one rope is close to having all these characteristics."

True enough; different ropes handle differently. How a rope behaves—its flexibility, how well it holds a knot—depends on its thickness and model. The more-flexible, softer ropes are easier to manipulate but tend to have a looser woven sheath and to fray faster than the stiffer variety. This is stuff you'll learn over time. The good news is that most ropes on the market today are quite user-friendly.

## Ropes Get Wet

A wet kernmantle rope is just as strong as its dry counterpart. The biggest difference is that it gets heavier and harder to handle. If you're an ice climber or climb alpine-style (on big snowy mountains), a water-resistant rope is the only way to go. The rope is more expensive, but your line will last longer and save you money in the long run.

Even if you climb in the Sahara Desert, using a rope treated with waterproof coating (silicone- or Teflon-based) is a good idea. "Dry ropes" are more abrasion-resistant than uncoated ones; the coating reduces the effect of ultraviolet rays, which are probably the single most destructive force your rope is exposed to.

**Hold On**

Waterproof-coated (silicone- or Teflon-based) ropes are 33 percent more abrasion-resistant than uncoated ropes.

# Constant Care

When I started climbing I quickly noticed how finicky experienced climbers were with their rope—so much so that it reminded me of the way socialites care for poodles. When I finally saw that a rope can (and probably will) save my life, I understood why it deserves such pampering. (Though, please, don't use baby talk with your rope. You'll make your climbing partners sick.)

Here's the skinny on rope care: A new rope is ridiculously strong, but shoddy treatment can weaken it in a hurry. Climbing ropes are both durable and fragile, since the flexible nylon material can be damaged easily.

### Cliff Notes

At times, treating your rope with respect can be trying. When I was climbing the icy Cotopaxi in Ecuador, I was initially very mindful about not stepping on the line with my crampons. As we made our way from 16,000 to 19,000 feet, however, my gait became more labored and my concentration about as good as a child after two bowls of Frosted Flakes. While I managed to avoid stepping on the rope all the way to the summit, I danced with two left feet around the cumbersome line much of the way up the mountain.

The following basic elements of rope care are obvious but critical:

1. Inspect your rope often.
2. Never step on the rope—especially with crampons!
3. Never lend your rope to anyone.
4. Never buy a used rope.
5. To keep your nice new rope as nice and new as possible, it's a good idea to use a ground cloth or rope bag.
6. When your rope gets really dirty, wash it in the bathtub or machine-wash it in cool or warm water with mild detergent. Avoid the dryer; either hang the rope in a shady place and let it drip dry or uncoil it on a clean floor and allow the moisture to evaporate for several days.
7. Keep your line out of direct sunlight whenever possible. UV rays are killers!
8. If the ends of the rope are fraying, fuse them with the flame of a match or cigarette lighter.
9. Make sure the ends and middle of the rope are well-marked according to the manufacturer's instructions. The middle marker is for identifying where to position the rope in a rappel in which the ends must be even.

## Storage

Over the years I've read some amusing tips about storing a rope, including: "Don't store your lifeline near toxic chemicals, terrorists, razor blades, or battery acid." Actually, the only really helpful hint in the obvious department is to be careful about stowing your rope in the trunk of your car. Corrosive substances tend to take refuge there. Gasoline is a pretty nasty solvent. Other than that, common sense should prevail.

Make sure your rope is completely dry and free of dirt before you put it away. Get rid of any knots. Coil it loosely and store it in a cool, dry area away from directly sunlight, nylon-eating mice, and other insidious forces eager to stymie rock climbers. Storing your rope in a rope bag or stuff sack is a good way to make sure your little brother doesn't stick his bubble gum in your precious line.

## Coiling and Uncoiling

It sounds like an obvious thing to avoid, but it's surprising how often climbers get to the base of a climb and simply toss their coil of rope onto the ground. This is potentially harmful to the rope since dirt and debris can work through the sheath and cut the core.

When you're setting up shop at a site, uncoil your rope and stack it in an orderly but random pile on a smooth surface; this reduces the amount of tangling that will occur as you sort the rope. When it's time to head home or to another site, recoil your line and away you go. I learned to coil from two military men—one a former Navy Seal and Marine—who coil a rope so symmetrically and tight that it seems as if it were done by a machine. (If you really want to be dazzled, you should see these guys make their beds.)

There are two basic ways to coil the rope for carrying or storage: the *mountaineer's coil and the butterfly coil.*

The mountaineer's coil involves wrapping the rope in a circular pattern so that it can be tied off and

**Hold On**

Never lend out your rope, borrow a buddy's rope, or buy a used one.

**Finger Tips**

Uncoil the rope one loop at a time, into a pile. If you simply drop the coils on the ground and start tugging at one end, you'll end up with a tangled mess that will resemble an 100-foot long telephone cord.

**Nuts and Bolts**

The **mountaineer's coil** involves wrapping the rope in a circular pattern so that it can be tied off and handled neatly. It's a convenient way to carry the rope but puts a lot of twist into the line.

The **butterfly coil** also involves wrapping the rope in a circular pattern. When the rope is tied off, the climber can wear the neat package like a backpack.

handled neatly. It works, but it also puts a lot of twist into the line. I prefer the butterfly coil, which also involves wrapping the rope in a circular pattern. When the rope is tied off, however, the climber can wear the neat package like a backpack.

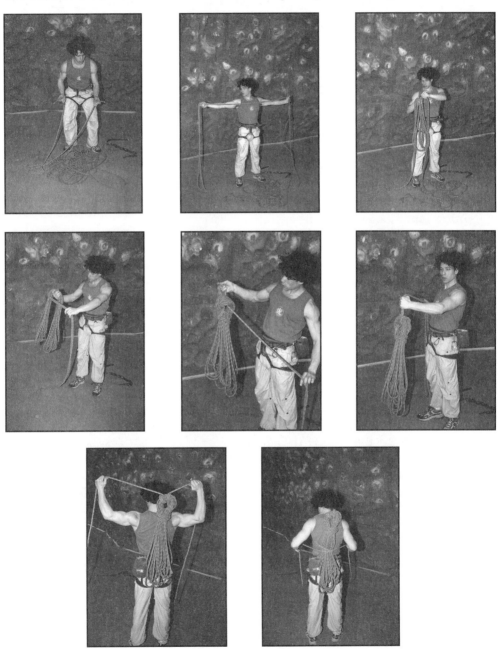

*Tying the butterfly coil. (Photo courtesy Mark Eller.)*

Here's the skinny on the butterfly coil:

1. Start by matching the two ends of the rope so that you have one double rope. If you're stacking the rope in your right hand, leave about 15 feet of rope free on the right side.

2. Lap the doubled rope over your right hand so that you have two equal lengths (or droopy butterfly wings) on either side of your hand. Do this until you get to the doubled end of the rope.

3. When you get to the doubled end of the rope, split the difference across your hand.

4. Wrap the free end several times around the coil below your hand, and then push a *bight* of the remaining rope through the eyelet formed by the wraps.

5. Thread the doubled free ends through this bight to secure the wraps. The rope is now ready to roll.

**Nuts and Bolts**

A **bight** is a double loop of rope. Knots are often tied "on a bight."

6. You can carry the coil on your back by laying each free end over a shoulder and then wrapping them back across the rope coils and your waist.

7. Tie the free ends in front of you with a square knot (which we'll cover later) and you're off.

# Retire That Rope!

Knowing when to retire your rope is a bit subjective since it depends on the type of rock you climb, how often you use it, and how often you fall.

The condition of the sheath is often the best indicator of a rope's overall health. If a crampon cuts the rope near the middle, put it on the shelf. If it's sliced near the end, you can cut off the damaged section and be back in business. If the rope is damaged by a falling rock or if some other natural force leaves the sheath looking ragged, however, you should seriously consider sending your rope to pasture even if it is relatively new.

**Hold On**

Get rid of the rope when the sheath is fuzzy—meaning sheath fibers are severed—or when you feel it's compromised in some way.

If the sheath looks fine, however, it's harder to know when to say "no mas" to a particular rope. The following guidelines will help you decide:

1. If you use your rope on a near-daily basis, it should be discarded after a year.

2. If you're a weekend warrior, figure about two years.

3. If you use it rarely, or not at all, it should be tossed after four years since nylon falls apart over time and its ability to absorb shock is greatly compromised.

4. A rope that has endured one very severe fall should be retired ASAP.

5. If huge moths fly out of the bag it's stored in, the rope is history.

---

### The Least You Need to Know

➤ The rope is your best friend, a safety net, and a security blanket.

➤ The rope has come to represent climbing and a climber's connection to another person.

➤ A rope approved by the UIAA has never snapped from a hard lead fall.

➤ Keeping the rope clean and storing it correctly are crucial to getting the most miles from your line.

➤ Knowing how to care for your rope includes knowing how to uncoil and recoil it.

➤ If the outside of the rope is frayed, it's probably time to retire it.

---

# Part 3
# Base Camp

*Okay, if you've read Parts 1 and 2, you have a good idea of what climbing is all about. Now let's get into the nitty-gritty of getting up the rock. Odds are that the first time you go climbing, you'll start on a top-rope. I'll give you a thorough understanding of what's involved as well as go over the crucial mechanics of belaying your partner. I'll also outline the mechanics of proper rappelling—a facet of climbing that intimidates many (if not all) beginners. Understanding what you're up against should help ease the anxiety.*

*Not only is climbing gear-intensive, it demands sound technique. While it's best to learn under the watchful eye of an instructor or knowledgeable (and patient) friend, I'll give you some helpful hints to think about when you find yourself perched on a narrow ledge of rock. After you've climbed once or twice, re-read this part of the book and it should make even more sense.*

*Finally, I offer my two cents on indoor climbing gyms—perhaps the single biggest factor in the recent explosion in the sport of climbing. Plus, you'll find out my thoughts on a subject that's near and dear to my heart: eating. So sit back with a bag of GORP and get your fill of information.*

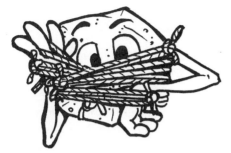

# Chapter 8

# Know Your Knots

---

## In This Chapter

➤ Single knots, retraced knots, and knots on a bight

➤ When a knot is not a knot, but a hitch

➤ The most commonly used climbing knots and how to tie them

➤ Learning when to use which knot

➤ Clove hitch, Prusik, double bowline knots—the best of the rest

➤ Checking and rechecking for safety

---

Although the most famous of Shakespeare's lines—"To be or not to be, that is the question"—had nothing to do with rock climbing, it could have. Without a proper knowledge of knots, a climber won't be around too long. (And come to think about it, the Bard did mention slings.)

Okay, so the analogy is a bit strained. Nevertheless, knots are to climbing what dialogue is to a playwright. These intricate twists of the rope are the basis of climbing safety; they keep you tied to the rope and ensure that the rope remains securely tied to your anchors. Simply put: Knots save your derriere. If you are to grow as a climber, you need to know how to tie them.

Here's the good news and the bad news: Knots aren't particularly difficult to learn. You need to get a knot just right, however, for it to be effective. Just as important is knowing which knot to use when. Do them incorrectly and you can die. The drawings and instructions in this chapter are intended as a refresher course to reinforce what you, the climber, have already learned from a competent guide—someone who can tie the most hideously complex knot while whistling Dixie in his sleep.

If you really get nutty about knots, of course, there are books dedicated to the subject. *The Book of Outdoor Knots*, by Peter Owens, for example, provides step-by-step instructions on how to tie more than 100 different ones. (I like the Highwayman's Hitch, which is excellent for robbing stagecoaches when you want to get away quick with your rope, though it isn't recommended for climbing.)

### Finger Tips

Knots tied on a bight—a doubled loop of rope—create quick and sturdy links. They are commonly used for clipping into anchors.

## Nuts for Knots

So as not to overwhelm you with too much information, I'll describe the handful of the soundest, most versatile knots climbers should have in their arsenals. A good way to practice is to take a short piece of rope and tie knots while you're on the phone, watching the tube, or traveling in the car (assuming that you're not driving).

You should get to the point that you couldn't forget how to tie a figure-8 knot if you tried.

One of my climbing friends says that to ensure he could do it in "full conditions," he stood on a two-by-four in the shower with the water running and the lights out and tied 20 wet ones. While this might be one of the most idiotic ideas I've ever heard, he did have the good sense to do it while wearing Gore-Tex.

If all this twisted rope talk seems confusing at first, remember the first knot you ever learned—the one to tie your shoes—once seemed all but impossible. Be patient, and tying knots will become second nature.

### Nuts and Bolts

A **single knot** uses one strand of rope to form one "simple" knot. To **retrace a knot** is to follow the shape of a knot with the tail of the rope to make a "doubled-up knot." A **bight** is a doubled loop of rope. Knots are often "tied on a bight." A **hitch** is defined by rock climbing purists as a loop involving a single strand of rope that is wrapped around something.

## Types of Knots

Knots fall into a few basic categories:

➤ **Single knots.** This doesn't mean that they can't get a date, but rather that the knot is tied with one strand of rope to form one "simple" knot.

➤ **Retraced knots.** This simply means that you follow the route of a single knot with a second strand. The figure-8 knot is the best example of a retraced knot.

➤ **Knots on a bight.** This involves tying any number of knots on a *bight*, or double loop, of rope. This is often done to make a solid link for clipping into an anchor.

It's worth noting the difference between a knot and a *hitch*. Whereas a *knot* involves a bend in the rope that alters its shape and function, a *hitch* is a single strand of rope wrapped around a tree, rock, or other immovable object.

Experienced climbers probably can tie close to two dozen knots. Most climbers, however, rely on six primary knots—even if they're climbing the north face of the Eiger. Of these knots, the most basic are the overhand, the figure-8, and the fisherman's knots.

**Cliff Notes**

To learn more about the north face of the Eiger, read Heinrich Harrer's *The White Spider*. Harrer details the harrowing first ascent of the Eiger's treacherous north face, which was done, mind you, decades before the advent of Gore-Tex.

## The Overhand

The *overhand knot* is probably the simplest knot of all. Done with a single strand of rope, it is usually used to secure loose rope ends after another knot has been tied. (This is known as a *stopper knot.*)

Using the overhand knot for joining two ropes of equal diameter in a rappel has been called "the European death knot." (The overhand is *not* a good knot for joining ropes of *unequal* diameter.) Despite the foreboding name, this procedure actually has an advantage over other knots because it is often easier to pull down the ropes after a rappel.

There are downsides to the knot. It can untie if there is not a lot of extra line left over once the knot has been tied. Also, it is not easy to untie after being loaded. Most experts recommend that you use a figure-8 or double fisherman's knot to join lines of equal diameter in rappel situations. (We'll get to those knots in a minute.)

A variation on the overhand knot is the *water knot*, which is good for tying the ends of webbing together. Essentially, it is simply a follow-through on an overhand knot. Beginners tend to use webbing for top-rope anchors, so it's good for them to learn this technique for use with webbing.

**Nuts and Bolts**

The **overhand knot** is a simple, easy-to-use knot that can be used to secure the loose rope ends coming from another knot, as well as to connect two ropes.

The **stopper knot**, also called the *overhand knot*, is used to secure loose rope ends after another knot has been tied.

**Nuts and Bolts**

The **water knot**, also known as a **retraced overhand**, is the knot often used with webbing since it symmetrical, strong, and allows the material to lie flat without folding. It is not very secure though, so check it frequently and leave at least a one inch tail after tightening.

Here's how to tie an overhand knot with a single strand of rope:

1. Make a circle at the end of the rope. Leave room for a *tail*.

2. Thread the tail behind and through the circle, and you're done.

The *overhand on a bight* is the simplest way to create a closed loop in the middle of a rope. You do this when you need to clip yourself or a piece of gear into the rope. To make an overhand loop, follow the preceding steps, using two strands of rope side by side.

There's just one small problem: The overhand on a bight is a bear to untie after it's been weighted by a climber. In fact, most climbers prefer to use a figure-8 knot for just this reason.

*The overhand on a bight.*

## The Retraced Figure-8

There are many ways to connect the climber to the end of the rope (via the climber's harness), but the *retraced figure-8 knot* has become the way among climbers I know—

**Hold On**

Most climbers use a figure-8 knot rather than an overhand on a bight, because the overhand is hard to untie after it has been weighted.

and for good reason. This knot is really strong and tends not to come untied. It's also easy to inspect. Like all *cinch knots*, the tighter you pull, the tighter the knot becomes. This all-purpose knot is probably the most useful of all climbing knots. It's certainly the one used most often.

Over time, the standard tie-in to your harness will become second nature. Remember to secure the rope through both the front loop and sling that bridges the leg loops of your harness.

Here are six simple steps for tying a radical retraced figure-8 knot:

1. Holding the end of the rope with your left hand, create a loop with about a three-foot tail that crosses in front of the main rope.

2. With your right hand, thread the end of the tail behind the main rope and back through the original loop. Pull on the tail a bit and—*voilá!*—you've got a figure-8 knot.

3. Run the tail through the leg loops and waistbelt of your harness. Now you're ready to retrace the line of the first knot.

4. Thread the tail back into the knot. If you've done it right, the two strands of rope will be parallel and under the bottom of the knot.

5. Take care to follow the line of the first knot, making sure the two strands are side by side and not crossed.

6. If you have a foot or more of rope left over, don't worry; just tie off the loose end with an overhand knot above the figure-8 knot so that it doesn't get in the way. In fact, it's standard practice to secure your knot with a double overhand or grapevine knot as a back-up.

Before you climb, make it second nature to check that your partner is tied in correctly to his or her harness. He or she should do the same for you. This is the beauty of the buddy system. Now you're ready to roll.

*The retraced figure-8 knot.*

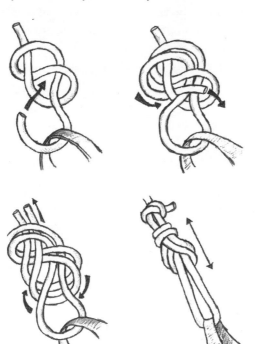

### Nuts and Bolts

The **retraced figure-8 knot** is the most commonly used knot to attach a rope to a harness. It is formed by tying half the knot, looping the rope around a harness or desired object, and "retracing" the shape to finish the knot. A **cinch knot** becomes tighter the more you pull on it.

### Finger Tips

The figure-8 and retraced figure-8 are strong knots that can be easily untied even after they have carried a heavy load.

### Finger Tips

Learn how to tie the retraced figure-8 knot in your sleep. A good way to learn is to practice the knot with your eyes closed.

# The Figure-8 on a Bight

The figure-8 on a bight knot is actually an easier knot to tie than the retraced figure-8 you use when securing the rope to your harness. Typically, climbers use this knot to tie into an anchor or when traveling as a rope team—say, through a crevasse field. While the figure-8 on a bight knot is easy to tie, you'll need to learn when to use it from an experienced hand. Here's how you tie it:

1. To form a bight, pinch a piece of rope in the middle of the rope (any place other than the ends) so that you have a loop with two strands side by side, with the top of the loop hanging down. Now you're ready to follow the steps outlined in the section on trying a retraced figure-8.

2. Instead of making one figure-8 knot and following through with the tail to make another, simply weave the two strands of rope into a figure-8.

3. Cinch the knot so that the strands are snug and neatly aligned—and there you go.

# The Fisherman's Knot

Originally used to join fishing lines, the good old *fisherman's knot* is the simplest way to joint two ends of rope together. All you have to do is tie two overhand knots. And no knot is easier to tie than the overhand knot. Many experts consider the grapevine a.k.a double fisherman's knot more secure and use it instead.

Here's the drill:

1. Overlap the two ends of the rope, leaving the tails long enough to tie an overhand knot.

2. Tie an overhand knot on one end and then another one on the other end.

# The Double Fisherman's Knot

The *double fisherman's knot* (also called the *grapevine knot*) is the most secure way you can tie two ropes (or slings) together, or a single line into a loop. This knot is often used for joining two lines together in rappelling situations. Along with this security, the good news is that it's easy to inspect the symmetrical double-X design. And it's easier to untie after a rappel than a figure-8.

Here's all you'll need to know to tie this valuable knot:

1. Overlap the ends of the rope or sling by about two feet.

2. Instead of tying a simple overhand knot, loop the rope around the opposing strand again before you thread the tail back through as you would a single fisherman's.

3. Snug the knots together and tighten.

### Nuts and Bolts

The **fisherman's knot** is the simplest way to join two ends of rope together. It's formed by tying two overhand knots.

### Nuts and Bolts

The **double fisherman's knot**, a.k.a the **grapevine knot**, is said to be the most secure knot around. It is typically the knot selected for tying the end of two ropes together for a rappel.

*The double fisherman's knot.*

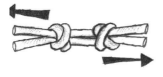

# Knot Satisfied?

Once you have the frequently used knots down, there are few more you should try: the clove hitch, the Prusik, and the double bowline. These knots aren't any more difficult to tie, but they are more specialized.

**Nuts and Bolts**

The **clove hitch** is commonly used for tying the middle of the rope into an anchor point.

**Hold On**

Securely cinch down the clove hitch; otherwise, it could ride up the carabiner and force the gate open. This is why you want to use two carabiners with a clove hitch loaded from opposite directions. The backward carabiners ensures that the strength of the carabiner is not compromised by being loaded out away from the "elbow" of the biner.

## The Clove Hitch

If you learn to climb from a guide, you're likely to notice how often he or she uses the clove hitch. "Easy" is the operative word with the *clove hitch*. It's easy to learn, easy to tie, and easy to adjust for length once you've tied it. While the clove hitch knot is a favorite among climbers for its simplicity and versatility—it's ideal when tying the middle of the rope into an anchor point—the tradeoff is that it's not that strong and can easily slip.

Here's the nitty gritty on the clove hitch:

1. Make two same-sized circles in the rope so that when you hold them side-by-side they look like Mickey Mouse ears.

2. Take the left loop (or ear) and match it up behind the right hand loop.

3. Without twisting the loops, clip a carabiner (attached to an anchor) through both loops.

4. It's important to make sure that the load-bearing strand of rope is next to the spine (or long side) of the biner, because if the knot isn't cinched tightly, it has a tendency to creep up and open the biner. To eliminate this possibility, it's a good idea to use double (and opposed) biners.

*The clove hitch.*

# The Prusik

Assuming you've got the double fisherman's knot down, the *Prusik knot* is a simple knot to tie. The Prusik does require a fair bit of know-how to make it work, however, because it is used to attach a secondary (thinner) rope to the main climbing rope. The Prusik works best on a standard climbing rope with a seven millimeter cord. Because it is *a friction knot* when the Prusik is weighted, it won't slide. When unweighted, it can be moved up or down the main rope. Once you've tied your cord in a circle using the double fisherman's knot, you're ready to roll with the Prusik.

Here's the low-down on the Prusik:

1. Place the cord that has been tied together using the double fisherman's knot behind the rope.

## Nuts and Bolts

The **Prusik knot**, developed by Austrian climber Karl Prusik, involves winding a thin rope around a thicker rope, thus creating a strong friction knot that prevents the thin rope from slipping while weighted. There are many variations on Prusik's design.

A **friction knot** won't slide when loaded, but it may move up and down the rope when unweighted.

### Hold On

When tying a Prusik knot, be neat and generous with your wraps (the loops you tie around the main rope). A neat knot is stronger than a messy one. The knot will slip with an inefficient number of wraps, leading to friction that can melt the thin cord.

### Nuts and Bolts

A **double bowline knot** is a spin-off of one of the original sailing knots, the *single bowline*. Because it can hold heavy loads and be untied easily, it is used to join the rope to the harness and to tie the rope around a natural anchor.

### Hold On

The **single bowline** is not typically used in rock climbing because it can easily come undone—a dicey proposition when your life depends on it.

2. Using the fisherman's knot as a guide, pass the cord around the rope and through the loop.

3. Do it again.

4. Tug on the fisherman's knot to secure the loops that you've made around the rope.

5. Climb on!

## The Double Bowline

With a *double bowline knot*, you can make a loop at the end of the rope in case you need to secure the rope around a tree or some other anchor. (It's highly advisable to tie off the loose end with a single grapevine instead of an overhand knot.) Some climbers use a retraced bowline for tying into a harness instead of a retraced figure-8.

Here's the skinny on tying a double bowline. (Just for the record: The figure-8 is stronger than the double bowline; it's just as versatile and a lot less easy to screw up.)

1. Begin wrapping the doubled-back (or bight) of rope around your anchoring point.

2. Make a loop on one end of the rope.

3. Pass the other end of the rope through the loop (or up through the "phantom bunny hole," as many say).

4. Move the loose end of the rope around the standing part (or "phantom tree").

5. Pass the loose end of rope back into the loop (or down the bunny hole).

6. Pull the double bowline tight.

7. Secure the extra loop with an overhand knot or a biner.

## Before You Tie On

Before you go nuts with the knots, remember the standard practices safe climbers follow:

1. Check to see that the tails—the lengths of rope left after you've tied the knot—are long enough. Around eight inches is fine.

2. Always make sure the knot is sound. Pull on the incoming and outgoing strands of rope and cinch them until they're snug. Tying off the loose ends with an overhand knot will up the safety quotient.

3. Check, double-check, and check again. Do this routinely. Remember: You're trusting your life to these little suckers.

---

### The Least You Need to Know

➤ Knots are the basis of climbing safety.

➤ The various types of knots include single-strand knots, knots on a bight, retraced knots, and hitches.

➤ The retraced figure-8 knot, frequently used for tying the rope to a climbing harness, is probably the most useful of all climbing knots.

➤ The double-fisherman's knot, often used for rappelling, is about the most secure knot around.

➤ After you've mastered the main knots, try your hand at the clove hitch, Prusik, and double bowline knots.

➤ It's crucial that you practice tying knots and that you learn from an expert when and how to use each one.

# Chapter 9

# Top-Roping ABCs

---

### In This Chapter

➤ Pushing your limits with top-roping

➤ Anchors aren't just for sailors

➤ Tying in to the rope

➤ The belayer as "ropemeister"

➤ Rock talk

---

Years ago, a friend was hitchhiking out West and found himself in northeast Wyoming at a campground near Devil's Tower, a towering monolith that juts into the sky like the world's largest tree stump. For those of you who haven't seen the movie *Close Encounters of the Third Kind*, Devil's Tower was the awe-inspiring landing spot for the Mother Ship. (Actually, scientists think it is the core of an ancient volcano.)

Standing near the tower one morning, my friend struck up a conversation with a climber who was complaining that his climbing partner hadn't shown up. My friend, a fit construction worker comfortable in high places, had been pondering how cool it would be to scale the daunting tower. When asked if he wanted to climb it, he barely paused and said, "Well, sure!"

The story is fairly unremarkable in climbing circles; strangers hook up on sites all the time—except that my friend had never climbed before. Fortunately, the story has a happy ending: They successfully climbed the 865-foot tower and lived to tell the tale, and my friend went on to become an avid and skillful climber. This, however, is a dangerous—some would say insane—way to learn how to climb.

And although it's true that most guide services will take beginners on an easy multi-pitch route to give them a taste of the thrills to come, the easiest—and safest—way to learn to climb is on a top-rope.

# The Setup

In top-roping the rope is tied to a climber at the bottom, fed up through an anchor at the top, and pulled back to the ground, where it is attached to a belayer. Compared to lead climbing, top-roping is rather straightforward. A basic understanding of anchor systems, however, is essential. Failure to rig the anchor correctly is likely to get someone killed.

The *slingshot* system is the most commonly used setup in top-roping. Basically, it's just a belay that gets directed down to a stance where the climb begins. Here are the basics:

**Nuts and Bolts**

In a **slingshot** belay, a rope tied to a climber runs up to a secure anchor above, through carabiners that serve as pulleys, and back down to the ground to an attentive belayer. As the climber moves up, his partner keeps the rope snug, ready at all times to lock off the rope if the climber falls.

➤ Two anchors should be involved, preferably stout trees with trunks greater than 12 inches in diameter. The two anchors should share the load or, in climbing terms, be "equalized." If no trees are available, a big boulder or a car can be substituted.

➤ The anchor slings should be tied with figure-8 knots for line, or with water knots for webbing. *Girth-hitching* the slings around the trees will keep the lines from sliding.

➤ The two anchors are connected to two locking carabiners, which are in turn connected to the climbing rope. The best choice for anchor slings is a static rope. Webbing is plenty strong but can be cut easily, especially under load. Sharp rocks under the anchor lines can be padded with shirts or a towel.

➤ The anchor should hang over the cliff line to avoid abrasion on the rope. Great care should be taken not to fall off while checking the position of the anchor. And be careful of knocking off loose rocks that can brain bystanders below. If needed, belay the person rigging the anchor from a higher point.

**Nuts and Bolts**

**Girth-hitching** refers to wrapping a sling or runner around an anchor or through your harness. Then slipping one end of the sling/runner through the center of the other end of doubled material and pull tight.

As the climber heads up the rock, the belayer takes in the slack in the rope; as the climber descends, the belayer pays it back out. The mindful belayer is ever ready to lock off the rope if the climber falls. (See Chapter 6 for more on belaying.) Remember: The laws of gravity are cruel even to the kindest climber.

The ideal top-rope site is 75 feet high (at most), has solid anchors near the edge of the cliff, and has no loose rock or dirt around the top that could rain down on you. It should follow a fairly direct line from the bottom to the top. Rigged correctly and done with an able belayer, this setup is a reassuring way to climb, because a fall can be arrested quickly and (usually) painlessly. If the belayer is doing his or her job, the biggest risk in top-roping is falling off the top while setting up or taking down the ropes. Be on guard!

Top-roping is not just for beginners; experienced hands often climb this way. It's a safe way to hone technique since you can focus on the choreography of the climb rather than finding and placing solid protection. Advanced climbers tend to climb with more slack in the line than antsy beginners, who prefer a more snug line that will reduce the amount of airtime in the event of a fall. Although you don't want your belayer to tug you up the wall, the gentle pull of the rope can be reassuring at first. Regardless, beginners should never climb with a slack line.

## From the Top—But Not for Starters

You can, of course, set up a top-rope so that the rope runs through an anchor at the top of the cliff and the climber is belayed by a partner standing above him at the cliff's edge. If the belayer is well fixed in his position, there is no problem with giving a belay this way. The key ingredient is making sure the belayer is anchored solidly from behind.

## To the Limit—Either Way

Either way, top-roping enables climbers to push their limits without worrying falling. Former American Alpine Club President John Case, a rock-climbing pioneer, did the vertical dance for 50 years and never fell. The current thinking is that if you aren't willing to take risks and fall now and again, you aren't willing to grow as a climber. Regardless how hard you push the envelope, you should know that falling shouldn't be taken lightly even if the top-rope setup is bomb-proof and the belayer is as vigilant as a Secret Service agent. Why? Falling scares the snot out of you, and you're liable to bang rudely into the rock.

**Finger Tips**

Because most climbing ropes are about 190 feet (60 meters) long, and the rope must run up and down the length of the cliff, 85 feet is the maximum practical height for a top-rope site.

**Hold On**

If you must belay from the top, be sure the rope and belayer are solidly anchored to securely support a hefty load. Because a top belay places a lot of stress on the belayer, beginners should avoid it and use a sling-shot instead.

### Hold On

Redundancy is the key to safety. Always use two top anchors, triple-check their security, and never trust your life to just one piece of gear.

### Hold On

Belaying can be uncomfortable and tedious—especially if your leader is having difficulty finding good cracks to place her pro. In any case, it is mandatory to maintain your concentration for two reasons. First, your partner's life depends on it. Second, watching skilled climbers in action is an invaluable way to learn.

### Finger Tips

It's better for a beginner to belay from the bottom so that an expert can examine his harness and knots and give climbing advice.

# Anchors Aweigh

Getting to the top of the climb to set up the top anchor happens in one or two ways. In places like the Shawangunks, you can often hike a trail to the top of the crag, in which case your guide or experienced friend will walk up, set up the top anchor, and have you belay him down from whence he came. He can also walk back, but it's less fun.

Professional guides use the acronym RENE (Redundant Equalized, with No Extensions) to describe their anchor systems. This makes up what they call a "bombproof" anchor. Redundancy is the key here; never trust your life to just one piece of gear. Always prepare for the worst possible scenario—that an anchor, for instance, is not stable—and anchor to two separate points.

If there is no trail to the top, someone must lead the route, setting up anchors (or "protection") along the way. As your leader heads up the rock, he or she uses a carabiner to clip the rope to a piece of pro. Once the lead climber passes the new anchor, any falls are limited to the distance between the climber and the last anchor—plus the distance again as the fall continues past the anchor before the rope finally pulls taut. Clearly, lead climbing is not the beginner's job. It's good to know the procedure, however, since you are likely to be belaying the leader. (See Chapter 17 for more on lead climbing.)

Once your intrepid leader has reached the top, he or she will anchor the rope to a tree, rock horn, or some other immovable object, and then walk or rappel down. After that, your top rope is set and you're ready to roll.

# Top Anchors vs. Bottom Anchors

Clearly, the bottom anchor isn't as crucial as the one on top, since the belayer's body weight is a natural anchor. While you often see climbers belaying without tying themselves in to an anchor, it really is prudent to tie the belayer to the ground—either with a rope or by tying the rear of the harness to a solid anchor.

Why? Anchoring your belayer ensures that he or she won't be flung into the cliff in the event of a fall. Also, if a rock is dislodged from above, it will keep the potentially freaked belayer from running. Although that may sound a bit far-fetched, it happens. The bottom line is that it's important that the belayer be positioned far enough from the wall so that the odds of being struck by a falling rock are between slim and none.

# Tying One On

Even if climbing deities Reinhold Messner and Sir Edmund Hillary could set up a top-rope for you, it wouldn't be worth a rocky hill of beans unless you're wearing your harness correctly and the harness is tied to the rope with a solid retraced figure-8 knot. Initially, these two basic facets of climbing will seem confusing. The harness might seem like a medieval pair of underwear and the knot a twisted trick best left to Harry Houdini. Don't fret. In time they'll become as automatic as tying your shoes. (For more on harnesses, see Chapter 5; for more on the retraced figure-8 knot, see Chapter 8.)

Even though you will quickly become accustomed to wearing your harness and tying in to the rope, experts do get careless and make mistakes that often end in tragedy. Always check your harness and knot, as well as those of your partner. It's called the "buddy system," and it works.

Here's what you should look for before leaving the ground:

1. Make sure the buckle on your harness is threaded correctly; that is, the waistbelt is doubled back on itself through the buckle.

2. Make sure the rope passes properly through your harness. Different designs have different specifications. Read the manufacturer's instructions carefully.

3. Make sure the retraced figure-8 knot is tied correctly and secured with a double overhand knot.

4. Make sure you check the integrity of your harness buckle and figure-8 knot throughout the climb. No matter how grumpy you or your partner may become, keep checking each other out.

### Hold On

Leave at least six inches of tail when tying the rope to your harness. This gives you enough to tie a back-up knot. If you fall, the knot will prevent the end of the rope from accidentally slipping through the knot.

*Top-roping indoors. (Photo courtesy of Mark Eller.)*

# Rope Wranglin': Belaying Your Partner

Although belaying your partner is a rather simple procedure, it requires practice and sensitivity to the climber above. Both the belayer and the climber must inspect their harnesses and knots before climbing begins. Check that the harness is doubled backed, that climber is tied in properly, and that the carabiners are loaded correctly.

### Nuts and Bolts

The **brake hand** stops the movement of the rope in the event of a fall. It should never leave the rope!

The **guide hand** directs the rope while you are belaying a climber and helps retrieve excess rope during the climb and rappel.

Once you are anchored securely, you'll decide which hand is your *brake hand*; that is, the hand that will secure the rope in the event of a fall. Usually, if you're right handed, your right hand will be the brake hand, though some people prefer it the other way around. The other hand becomes the *guide hand*, which will, well, guide the rope to the climber or help take in any slack.

Here's an important thing to remember at the indoor gym as well as at the popular outdoor crags: When you find yourself at a crowded venue, it's only natural to check out the other climbers. Remain vigilant; don't let your eye wander while you're belaying. Spacing out at the wrong moment can mean the difference between an "innocent" fall and one with dire consequences. As my first-grade teacher, Mrs. Wright, said, "Pay attention!"

## Flying Kites and Milking Cows

I know I keep hammering this point, but it's crucial: The first thing to remember when learning how to belay is to never let go of the rope! This is a tad tricky and requires time and practice before it becomes ingrained. At first, it's best to watch your hands, not the climber. Soon enough, you'll be able to do both. Once the practice becomes second nature, you can watch your mate as intently as you like.

Here's the nitty gritty on belaying:

1. While the left (guide) hand reels in the rope to maintain tension as the climber heads up the rock, the right (brake) hand pulls the rope through the belay device. If your partner is climbing well and you're in sync, this should be a smooth, nearly rhythmic movement—a cross between flying a kite and milking a cow.

2. To get back to the best position to reel in more rope, slide the guide hand up the rope and reach a couple of fingers across to grab the brake side of the rope ahead of the brake hand. Without letting go with the brake hand, slide it back down to the belay device.

   Now you're ready to do it again. Continue to reel in more rope until the climber shouts, "Off Belay!"

3. If your partner falls, bend the rope as quickly as possible across the belay device with your brake hand.

As usual, you should have a seasoned climber show you how to do this. The rest is practice, practice, practice.

### Hold On

When belaying your partner, don't be tempted to watch other climbers or to strike up a conversation with spectators or your neighboring belayer. Even a slight delay in braking can allow several feet of rope to slide through your belay device, resulting in a potentially painful fall for your partner.

### Finger Tips

It takes a while to get the hang of belaying. Don't fret if you feel spastic at first. Time and repetition will—and must—make belaying second nature. Your goal is to watch your hands, not the climber. Listen to the climber's needs.

## The Big Letdown

When your partner wants (or needs) to be lowered, you should keep the following tips in mind. (Although this is a simple procedure, accidents often happen.)

1. Communication is key. The lead climber will yell, "Lower!" or "I'm done, fried, finished," or any other pithy comment that gets the job done.

2. To lock off the rope, bend it across the belay device.

3. Lean back to establish good balance. Don't let out any rope until the climber's full weight is on it.

4. Put both hands on the brake side of the rope and slowly and steadily lower the climber by letting the rope play through the device. To monitor the speed of the descent, watch the braid of the rope as it passes through the belay device.

5. Only when the climber is standing safely on the ground should you take tension off their harness. Even then it's good form to wait for your mate to say "Off belay!"

**Hold On**

If there is notable danger of rockfall, you should belay from the shelter of an overhang or bulge. If none is available, wear a hard-shell, UIAA-approved helmet. In fact, most safety-oriented climbers will tell you that helmets should always be in use.

## *Vertical Tug of War*

Finding a solid and comfortable stance is important when you're belaying. Think of yourself in an imaginary tug of war. Stand with your feet a bit past shoulder width, with one foot forward, the other back and to the side as if you were fencing. Your center of gravity should be over your hips.

If your partner falls, your body will absorb the initial impact and lessen the impact on the anchor behind you (the last line of defense). If the system is set up correctly and you've been on guard, you'll be surprised how easily you can catch a climber who weighs as much as an NFL middle linebacker.

## Say What?

Communicating effectively while climbing is crucial. Without a verbal understanding of what's up, you might as well be climbing in the dark. If you are belaying and can't figure out what your mate has said, remove any slack from the rope and ask again. There will be plenty of times when you'll be near a raging stream or in a wind that can muffle your words like heavy blanket. When in doubt, shout like your house is on fire.

**Finger Tips**

Whether you're climbing or belaying, keep your comments short and simple.

Furthermore, in areas where climbers are often within earshot of each other, follow each cue with your partner's name to avoid confusion. "On belay, Moe?" "On Belay! Curly." (Although if someone named Joe or Shirley is nearby, it could get confusing.)

Heading back to my car on a windy but otherwise perfect fall day in the Gunks, I nearly had a heart attack watching a woman perched on a ledge 50 feet off the ground with no protection. What happened? Her belayer heard a nearby climber say "Off belay!"

Fortunately, he realized his error and was fine, but the misunderstanding had disaster written all over it.

Finally, don't shout long detailed comments between climber and belayer. Keep them short and clear, and if you aren't sure what you've heard, ask again. It's better to keep the rope on belay and to remove any loose slack than to assume that the climber no longer needs the belay.

## The 15 Commandments

Climbers have their own lingo, born over time and out of necessity. (I've put an exclamation mark after each command to emphasize the importance of speaking loudly and clearly.)

1. **"On belay!"** A sacred phrase that means the belayer has checked the harness buckle, anchor, knots, and belay device setup, and is in position to accept responsibility for the lead climber. Again, check both your partner's harness and tie-in knots.

2. **"Climbing!"** The climber, poised at the base of the rock, makes sure the belayer is ready. When all is right with the universe, he or she utters this magic word.

3. **"Climb!"** or **"Climb Away!"** This is the belayer's way of telling the climber to have at it.

4. **"Up rope!"** The climber wants the belayer to reel in some of the slack in the rope.

5. **"Slack!"** The lead climber feels the rope is too tight.

6. **"Take!"** or **"Tension!"** or **"Hold me!"** The person above needs to hang on the rope. The belayer should lock off the rope and hold the climber's weight until otherwise noted.

7. **"Watch me!"** If the climber feels gripped by fatigued or is worried that the next move is risky, this command alerts the belayer to be ready to break a fall.

8. **"Falling!!!"** Need I say more?

9. **"Rock!"** When a rock takes to the air, this is the call.

10. **"Off belay!"** The leader is on firm ground at the top, anchored, or tied up by a band of masked men. In short, your job as a belayer is temporarily on hold.

11. **"Belay off!"** The belayer is taking the climber off belay. Make sure you use this command before you actually perform the task.

### Hold On

When you finish the route, remember to make eye contact with your belayer and to shout "Got me?" Get a definite confirmation that she has the brake securely on before you sit back and begin your descent.

12. **"Got me?"** The climber wants to come down. Before you put your weight on the rope, you darn well want to make sure you've got a friend.

13. **"Lower me!"** Once the climber is in good hands, he or she has a free ride to terra firma.

14. **"Again?"** If either of you can't hear what the other has said, don't be coy.

15. **"Thanks!"** or **"Thanks, dude!"** When all is said and done, a little gratitude goes a long way.

## Safety Review

When you read reports of climbing accidents, it becomes clear that the majority stem from human error. Climbers often are so jazzed to get to the rock that they rush through the standard safety procedures. Keep the following oft-repeated tips in mind, and your day at the crag will remain another good memory:

1. If you have any doubts about your belay system, keep tinkering with it until it's fail-safe. And remember to double-check all knots, biners, and harnesses.

2. Check your partner's harness and knots as well as your own.

3. When belaying your partner, be attentive. A life (and your conscience) depends on it.

4. When you reach the top, make sure the belayer below is ready to take your full weight. "Got me?" is the thing to say.

---

**The Least You Need to Know**

➤ Climbing on a top-rope is the way most (sane) beginners begin.

➤ The anchor at the top of a top-rope climb is the linchpin of the climb.

➤ Though tricky at first, tying in to your harness will, in time, become second nature.

➤ Handling the rope and staying alert are the belayer's primary tasks.

➤ The climber's lingo is a concise one, dude!

---

# Rappelling: What Goes Up Must Come Down

Whether it be *The Eiger Sanction* with Clint Eastwood or *Jagged Edge* with Sylvester Stallone, virtually every climbing movie I've seen has a similar scene: A manly man (often in a tanktop despite the weather) is seen rappelling down the side of a cliff, bounding prodigiously like a gazelle on amphetamines. Of course, if someone were firing an automatic weapon at me, I'd hurry as well. But the basic lesson here is this: Take that image and leave it on the editing room floor! Heroic rappelling might look cool, but such herky-jerky movements stress the whole system and can singe a rope's sheath.

Although thrilling, rappelling isn't suited for adrenaline junkies or tough guys on a mission. If you want to simulate a near-death experience, dash down to the nearest bungee-jumping outfit and free-fall from a crane. If you want to "walk" efficiently down a sheer rock face, however, you need to learn to rappel properly—which means prudently.

# Going Down?

"Getting to the top is optional; getting down is not!" is a popular saying in climbing circles. *Rappelling* (or *rapping*) is the process of sliding down a fixed rope, using friction on the rope to maintain control of the descent. Think of an elevator moving down a fixed cable—only you're the elevator as well as the elevator operator. Remember to lean back while rappelling. Keep your feet a shoulder's width apart and look at your feet and where you are going. The harder you lean back, the more your feet will stick to the rock.

## Nuts and Bolts

**Rappelling** (or **rapping**) is the act of sliding down a stationary rope, applying friction to the rope to control the speed of the descent.

The word *rappel* comes from the French verb *rappeler* (to call back). This is significant because rappelling is practical only if the climber can retrieve the rope when he's back on the ground or a ledge en route to the bottom. This happens by doubling the rope around or through an anchor, rappelling on both strands, and then pulling one strand through to call back the rope.

You can rappel on a single strand of rope, of course, but this will get expensive and—if you're more than one rope length off the ground—impractical, because the rope will stay tied to the top when you're far below. (If this does happen, you can use another all-purpose term French climbers and taxi drivers use often: "*Merde!*")

So, barring unusual circumstances, you'll be rappelling on a double rope (or ropes that you've tied together with a figure-8 knot), which you retrieve by pulling through the anchor slings. The double-rope rappel is similar to the top-rope setup; the same concerns about anchors apply. The most common way to put it is that you never trust your life to just one anchor. Two "fail-safe" anchors (preferably towering ponderosa pines) are the minimum. If you don't have solid placement like that, three or four redundant, equalized, non-extending placements are the only alternative. (*Non-extending* means that if one of the anchors fails, there is no slack in the system to allow the rappeller's body weight to *shock-load* the remaining anchors.)

## Nuts and Bolts

**Shock-load** is to stress the rope when you suddenly fall.

Statistically, rappelling is the second most dangerous aspect of climbing, just behind leader accidents. You must pay careful attention to detail on every aspect of the procedure. Faulty anchors result in dead climbers.

It goes without saying that you must be sure that the rope reaches the ground (or the next anchor). If you have any doubt, tie a "stopper knot" in the end of each rope so that you won't rappel into thin air. In fact, most climbers do this automatically. Since stopper knots tend to get caught on natural rock features, many climbers tie the ends of the rope together with a figure-8 knot.

# Nothing to Fear but Fear Itself

Stated simply, rappelling is scary—and for some, terrifying—until you get used to it. My biggest obstacle was learning to trust my harness. While I had no problem thinking my harness would hold me if I slipped on the way up, somehow sitting all the way back into something that basically reminded me of a jockstrap made of webbing left me uneasy.

Even though human instinct tells you not to lean backward on a sheer rock face high above the treetops, once you do it a few times, it seems much more natural and soon becomes pleasurable. (I know folks who head to cliffs not to climb but just to rappel.)

Many guides belay their clients on their first rappels because it reassures them that they'll be fine even if they panic. Similarly, beginners can easily belay each other on rappels. The procedure requires someone on the ground who can pull the rope tight if the rappeller lets go with his brake hand. A firm tug on the line from the ground will stop a potential disaster.

## A First Time for Everyone

The rappel that got me over the fear hurdle took place on a cliff on Big Rock Mountain in China. The rappel was the first event on the last day of a four-day adventure race called the Mild Seven Outdoor Quest. While the rappel was "only" 300 feet, staring up at my nemesis from below made it seem three times that size. Playing disaster scenarios over in my mind, I fidgeted in my sleeping bag most of the night, trying to calm my jangled nerves. (Clearly, Clint and Sly didn't toss and turn like this before their big descents.)

Edging backward over the cliff the next morning was like stepping into the mouth of a fire-breathing dragon; the villagers below looked like figures on a train set, and my tent like a hotel on a Monopoly board. Yet once I cleared that nasty ledge, it was as though a switch had been flipped. I loosened my death grip on the rope and grinned like a pardoned prisoner all the way to the ground.

**Hold On**

For an emergency backup to fixed rappel anchors, bring along a couple of one-inch tubular webbing slings tied with a water knot. (You can learn how to do this from *The Book of Outdoor Knots*, among others). In most cases there will not be a separate fixed anchor near the rappel station, so the rappel will have to backed up by placing gear if the anchor is suspect. This is a tricky, but common, situation because the gear will be difficult to retrieve unless it is looped around a flake or threaded through the rock. Beginners beware!

**Hold On**

Footholds and ledges should not be used while rappelling. They cause you to stop and jerk down the rock.

113

Joe Glickman, my co-writer, had a similar experience in a very different setting. Even though he had rappelled many times on rock, during a five-day climb on Mt. Rainier in Washington, he and his mates rappelled into a massive crevasse in the Nisqually Glacier to do some ice climbing.

Here's what he wrote about it for an article on ice climbing for *The New York Times*: "This yawning chasm—an eerie, hauntingly beautiful place—vanished under a bulge hundreds of feet below my crampons. After several deep, audible breaths, I quieted my mind and started down as fast as possible."

In other words, he was as calm as a cornered squirrel. After several more trips into the icy cavern, he warmed to the task and even enjoyed it.

## The Stance

What's the best way to do this downward dance? The most important—and hardest—thing to do is leaning back far enough to keep your feet in contact with the rock. Why? The more you recline, the better your feet will adhere to the wall. Picture water-skiers sitting back in their harnesses and you've got a good picture of your backward lean. Actually, the position is closer to someone sitting in an easychair with his or her feet up—only far less relaxing.

The second most important thing to remember is to keep your legs a bit wider than shoulder-width apart. This stance will keep you properly balanced. Twisting slightly to the side to look down is the best way to travel. The first time I rappelled, I was so intent on feeding the rope through my friction device that I nearly impaled myself on a tree rooted in the side of the cliff. Furthermore, resist the urge to stop on ledges; it takes weight off the rope and makes it hard to get back into that proper rear-lean position.

*Rappelling. (Photo courtesy of Mark Eller.)*

## The Glove

Some climbers carry a thin leather or cycling glove when they rappel to protect their hands from rope burn. Since I lack the calluses to protect my hands, I'm in the Michael Jackson camp and usually stuff a glove in my harness. It's up to you; some climbers consider it overkill (read: wimpy). You be the guide. If you have a promising violin or piano career, go with a glove.

### Cliff Notes

Mentioning the glove reminds me of a comical scene that occurred during a Hi-Tec adventure race I did in Miami in 1998. These multi-sport events usually involve climbing skills. During the race each competitor was handed a work glove and a life preserver (or PFD—personal flotation device). On this hot, muggy day, my teammates and I reached the top of an overpass, donned our gloves and PFDs, and rapped 50 feet down the side of a bridge into the causeway below. Halfway down I started to laugh, imagining what unsuspecting spectators were thinking as waves of frenzied, mud-splattered people—each wearing a bulky, bright orange PFD and one glove—sped down a rope off a bridge. "Look, Martha, must be escapees from the nut house."

## Hanging Out Big

The funkiest side of rappelling occurs when you rap past an overhang into thin air. The first time this happens you might feel a big hole in the pit of your stomach. Fret not. When this happens, place the rope between your legs, under one leg, and up to your brake hand. This way the added friction of the rope rubbing under your leg slows the descent. Assuming everything is set up correctly, you can stop in midair by folding the rope over the leg.

The key thing to remember is to maintain a smooth and steady pace. If you freeze up and inch your way down, you tend to twirl on the rope. Keep the same position you would if you were sitting in a lounge chair. Holding the line with

### Finger Tips

Dig your heels into the rock while rappelling. This places your body in a solid sitting position. Then walk slowly down the rock to avoid major friction and heat build-up on the rope. Always move in a straight line; moving from side to side often causes abrasions in the rope near the anchor points.

your guide (uppermost) hand will help keep your upper body upright. When you come back to the wall, stick your legs back on the rock and breathe a sigh of relief.

# Rappel Gizmos

Done correctly, rappelling isn't arduous; you can easily control your descent with one hand. Although the act of rappelling isn't too difficult, setting up the ropes and anchors is clearly the domain of a guide or seasoned climber. The same is true for selecting a *rappel device*—the metal gizmo that slows your descent down the rope.

The figure-8 descender and various tubular devices are the most common rappel gizmos. The other methods I'll mention are excellent to know as well; they will serve you well if you lose or break your belay device.

## Go Figure

The *figure-8 descender* was, and probably still is, the most popular of rappel devices, though flat plates like the Sticht are frequently used. (See Chapter 6 for more on flat plates.) The figure-8 device is shaped more like a two-tiered snowman than it is an "8." A bight of rope passes through the bigger bottom ring, loops around the stem, and then clips through the small hole into your harness with a locking carabiner or two regular biners with the gates opposed.

The upside with this device is that it's extremely ease to rig and quite safe to use. The downside is that it's heavier than other devices you can use and often puts a twist in the rope that causes kinking. Still, it's the device I'm most comfortable with and probably the one you'll use as well.

## Tubular, Man

The other option to use is something that's already on your gear rack: a lightweight, tube-shaped belay device, such as the Black Diamond ATD, the Lowe Tuber, or the Trango Pyramid. Again, ask your local climbing expert which is best and how to use it.

# The Art of Anchoring

It goes without saying that to rappel safely, the anchor (or anchors if it's a multiple-pitch climb) must be rock solid. If you have any doubt about an anchor, find

**Nuts and Bolts**

A **rappel device** is a metal gadget used to slow your descent down the rope. It functions by applying friction to the rope.

**Nuts and Bolts**

A **figure-8 descender** is a metal device shaped like a figure-eight, with a small circle on top of a larger circle, used for rappelling.

**Hold On**

Some climbers use the Gri Gri belay device (discussed in Chapter 6) to rappel. The Gri Gri device is *not* designed for rappelling, however. Use a figure-8 descender instead.

another; faulty anchors are usually fatal. Again, this needs to be left to an expert. Individual lessons or classes in lead climbing will cover anchor safety in detail.

There are two types of anchors: *natural* and *artificial*. Natural anchors are trees, rock horns, or holes in the rock that you can thread a sling through. Artificial anchors refer to something placed in the rock, either wedged in a crack or drilled into the stone. If the gear is left in place, as with bolts, it is called a *"fixed"* anchor.

Because you want to retrieve it, the rope must run through a locking biner (or two non-lockers with the gates opposed) attached to an anchor sling, which, in turn, is attached to a solid natural feature or artificial piece of pro. In addition, many rappel anchors feature "rappel rings," closed metal loops with no gate. Many routes have rappel anchors already threaded with several loops of webbing left by previous climbers. While the temptation is to use these anchors, you don't know how long the slings have been there. The rule of thumb is to check 'em out to make sure they haven't been bleached by the sun or chewed by renegade rats. Replacing suspect slings, including cutting away the old gear and cleaning up the mess, is a good public service, but a job for experienced climbers.

Adirondacks guide Don Mellor says that he once leaned back on an old sling and it snapped. The $2 backup he used saved his life.

Another word of caution: Occasionally, you'll find rappel anchors made of slings tied around large rocks that have been jammed against each other or wedged into cracks. While such a setup just might be able to hold a Roman statue, you can't be sure of its integrity, and you don't want to find out the hard way. Anchors aren't fixed by the Department of Rappelling Safety. In fact, a bold beginner might have rigged the setup you stumble upon.

Because rappelling is relatively easy, climbers often rush through their safety checklist—especially

### Nuts and Bolts

**Natural anchors** are trees, rock horns, or holes in the rock that you can thread a sling through. **Artificial anchors** refer to gear that is placed in the rock. It can be either wedged in a crack or drilled into the stone. **Fixed anchors** are gear, such as bolts, that are left in place.

### Hold On

Never rap (rappel) on a suspect anchor that has been left by previous climbers. You have no way of knowing how well it was secured or how long it has been there. Your life depends on it.

### Finger Tips

Use gear anchors (bolts, for example) only as a last resort. You'll have to leave them behind when you rappel.

117

since rappelling often occurs at the end of the day when they're really tired. Like a racecar driver, make sure everything is in place before you head into the danger zone. With a little care, you won't become a statistic.

# Look Before You Heave

It sounds too simple to be good advice, but it's important to eyeball the rappel route before you toss your rope down from your anchor site. First, you don't want to nail someone under you. Second, you want to avoid snagging the rope on trees or outcroppings of rock. If you don't visually inspect the route first, you inevitably end up wasting time by having to do things twice.

### Hold On

Leave the rappel setup to an expert. Watch the expert carefully to see how they rig their set up. Ask questions and when you finally set one up yourself make sure it's been inspected by a pro.

Once the route is clear, the procedure is simple. Coil the rope, shout "Rope!," and heave-ho. (I find it enormously satisfying to watch the coil slowly unfurl and slither like a dying snake down the side of a cliff.)

# Back It Up

Rappelling often comes at the end of a tiring day of hard climbing or in funky weather when you're eager to get down ASAP. Again, resist the urge to skirt safety procedures. It's crucial not to let your guard down or to think that since rappelling is "easy" it isn't also dangerous. Stated simply: A lot can go wrong—and if it does, it can be disastrous. For example:

1. Your anchors could be set up improperly.
2. Your brake hand could slip or cramp.
3. The rope might not reach the next anchor spot.

### Finger Tips

Climbers sometimes need to rappel with a heavy pack that can cause them to flip during the descent. The most common solution is to suspend the backpack below you from the rappel carabiner or to wear a body harness to keep you upright.

For these reasons (and others), it's important to use some kind of backup while rappelling. Beginners are commonly belayed from above. If there is a problem or the climber panics or can't find a rhythm, he or she is protected. Typically, after a few belayed rappels, the climber finds a comfort level and is ready to go it alone—provided some of form of protection is in place, of course.

# Enter the Prusik

This is where the Prusik knot comes in. As you saw in Chapter 8, this neat little knot (tied with an 8-millimeter cord) binds on the rope when weighted but can be easily slid along the rope when it is not. Although the Prusik works well, it can jam or slip, and it takes a bit of practice to slide the knot smoothly down the rope.

Although most people rig the Prusik above the belay device, this is not very safe. The American Mountain Guides Association teaches all it's students to rig the Prusik below the belay device from the climber's leg loop. The Prusik is used as a backup for the brake hand rather than a backup to the rappel device. Again, have an instructor show you the ropes about this rope-on-a-rope maneuver.

# Rope Retrieval

Retrieving the rope isn't complicated, but it must be done properly when you are safely on the ground or a ledge connected to an anchor. Here's what you need to keep in mind:

1. Ensure that the rope is knot- and tangle-free and that you are pulling the correct end.

2. If you're on the ground (or a very large ledge) it's helpful to walk away from the cliff.

3. When pulling the rope, shout "Rope!" when it comes free from the anchor.

4. Before doing any of the preceding, learn the X's and O's from a guide.

5. If your rope gets stuck, don't climb up it to retrieve it. This is a disaster waiting to happen; if the rope gets "unstuck" mid-way up the ascent you're toast. The only safe option is to re-climb the pitch using a different rope.

**Finger Tips**

To simplify rope retrieval, remember on which side of the anchor the knot that joins the two ropes is placed.

## *Eight Ways to Stay Alive*

As stated earlier, rappelling isn't hard. It is dangerous, however, and you must be ever careful to run through a mental checklist to ensure a safe journey back to solid ground.

The following list is filled with the obvious, but you'd be surprised how easy it is to neglect proper procedures after a long and tiring day of climbing:

1. Make sure the anchors are dead solid perfect and the rope is attached to them properly.

2. Make sure no clothing or hair can get caught in the rappel device. Anything that's sucked in will bring you to an abrupt and possibly painful halt. If this sounds unlikely, think again; it happens more than you might think.

3. Make sure both ends of the rope reach the ground.

4. Guard against rappelling off the end of the line by tying the ends of the rope together in a figure-8 knot. As odd as it may seem, it happens all the time.

5. Ensure that the rappel devices are rigged correctly.

6. Check that your harness fits securely and is properly fastened. Check your partner's harness as well.

7. Make sure the locking carabiners are locked.

8. Retire any gear that appears compromised.

Finally, according to author and expert climber Jeff Lowe, a good way to make sure that you do a thorough check of your safety chain is to check your "BARK" (Buckle, Anchor, Rappel device, and Knot). Not only is this a good way to cover your behind, but it harkens back to the early days when the only real climbers were mad dogs and Englishmen.

---

### The Least You Need to Know

➤ Movie images of action heroes teach you how *not* to rappel.

➤ Rappelling, though not physically difficult, must be done properly to be safe.

➤ Leaning over the cliff is the hardest part of rappelling. Breathe deep, sit back, and walk down the rock.

➤ Knowing how to use the rappel device—the metal gizmo used to control the friction on the rope—is a big part of getting down.

➤ The Prusik knot is your emergency brake.

➤ "BARK" for safety. Check the Buckle on your harness, as well your Anchors, Ropes, and Knots.

---

# Keep It Indoors

In the past five years indoor rock-climbing gyms have multiplied like gourmet coffee shops. There are six indoor walls in Manhattan alone and a handful more within a 50-mile radius. It's just a matter of time before Starbucks puts a climbing wall in one of their stores.

These indoor walls are plywood or (if you're lucky) fiberglass, from 20 to 50 feet high, with movable handholds that can be changed to create new routes. The walls offer hassle-free climbing; you won't get cold or dehydrated, menaced by lightening, wind, falling rocks, rain, hail, sleet, snow, or anything else I left out. And if you're a city slicker you won't get bogged down in the logistics of getting to the rock. The gym is a great place to practice top-roping as well as bouldering. It's also a fine place to meet people (read: boy meets girl, girl meets boy), and a better place to improve your technique and fitness. And the climbing is extremely safe. What's not to like?

# The Phenomenon

Madison Avenue has noticed the explosion in climbing; now more than ever people see images of climbers in ads for everything from automobiles to beer to life insurance. Perhaps the biggest reason for the climbing boom is the indoor rock gym. Today, nearly every city in the country has at least one climbing gym. For that reason (and others), artificial walls have changed the face of climbing.

## Way Back in the 1980s

The first artificial climbing walls were simple handholds and footholds nailed, glued, or bolted to plywood or concrete in basements and garages. New York City's first rock gym, the City Climbers Club, opened in 1989 in a converted handball court in a run-down New York Department of Parks and Recreation building. A windowless gym with a shredded-tire floor for padding, it was started by dedicated climbers who wanted to train during the winter.

Before such spaces were available, climbing devotees improvised with various strategies. Ivan Greene installed handholds in his apartment and literally climbed the walls. When his rock withdrawal became too intense, he would take his "psychosis and meager savings" to the south of France and climb until his francs ran dry. Today, the sport is so trendy that if a climbing fanatic like Ivan Greene is climbing the walls at home he either needs to see a shrink or spend more time working out in the gym.

### Cliff Notes

During World War II the British army used climbing walls to train mountain troops. Years later, in the mid '70s, climbing walls were used for climbing competitions in the former Soviet Union and Eastern Europe. This concept then migrated to the United States in the '90s in the form of wooden handholds bolted onto a simple plaster wall. The first commercial rock gym in the United States was Vertical World in Seattle, Washington.

## The State of the Hold

These days the better facilities feature overhanging walls, *slabs*, *roofs*, crack systems, *aretes* (outside corners), bouldering walls, and *hangboards* (apparatuses with finger depressions mounted overhead like a pull-up bar that are used to improve hand strength.) (You haven't lived until you've seen someone do a one-finger pull-up.)

Long gone are the crude wooden holds fashioned by climbers 25 years ago. Today, these state-of-the-art fixtures are made of epoxy or resin and sand, and are attached with bolts that screw into threaded inserts called *T-nuts*. The holds have come to approximate the actual feel of climbing on real rock, and the seemingly endless variety of multi-colored holds gives instructors a variety of routes to set. Indeed, setting routes has become an art unto itself.

## Chelsea Piers: Jackson Pollock with Play-Doh

Take the wall at the Sports Center at Chelsea Piers on Manhattan's West Side adjacent to the Hudson River. Part of a sprawling sports center and gym, the 100-foot-long wall is a bizarre-looking creation. Brightly colored handholds of all shapes and sizes are spattered in random patterns on the textured wall with an overhang that makes the wall 60 feet high. Picture Jackson Pollock working in Play-Doh and you begin to get the idea.

Ivan Greene, the head instructor at Chelsea Piers, calls indoor gyms "the world's greatest jungle-gyms" and considers his French-made, textured-fiberglass model the best in the country. Opposite the towering wall is a low bouldering wall where climbers can warm up or work on a difficult sequence of moves without roping up.

**Nuts and Bolts**

A **slab** is a large, smooth, inclined surface of rock or simulated material. A **roof**, is an overhanging horizontal section of rock or wall. An **arete** is a sharp outside corner of rock or wall. A **hangboard** is a training apparatus with finger grooves that gets mounted overhead like a pull-up bar.

**Nuts and Bolts**

**T-nuts** are the threaded inserts to which bolts attach to secure artificial holds to climbing walls.

When the regular patrons of this hip Manhattan gym—city folks used to the "traditional" routine of weights, aerobic classes, and stationary bikes—wander over and see this funky-looking playground, many of them inevitably want to try it.

**Cliff Notes**

Revamping a flock of abandoned grain silos in Bloomington, Illinois, Chris and Pam Schmick created the tallest climbing gym in the world. There are 80 routes, and one of the house specialty routes is 145 feet off the ground, five times higher than most indoor walls.

*Ivan Greene climbs the walls at Chelsea Piers, Manhattan. (Photo courtesy of Mark Eller.)*

Before they can say "Patagonia," many people are struck by the one element largely missing from their fitness routine: fun! Once they realize that they can get an excellent workout without the drudgery of the standard exercise routine, an indoor climber is born.

## The Indoor Advantage

How good a workout is it? Climb hard in a gym for an hour or two and your hands and forearms are blitzed, your legs are sore, and your upper body longs for the nearest masseuse. What hooks so many people, however, is the comprehensive mind/body nature of the sport. Not only are you working your upper and lower body, you're developing balance, agility, flexibility, and concentration.

Serious climbers (those willing to sleep in their cars to be near great slabs of rock; rock hounds I call "enlightened dirtbags") train indoors like Navy Seals during the winter, and then go outside to probe the limits of gravity. But indoor climbing has taken on a life of its own. People who start out climbing a lot indoors often improve their technique quicker than their counterparts

**Finger Tips**

You can play countless games on an indoor wall. One of my favorites is H-O-R-S-E, a spin-off from my childhood basketball days. To play, you challenge your partner to follow your exact moves on a selected route. If you make three moves on green, one on red, and stay on blue to the top, for example, your partner must do the same. If she fails to do so, she gets an *H*, and so forth. The first climber to spell "horse" loses.

who learn outdoors. Why? Indoor gyms offer more consistent, sustained climbing. You tend to get more bang for your buck when you climb indoors.

Part of this is simple physics. Unlike real rock in the great outdoors, the spacing of the handholds and footholds in indoor gyms is set up with Homo sapiens in mind. If you can't find a hold outdoors, it doesn't matter how skilled you are—you ain't going nowhere. Indoors, it's obvious where the holds are; they're color-coded and stand out like a sheep on a lava field.

That's where a good instructor comes in. Climbing indoors is more like being in a classroom than the "real" world. Instead of bombarding you with a lot of information about positioning your body, an instructor will give you a few basic ideas and tell you to go play. This way you get just enough feedback to figure things out for yourself. Climbing is, after all, a sport about problem-solving. The more you learn, the more specific the teacher can be in correcting specific flaws.

**Finger Tips**

An indoor wall is a terrific place to learn basic climbing techniques in a safe environment. Even if you've never climbed before, you can visit just about any climbing wall in the country and be scaling the wall in a matter of minutes—under the guidance of a knowledgeable instructor.

## Young At Heart

There is now a whole new group of people who never leave the safe haven of the indoor scene—to which I say, "Climb on!" Controlled-climate vertical types are part of the rich tapestry of the climbing world.

Whether you're 5 or 55, indoor gyms are a perfect place to learn the proverbial ropes about climbing. Youth climbing programs are becoming more popular. In fact, the generation of climbers that has grown up climbing indoors is climbing some of the most radical, technically difficult routes out there today.

**Cliff Notes**

The indoor climbing gym can be a user-friendly form of child care. While working out at the Manhattan Plaza Health Club one afternoon, I found myself climbing next to two 40-ish men in yarmulkes who were taking turns on the wall while minding a 17-month-old girl. She sat at the base of the wall, mesmerized by the moving gate on a carabiner as they did their thing.

Kids thrive in these indoor jungle gyms—unlike in Little League Baseball, which is more about standing around and trying not to screw up. It's quite common for parents to eschew the magician or clown, and host birthday parties for their kids at climbing gyms.

# What to Wear?

After good friction shoes and a harness, the decision about what to wear indoors is basically yours. Shorts and a T-shirt or tank top are the mainstays. Tights and thin bike shorts work well. I prefer lycra tights and a zip-neck poly-propylene turtleneck. The shorts stay snug when I'm climbing, and I can zip up the top to stay warm while belaying.

Dress in clothing that allows easy movement. Some climbers like lycra tights, whereas others go for baggy shorts. The fashion police are not strict. Bring an extra top layer to wear while belaying and just say no to cotton base layers. Cotton absorbs moisture (a.k.a. sweat) and holds it near and dear to your body.

### Cliff Notes

Some people say climbing is in their jeans. Shena Sturman, a 17-year old from Cottage Grove, Oregon, loves her Levi's 501s so much that she competes in them. It doesn't seem to be slowing her down. This gymnast-turned-competitive climber, known for busting through impossible problems, was ranked sixth in the 1999 women's competitive climbing division.

### Hold On

Avoid wearing extremely loose or floppy clothing while climbing. Extra fabric can easily get caught in gear.

Basically, any garment that allows freedom of movement is the ticket. A tuxedo made of lycra will work as long as it's comfortable and the tails have been removed. Avoid wearing very loose-fitting clothing, which can snag on the wall or in the rope. I once wore a baggy T-shirt that drove me batty because the darn thing kept dropping off my shoulder and messing with my concentration.

# Indoors vs. Outdoors

So what's the difference between climbing a wall indoors and a rock outside? After all, you use the same equipment and the same techniques, and the same physical demands are made on your body.

One climber I know compared it to the difference between a rehearsal and a live performance. It's the adrenaline factor. Outside, knowing you're 10 stories above the ground is like realizing there's a full house of snarling critics in the audience.

While it's true that climbing outdoors is far more dangerous than climbing indoors, don't take the relative safety of the artificial wall for granted. If you haven't buckled your harness correctly, tied a proper figure-8 knot into your harness, or made sure your carabiner is locked, a fall from 20 feet onto a paddled floor can cause serious damage.

Conversely, just because you can climb indoors like a monkey doesn't mean you can do the same outdoors. Not only must you deal with the weather and finding routes, you need to have a thorough knowledge of anchor systems and self-rescue techniques. And just because you can lead climb indoors doesn't mean you can do the same outdoors. Most indoor gyms space their protection bolts often less than five feet apart. In many ways lead climbing indoors is like moving your top-rope higher and higher as you go and can give you the impression that leading is no big deal. Wrong!

No matter what level of proficiency you've established indoors, when you move to the real thing, assume a beginner's mind. Humility and respect for your environment, sport, and fellow climber are a time-honored part of life in the hills.

# Bend, Don't Break

Passion and energy are wonderful qualities to bring to the gym, but they must be tempered by good judgment. Part of the indoor phenomenon is the tendency to overtrain. Overtraining and overstraining are the biggest causes of injury. Even if you've been pumping iron religiously and look like a young Arnold, your muscles develop faster than tendons. So while your arms, shoulders, and back might be able to do pull-ups till the cows come home, the tendons in your hands and elbows might not be up to the strain.

Here are a few hints to keep you climbing longer and, ultimately, harder:

➤ Don't climb every day. Three or four times a week is fine. If you need to get an endorphin fix, cross train. Since I have a triathlete's background, I swim, bike, and run.

**Hold On**

Regardless of the level you've reached on an indoor wall, start as a beginner when you move to the great outdoors. Hire a guide, take a class, and learn the specifics about outdoor techniques and safety. Climbing outdoors is much more complicated and dangerous than climbing in the controlled indoor world.

**Finger Tips**

To build hand and body strength, do one-arm pull-ups on an indoor wall. Grasp a hold with one hand and pull yourself up, and then repeat with the other hand. The goal, unlike the recommended rock-climbing technique, is to use your legs as little as possible.

➤ It's preferable to let go of a hold that's about to pull your pinky from its socket and to fall than to fight furiously and risk injury. (Remember, you're on a top-rope.) This isn't to say that you shouldn't push to your limit, but you need to recognize the difference between strain and pain. Hand injuries are notoriously slow healers. Even a minor tendon pull can take two weeks to heal.

➤ It's natural to be sore after a hard climbing session, but if the pain persists after a few days, don't climb again until it subsides. "No pain, no gain" is a catchy phrase that has probably done more harm than good.

**Hold On**

Beware of straining your muscles when climbing in an indoor gym. Although an indoor gym is a fun and social environment, it is conducive to overworking muscles and tendons.

➤ When in doubt about an injury, see a doctor. I strongly recommend seeing a physician who has a background in sports medicine.

➤ Warm up before you do any dynamic climbing moves. I often do a few "laps" on an easy route, moving deliberately and stretching into the move with as much flow as possible. Picture a cat waking from a nap while you reach gracefully for the next hold.

➤ Leave the single-digit finger-pocket holds to X-Game competitors and teenage climbing prodigies.

# Climb the Walls at Home

If you have the space and basic carpentry skills, you can build a wall in your own home. All you need is ³/₄-inch plywood and the holds. You can make holds out of wood, but it's far better to buy them from a climbing store or a company listed in a climbing magazine. It's also a good safety precaution to cover the floor with an old mattress; even a fall of six feet can cause injury if you land awkwardly.

Nels Akerlund, one of the photographers for this book, has set up the best indoor home wall that I know. After climbing indoors during college, he returned to his hometown of Rockford, Illinois and suffered a severe case of "plastic wall withdrawal." With no medication readily available for this little-studied disease, he removed the second floor of his parents' two-story garage and dotted all four walls with at least 100 holds that he bought or made. From floor to ceiling it was more than 20 feet high, and the pitch of the roof added another 10 feet.

A word to the wise: No matter how gung ho your parents are about climbing, it's proper climbing etiquette to ask them for permission before you remove the floor of any building on their property.

# Plastic U.S.A.

Appendix C gives you a list of indoor walls in North America. As I said earlier, Ivan Greene considers the wall at the Chelsea Pier Sports Center in New York City to be the best in the country. Several climbers I've talked to, however, say this is a very " New York-, Ivan Greene-centric view of indoor climbing." While I've seen none better, I'll take their word for it and be content knowing that the indoor boom continues to grow.

---

### The Least You Need to Know

➤ The proliferation of indoor climbing walls has led to a climbing explosion.

➤ Indoor gyms offer a climate-controlled environment to improve your technique and fitness.

➤ Climb hard and climb often, but guard against overtraining.

➤ If you don't have access to an indoor wall—or are just plain antisocial—build your own wall.

➤ Let your fingers do the walking; find an indoor gym near you.

---

# Chapter 12

# Look Before You Leap

## In This Chapter

➤ Learning the rules—and breaking them

➤ Hand grips to get you to the top

➤ Smearing, edging, and more on fancy footwork

➤ Downclimbing

➤ Success through failure

To quote an old joke: "How do you get to Carnegie Hall? Practice, practice, practice." In short, good climbers climb a lot; very good climbers tend to climb more than good climbers; and so on.

Whereas strength and technique improve rather quickly with proper training, one of the most difficult things for even the strongest new climber to acquire is the ability to see a route and solve its problems mentally before moving up the rock. It's like learning to play chess: You might know how all the pieces on the board behave, but until you can anticipate a few moves ahead, you're stuck at the beginner's level.

The bottom line is that learning to read and react to the rock takes time and patience. Sound technique accelerates the learning curve and allows you to feel freer on the rock. Unless you're a prodigy like Chris Sharma—the super-mutant climbing version of Mozart—you should learn the basics from a qualified instructor.

Here's the point: While Sharma "hates to train" and climbs with a seemingly haphazard technique (compared to the top Europeans), he has a fearless, intuitive style, honed from countless hours on the rock. "I love to climb," he says, "and I climb as much as I can. I feel that's the best way for me to improve."

**Cliff Notes**

Chris who? In 1995, less than a year after picking up the sport, the then 14-year old from Santa Cruz, California notched the top spot on the men's open sport climbing circuit. At 15, he climbed a 60-foot high wall averaging 45 degrees of overhang that had been previously scaled by only three others. Now 17, this wiry MTV-speak teenager with hands of steel has climbed some of the most ridiculously hard sport routes ever made. Forget about drug testing; climbers wondered if this "kid" was from this planet.

Few of us mere mortals will ever do a 5.14 route like the Super Tweak in Utah. The best ways for you to improve your style and technique is to learn the basic hand- and footholds, understand the principles of body positioning, study the experts, and do what a prodigy like Chris Sharma does: Climb as much as you can with as much enthusiasm as you have. After all, passion is the best learning tool in any classroom.

# Bone Up

What's so interesting about climbing is that when you start out it can feel both natural and foreign at the same time. "Cool," you think, "I'm climbing." Or, "Holy horse hockey, I'm hanging off the side of a cliff, and my arms feel like cast iron."

To put that unfamiliar feeling into perspective, think again about how weird and seemingly impossible your first bicycle was. From the moment you removed your training wheels to the last time you cruised down the trail on a mountain bike, a million minutes of kinesthetic training have been ingrained in your brain. Climbing is much the same: You need to master the basic techniques until you no longer have to consciously think about each individual move.

**Finger Tips**

Beginners should start with short climbing sessions and progressively build the power and strength necessary to play on the rock for hours at a time. It's easy to overdo it and not be able to get out of bed the next day. Take it slowly.

Here are three tips to keep in mind when starting out:

➤ Learn in a climbing gym, on a top-rope, or by bouldering—in other words, in a safe environment where the fear of falling is minimized. If you're a mental mess, you'll slip back to your most basic instinct of clinging to the rock and crying for your mommy.

➤ Practice one or two moves each time you hit the rock and repeat them until you're too tired to continue. Once lactic acid has built up in your muscles, the learning curve heads south.

➤ Climb with good climbers. Not only will you get valuable feedback on what your doing wrong, but you'll improve by observing what works. Reinforcing good habits at the start of your climbing career is important; unlearning bad habits later is tough.

Once you learn a move or sequence of moves, push it until you can't climb with sound technique any more that day. Practicing like this will help you recall the move(s) when you really need to.

### Finger Tips

New climbers tend to overdo it. Stop immediately if you feel a muscle tweak or pop. Ice the injury for 20 minutes to combat swelling, and then continue the 20-minute ice sessions for the next 24 hours. If the pain doesn't go away, see a doctor.

## Form vs. Content

Once upon a time, climbers were told to (1) keep three points of contact on the rock at all times, (2) maintain balance and, (3) never use their knees. While this was sound advice, today the first rule about technique is that there are no absolute rules. Climbing gracefully is the best way to travel, but looking pretty won't always get you from point A to point B.

### Hold On

Expect to take some falls when you are pushing your limits. Just make sure the safety system is sound.

When Chris Sharma first popped on the scene and started blowing the doors off some ridiculously hard routes, experts said his technique, which included an unorthodox leg swing, was rough, even ungainly. What other climbers (at least the ones who studied him carefully) discovered, however, was that his leg swing gave him the momentum to link moves. Had he heeded the three Golden Rules, he wouldn't have done the outrageous stuff he did.

### Cliff Notes

In the 1970s, "Hot" Henry Barber became a climbing legend, crushing climbing records throughout the decade. His secret? Monkeys. Barber spent days at the Franklin Park Zoo in Boston intensely studying the primates' movements, body positioning, grips, and straight-arm hangs. He then applied them to his own climbing technique, and voilá!

So as the saying goes, "If it ain't broke, don't fix it." Depending on the route you're on, your body type, reach, or level of fatigue, a lunge might be preferable over a controlled

reach; using your knee or derriere might be more effective than using your foot; or your elbow might be better utilized than your hand. Sometimes, one (or no) point of contact is just the ticket for making a move that's been kicking your behind. I've seen climbers use their helmeted heads to secure a hold. In other words, don't be afraid to be creative. As long as you stay relaxed, the best technique is one that allows you to climb your best.

Having said that, sound body positioning is a must for any beginner to advance. Keep the following in mind before you start improvising like a vertical version of Charlie Parker:

### Finger Tips

To climb efficiently on fairly low-angled rock, bend forward at the waist and lower your hands. You should also look at your feet from time to time, not just your hands.

➤ Climb with your feet first. Try to move up the climb with leg power by keeping your feet high and hands low. Climbing like this teaches you to balance on the footholds. If your hands are near or below your head, it is impossible to yank yourself up the wall.

➤ Keep your hips over your feet. Push your hips away from the rock slightly on less-than vertical terrain and suck them in when the going gets steeper.

➤ Keep your arms slightly bent. Don't extend them so high that your weight comes off your feet.

➤ Use your hands lightly for balance, not to claw your way up the wall.

➤ Constantly be on the look out for footholds instead of becoming fixated on handholds.

➤ Rest every few moves. Don't pull on the holds during your rest periods. Instead, hang from a straight arm while you lower and shake out the other, like a swimmer loosening up.

### Hold On

If you do chose a one- or two-finger hold, try to keep your fingers straight in the open-grip position so that you can hang from the bone as much as possible. Too much tension (too soon) on your untrained fingers can lead to tendon and ligament problems.

## Get a Grip

Whether you're in the gym or on the real thing, a handhold can be anything from a deep bucket that you can grab like the rung on a ladder, or a little nubbin that requires cement to stick to. In other words, you'll have to adjust your grip for each hold.

The key thing to keep in mind is that you don't need to use all your fingers to take advantage of a hold. Nor do you need to lock on to it with your digits as though your life depended on it. It's like speeding down a hill on a bike; squeezing the handle-bars with all your might does little except tire you out and make the ride rougher.

Experiment to see how "lightly" you need to grab the hold before you decide to squeeze tight. In most cases, your grip is an important contact point, not the glue holding you to the rock. By this, I mean that your arms, shoulders, and legs should do the climbing, not your hands.

The basic grips available to you are the wrap, crimper, open, and pinch grips, as well as various finger holds.

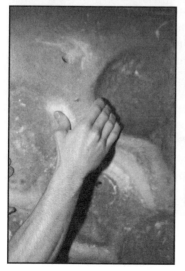 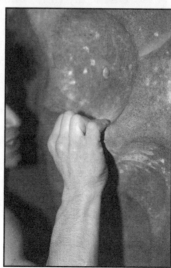

*Hand grips. Wrap (upper left), open (upper right), pinch (lower left), and crimper (lower right). (Photos courtesy of Mark Eller.)*

### Hold On

*Although the crimp grip might seem like a good idea for smaller holds, it's abusive on the finger joints. You're better off using an open grip and saving to the crimper as a last resort.*

### Nuts and Bolts

*The **open grip** involves loosely holding the rock. **Crimping** is grasping small holds with your fingers together and bent at the first knuckle. The **thumb stack** is the method of holding on to the rock by grip-wrapping your thumb over the top two knuckles of your index and middle fingers.*

### Hold On

*Even though the open-hand technique puts more stress on your bones and less on your tendons, your fingers and elbow still get pumped. Don't be a hero; rest between each climb.*

## It's a Wrap

The wrap grip is so natural that it's self-explanatory: simply wrap your hand around a knob-like hold. You have such a large contact surface and can use all the muscles in your hand. When possible, press the pinky side of your hand against the rock; it provides a more balanced body position.

## Cling On

With the more-advanced *crimper*, also known as the *crimp grip*, only your fingertips are in contact with the rock. This grip is best suited to flat-topped and small, sharp edges. The good news is that it works. The bad news is that, since your knuckles are hyperextended, the tendons in your fingers are under terrific strain. Use this grip only when necessary.

A kinder, gentler alternative to the crimper is something called a *thumb stack*. To do this practical grip, lock your thumb over your fingers when crimping. Essentially, what you have is a reinforced hanger. Seen from the side, it will look like you're making a scrunched-up hand puppet.

## Open Wide

One of my early climbing mates once told me, "When in doubt, stay open." He meant that whenever possible, use an "open" grip instead of a "crimp" grip, since it's less likely to cause an injury. The way to distinguish between the "crimp" and "open" grips is to focus on the angle of your fingers. If your knuckles are sharply up (forcing the fingers down), the hand is crimping. If the knuckles are low and under the hold, it's an open hand position.

## Just a Pinch

Whether you're a fine Italian cook or a hot climber, a "pinch" is a standard part of your repertoire. The *pinch* involves squeezing a hold between your fingers and thumb. This is usually required on large holds, which require a fair bit of hand and finger strength. It's not particularly painful, however, especially compared to tiny crimps.

## Pocket Man

The *pocket* is a hold where only a few fingers can fit into a hole. These holds are very common in gyms and at some outdoor areas, where they are often the exclusive feature of the rock. Pocket holds cause more injuries than all the other types of holds combined.

## Rest 'Til It Hurts

A great drill for practicing grips is to traverse the bottom of a wall (either indoors or out) until your arms feel like quivering arrows. Then pick a hold and perch there for as long as possible. Quickly, you'll find that there are several "rest" positions that you can take advantage of. As you cling to the wall with one arm, dangle the other and shake out your fingers like a swimmer on the starting blocks. This lets the blood return and, with it, the strength in your arm. (An appendage held high is drained of both.)

**Nuts and Bolts**

The **pinch** is a hold that must be squeezed between the fingers and the thumb. It's usually required on large holds.

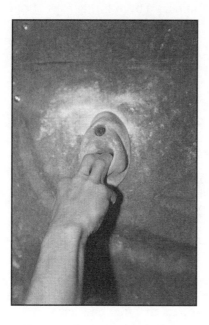

*A finger hold. (Photo courtesy of Mark Eller.)*

While you're "resting," think about what your hips are doing. Experiment with a shift here or tilt here and see how it affects your heartbeat and muscular discomfort. Listen to your breathing. If it's high up in your chest, take a deep breath from your belly and allow your body to recover. Bring full awareness to your climbing, even when you're two feet off the ground. The benefits will spill over into other aspects of your life.

### Finger Tips

Avoid pulling on holds during rests. Instead, hang from one straight arm and lower your other arm, shaking it out to generate blood flow.

### Finger Tips

After stepping on a hold, gently wiggle your heel. It's a good way to stay in solid contact with the rock.

### Nuts and Bolts

**Smearing** is a foot position on the rock that uses the maximum surface of a shoe's sole to adhere to a rock's surface.

Typically, beginners climb like mummies, using far too much muscular tension no matter how easy the move. The culprits here are inexperience and fear. Relax the muscles that aren't needed and you'll be fresher longer. Remember: This isn't a race, it's a dance. Think "flow."

# Fancy Footwork

While it's extremely important to lean away from the rock, to take small steps between holds, and to "climb with your feet," the best advice on footwork I've ever received is to look at the rock as one big foothold. Indoors, you can get used to using specific color-coded holds. Outdoors, however, you can use the whole surface to work with your feet; the rock is little more than a rough spot.

The first few times I climbed, I fixated my eyes upward to find the next handhold. This most basic error is why I felt as though I'd been lifting bags of cement all afternoon. Halfway up the wall, I was toast. Once I learned to look down and to trust my feet, my climbing life changed. As climbing ace Steve Ilg says in his book *The Winter Athlete*: "Fluid expert climbers often look down, not up, seemingly contradictory to their goal of attaining the top of the route.... Handholds are secondary. It's the feet that dance with the rock."

## *Smear Campaign*

When you're climbing a low-angled rock that lacks such features as edges or knobs, *smearing* is the way to go. To get a good hold, you must *smear* the sole of your shoes at the base of the toes onto a rounded bump. It's like spreading cream cheese on a bagel or scraping mud off the bottom of your shoe.

However you think about it, your aim is to maximize the contact between rubber and rock. Putting your weight over your planted foot makes the hold more secure. This technique works like a charm, but beginners are often hesitant to use it, preferring instead to find a small edge or crack to stand on. Learn to trust the integrity of this smearing method; it's an essential technique in any climber's arsenal.

Practice smearing on a variety of angles. (The technique works well on steep rocks.) Look for small indentations and bumps and experiment with a variety of foot positions.

Smearing is most effective when the majority of your weight is placed over the foot. Keep your hips away from the rock. Your upper body may need to lean forward to maintain contact with the rock, but resist the desire to "hug" the wall, which will cause your feet to slip and increase the load on your upper body. The key is to push your foot into the wall—hard.

The steeper the wall, the closer you'll need to bring your hips to the rock. This makes the balance point on your feet more precarious. Try to keep your hands around shoulder level whenever possible, especially on the steep stuff.

Because the rough "sandpaper" crystals in the rock can dig into the soft rubber of your shoes, place as much rubber on the rock as you can. If you hear a gritty noise from under your foot, clean the sole of your shoe by wiping it against your other leg. You might look like a two-year old after a day in the backyard, but you'll climb like a star.

## On the Edge

When you're on a steep rock face and need to hang out on a tiny hold—the serrated edge of a flake, a cluster of crystals, a pronounced wrinkle—there are several ways to use the edge of your shoe. Edging requires precision, patience, and feel. Once your shoe is weighted, it's important not to change your foot position, since you're more than likely to pop off the wall.

Learning to isolate the movements of your legs and upper body from this fixed foot position is one of the reasons climbing is such a phenomenal exercise in concentration and kinesthetic awareness. To find a rhythm, you need to scan the route the way a mountain biker scans a precipitous trail. Breathe from your belly and relax. If you get stuck or scared, return to your breathing and focus on your technique. The lesson here is that slowing down helps you speed up.

### Finger Tips

Climbing shoes loose their tackiness when they are caked with grit and mud. Bring a towel or tarp to wipe your feet on before you start climbing. If you're on a rock and need to clean your shoes without using your hands, wipe the soles against your calves and shins.

### Hold On

Place each foot deliberately and watch it land on the exact spot you have chosen.

### Finger Tips

Footwork finesse and balance are essential to quality climbing on less-steep terrain. Arm power and endurance should be saved for the steep stuff.

*Edging. (Photo courtesy of
Mark Eller.)*

The following techniques will help you live life on the edge with a minimum of stress:

➤ **Inside edge**   This is the most common type of edging maneuver. Use the inside
of your feet at the base of the big toe to maximize the strongest part of your feet
(and shoe). As with smearing, align your body over your feet to maximize friction. Vary the angle of your heel depending on the type of feature you're standing on. The sharper the feature, the higher you heels should be. Again, experiment to see what works best.

➤ **Outside edge**   The outside edge of your feet is weaker than the inside. Knowing
how to use the outside edge is extremely helpful when you need to move one leg
inside the other, especially when traversing. Outside edging is almost always
done using the flat are of your foot, just behind the little toe.

➤ **Front-pointing (or toeing-in)**   This technique speaks for itself—sticking your
big toe into a hold. You're likely to use this move when you're climbing on
limestone or volcanic rock that features pockets. Beware: It's tough on your big
toes.

## The Heel Hook

You often see pictures in climbing magazines of cat-like climbers hanging off a ledge
with the heel of their outstretched legs parallel to their hands. Welcome to the *heel
hook,* a strenuous move that uses the foot as a third hand and requires flexibility,
know-how, and moxie.

The perfect time to practice heel hooks is while bouldering indoors. Once you get that down, try it on the wall. Many indoor overhanging routes aren't possible without using this move. For now, just know that it exists and why it's used. Remember: If you're going to practice it, limber up first.

## Look Down

Climbing is a curious combination of thought, feel, and intuition. As you climb, scan the rock for the best footholds the way a chess player studies the board before making his next move.

**Nuts and Bolts**

The **heel hook** is used on steep, layered rock. Hook your heel over a sharp hold above your head and imitate a chimpanzee by using your foot as a third hand.

Looking down enables you to relax—a key ingredient in speeding your progress. Once you lean away from the rock, let your bones (not your muscles) bear the load, and survey what's available, your options expand exponentially.

Here's another pearl of wisdom from Mr. Ilg:

> When the climber looks down, peripheral and kinesthetic vision increases. Suddenly, a world of microedges and ripples emerges near the feet and hips. Look down as you climb. This oxymoronic hint will reward you with an emerging sense of resourcefulness and sensitivity on the way.

(And you thought you were just getting a good workout.)

Consider the following tips:

➤ Look down as often as you look up.

➤ Don't move your feet until you spot the next hold you want to stand on.

➤ Watch your feet land on the hold as carefully as a target shooter watches a clay pigeon fly through the air.

Starting out, the tendency is to use your hands to deliver you from your precarious perch. Whenever possible, place your feet directly below your hands to reduce the strain on your upper body. Cultivate your vision and learn to recognize "insignificant" features as potential holds. Holds you initially thought to be useless can, in fact, be quite useful.

Push your footholds to the max. When you feel secure on a stab, experiment to see how far away from the wall you can lean. If your weighted leg starts vibrating like a sewing machine needle, lower your heel to ease the tension on your leg muscles.

**Finger Tips**

It's natural for beginners to search "up" the wall for the next handhold. It's actually better, however, to keep your eyes on your feet and only occasionally to glance up.

**141**

# Down the Up Staircase

Many climbers hate downclimbing. The holds are hard to see and the sense of uncertainty is unsettling—all the more reason to practice this skill in a controlled environment. Downclimbing is often safer and faster than rappelling and, in some cases, can save your cookies. When you find yourself off a route or on a section that is over your abilities, downclimbing enables you to get back to your prior position to try again.

# Check Your Head

In his book *The Winter Athlete*, author/climber Steve Ilg details a conversation he had with Will Gadd—a world-class ice climber who also competed indoors on the World Cup circuit—about the importance of learning from mistakes. Keep the following words in mind the next time you climb:

Here's Gadd on taking risks:

> Fail lots. A good, successful failure is when you learn something. Sometimes it's physical, like a new way to drop your knee or move, but the best failures enlarge your mind and tell you what to do differently in life or next time in order to succeed.

> Many climbers will fail climbing because they can't figure out how to do a move or a route, rather than really analyzing a nice failure and developing their minds or technique. For example, if you fall off 'cause you're pumped, it's easy to think, "Hey, I'll just get stronger," rather than, "I failed because my technique sucked, and I got pumped out of my mind as a result." Those who fail to analyze their failures are doomed to repeat them.

### Cliff Notes

Bobbi Bensman, a twelve-time winner of the Phoenix Bouldering Contest and a semi-finalist in five World Cups, uses visualization to prepare for her bouldering and climbing adventures. *Visualization* is a mental dress rehearsal and is used by athletes in all sports. Bensman sees the climb in her head and takes herself visually through the sequence of moves she needs to perform. When she starts climbing for real, her muscle-memory takes over and helps her move over "familiar" territory.

On technique:

> As I climbed with the best climbers in the world…I had a near-religious revelation: All climbing is fundamentally based on technique and mental skill, not strength!…My wife can do exactly six pull-ups on a good day, but **she climbs overhanging 5.11** better than most people who can do thirty. It's technique, not strength, that will take you there.

And on keeping an open mind:

> Sometimes I think climbing is the process of forgetting everything society has taught us as "adults" and just remembering how it was to climb as a child. Children often have near-perfect technique and flexibility, but we somehow lose those abilities as we age.

## The Least You Need to Know

➤ The only way to the top is to practice, practice, practice.

➤ Technique is more important than strength.

➤ The wrap, open, crimp, and pinch are the handholds to know.

➤ Smearing and edging are the two footwork techniques you'll use most.

➤ Don't be afraid of failure—or of learning from it.

# Chapter 13

# Gnarly Noshing

## In This Chapter

➤ Carbs, proteins, and fats: a nutrition lesson

➤ What to eat before, during, and after a climb

➤ What and how much to drink

➤ A question of java

You might think that a chapter on food has no place in a book on rock climbing. Eating the right food at the right time, however, can make the difference between a great day and a miserable one. The longer you're out, the more important food becomes. Joe, my co-writer, tells a story about a five-day climb of Mt. Rainier in Washington.

To simplify his menu planning, he decided to have the same thing for lunch every day: "good old raisin and peanuts," or GORP. Meanwhile, the head guide, Kurt Wedberg, who's climbed the mountain more than 85 times, had no fewer than five different items for each lunch, including gourmet pickles—with mustard! (When Kurt climbed Mt. Everest in 1995, he brought enough mustard to cover a baseball stadium worth of hotdogs.) After four days of GORP, Joe would have nudged the guide into a crevasse if he thought he could have nabbed the guy's pack on the way down.

Even an afternoon at a rock gym will be more productive—and more fun—if you eat and drink what your body needs to perform at its best. Check out Appendix F for additional nutritional resources.

# Fast-Food Facts

Like most kids, I was introduced to the fundamentals of diet and nutrition in high school. Also like most kids, I forgot what I learned before I graduated. But as my sports career got under way, I evolved into a true nutrition geek, with a calculator, food scales, the whole works. I do more than just count calories; I keep track of what percent of calories come from protein, fats, and carbohydrates—except for wine and European chocolates, which I just leave out of the equation. I view eating right as the key to optimal health and performance—and, I admit it, optimal appearance.

Many theories on nutrition are floating around out there, some of which contradict each other. I've read and experimented a lot, and I'll pass on what makes the most sense to me. Ultimately, however, your body will make the call.

**Hold On**

Eat before you're hungry and drink before you're thirsty. If your stomach is empty, so are your muscles. Eat and drink frequently throughout your climbing day.

## To Eat Is to Energize

Calories are a measure of energy. How many calories you need depends both on you (your age, sex, weight, and body composition, for example) and on what you want to do (the intensity and duration of your climb, for example).

To use food to enhance your performance, you really need a basic understanding of how the body converts food to fuel; memorizing lists of "good" and "bad" foods will only take you so far. Here's a quick science lesson: Cells in the body convert food elements—carbohydrates, proteins, and fats—into *glycogen*, a source of energy delivered to demanding muscles. Glycogen must be available to feed muscles while they are exercising or they will quickly fatigue and even cramp. Carbohydrates, proteins, and fats are converted into glycogen at different rates. Eating the right mix of the three will help keep your energy level constant throughout your climb.

**Nuts and Bolts**

Glycogen, which fuels muscles, is a polysaccharide (a complex carbohydrate that the body can easily brake down into simple sugars) derived primarily from carbohydrates stored in the body's tissues.

## Crazy for Carbs

Although experts quibble about the exact ratio, most agree that carbohydrates, or "carbs," should constitute the largest percentage of calories in your diet. That's because they're the easiest for your body to convert into energy. Carbohydrates begin to break down right in your mouth from enzymes in your saliva. They then move quickly through your stomach and into the small intestine, where they are converted into simple sugars (such as glucose) that can be absorbed into the intestinal cells and moved into the bloodstream, ready for action. In just seconds, glucose reaches the muscle cells, where it's converted into ATP (remember your high school biology—that's adenosine triphosphate) and used for energy. (My high school biology teacher had us remember this by recalling where Native-Americans lived—a teepee.)

How long does this process take? It depends on your body weight, but the typical oatmeal-and-fruit breakfast—about 360 calories of carbohydrates—is available to fuel your muscle cells about an hour after you eat. Any glucose not used is stored as glycogen in your muscles and liver, and can be quickly reconverted to glucose, as needed.

The best sources of carbohydrates are fruits, vegetables, beans, and whole grains. These foods are good sources fiber and the vitamins and minerals that boost your energy and your immune system. Avoid products made with white flour. Yes, bagels, pretzels, and pasta do pack a lot of carbs, but most of the useful fiber, vitamins, and minerals have been lost to processing. I come from New York, the Bagel State (or at least the bagel city), and I know many people who cannot imagine life without the big bread doughnut. Instead of the "empty" white variety, you should eat the whole-wheat—or even better—multigrain variety. It's really not much of a sacrifice; whole-wheat bagels taste better than "plain" bagels and are much better for you.

Products high in processed sugar—candy, soda, Twinkies—have no place on a climb. Processed sugar is such a concentrated source of carbohydrates that it plays havoc with your hormone levels, giving you a short-lived energy spike followed by a collapse. To keep your energy level constant, make like Nancy Reagan and just say "no" to jelly beans.

It's time to acknowledge that we are human and often have the willpower of a tower of Jell-O. When you've just got to have something sweet, let it be something with some redeeming value. During the holidays, my friend Ben brings his mother's special fruitcake on our backcountry excursions. It's wonderfully sweet, but it's also

**Finger Tips**

Because your body finds it easiest to convert carbohydrates into quick energy in the form of glucose, complex carbs should be a part of every meal. Foods high in carbs like fruit and vegetables provide vitamins, minerals, fiber, and water.

**Finger Tips**

Good sources of carbohydrates are whole grains, brown rice, yams, and fruit juice. Eat small amounts—but often—for constant energy.

**Finger Tips**

Eat fresh fruits rather than foods high in processed sugar. Fresh fruits satisfy your sweet tooth and give your body a source of fibrous carbohydrates to draw on during your workout. (Bananas come in their own yellow wrappers, and pears fit snugly into a Ziploc bag.)

**147**

packed with raisins and nuts. If chocolate's your thing, don't pack candy bars—spike your trail mix (for example, GORP) with a handful of M&Ms.

### Hold On

Don't overload on protein; your body can't store it. Once your body's demand for it is met, the excess protein is either converted into energy for long endurance efforts or stored as fat.

### Nuts and Bolts

Your body is said to **bonk** when you're dehydrated or don't have enough fuel in your tank. In running circles, this is called "hitting the wall."

### Finger Tips

Egg whites or protein powder mixed with yogurt or into a "smoothy" fruit shake is a quick, tasty way to start off your athletic day.

## Proteins for the Long Haul

An essential part of your diet, protein is used in many vital functions, including creating and maintaining muscle. However, only small quantities are needed for these functions. Once this requirement is met, excess protein is either converted to energy or stored as fat. Again, experts disagree on how much protein we need. Some say we get all we need from simply eating a good mix of vegetables and grains, even without eating meat and dairy products. That might be true most days, but when you're pushing your body into overdrive for an entire day (or more), downing protein-rich food will help speed your recovery.

Years ago, I used to carbo-load for long bicycle races and triathlons. I found that my body would often *bonk* early, however, turning the event from an athletic contest into a grim exercise of putting one foot in front of the other. Now I make sure I get protein as well, for constant, stay-with-me energy.

In Ecuador, during the Raid—a multi-sport, multi-day race in the wilderness—my staples were Balance Bars (which have a fairly high level of protein), nut-filled trail mix, and turkey jerky. Other good sources of protein include tofu, egg whites, yogurt (preferably low-fat), cottage cheese, fish, poultry, cheese, and meat (preferably lean). High-protein foods tend to be high-fat foods as well, however, which is why cheese and meat are at the bottom of my list of good sources of protein.

## Fats for Fun

First the good news: Fat is good. You need fat. It's an important energy source; about 20 percent of your energy comes from fat. Stored body fats protect your vital organs and act as insulation against the cold. And fatty acids help maintain cell walls and protect your skin.

Now the bad news: You get all the fat you need from the small amounts in green or yellow vegetables, beans, and grains. If you also eat fish, poultry, and red meat, your fat needs have been easily met—without resorting to butter, cheese, and chocolate.

Fatty acids are an efficient, slow-burning fuel, and most of us already have a virtually inexhaustible supply stored in our fat tissues.

There are a few exceptions, of course. In Xichang, China, where I traveled for the Mild Seven Outdoor Quest, good sources of dietary fat were few and far between. At breakfast one morning, I watched top triathlete Mike Pigg, whose body fat must be around 6 percent, use nearly an entire stick of butter on a couple of rolls—desperate for the fat to keep his body working at 100 percent. (For the record: A fit male has roughly 10–12 percent of body fat; a comparable woman, 18–20 percent.)

Of course, he's Mike Pigg, the winningest triathlete ever, and we're not. So, unless you train 30 hours a week like the Pigg Man or expect to ski to the North Pole, go light on high-fat food. It's the hardest food to digest, taking about four hours to change into burnable fatty acids. A big high-fat meal can leave you feeling sluggish and sleepy.

### Cliff Notes

In 1983, Brian Maxwell, a Canadian marathoner, created a special energy bar, called the "PowerBar," for endurance athletes. PowerBar, now a multi-million dollar company, revolutionized the energy-food industry, offering athletes a prepackaged, easily digestible nutrition source. One PowerBar packs a walloping 230 calories, 2 grams of fat, 45 grams of carbohydrates, and 9 grams of protein. Wash it down with a glass of water and you're good to go.

## Time to Eat

To perform at your best—not only on the rock, but the next day when you drag yourself back to the office—you need to think about what you eat before, during, and after your climb.

## *Before Your Climb*

There are many good reasons to eat the right stuff before your climb. You'll avoid low sugar levels in your blood and the highly inconvenient feelings of weakness or even dizziness that can result. You'll top off your muscles' glycogen stores, giving you the fuel for an intense workout. You'll settle your stomach by absorbing gastric juices. Finally,

### Hold On

Starting a climb without a nutritious meal is like running a car without gasoline; you'll soon sputter and gasp. Low blood sugar levels can lead to a sluggish performance and poor decision-making skills.

you'll prevent hunger, which means you'll be able to concentrate on the task at hand (or foot). You do not want to be thinking about a bacon cheeseburger as you're tying into your harness.

Don't skip breakfast. Allow your meal an hour to digest before you begin any aggressive activity; you won't be hungry, but you won't feel uncomfortably full either. I do best when I start the day with foods high in carbohydrates and protein, such as yogurt, fruit, scrambled egg whites, and wholegrain bread.

### Finger Tips

Stash a pack of Gu, a carbohydrate gel, in your pocket for a quick energy hit. It packs 100 calories of pure carbs and won't freeze in the cold or turn to mush in the heat.

## During Your Climb

Your body can maintain glycogen stores for up to an hour. After that, it's time to refuel. If your planning to be at the rock or wall for more than an hour, bring something to keep your energy going: a piece of fruit, or an energy bar or gel. Again, stay away from snacks with processed sugars, such as candy or soda. They'll send your blood sugar level soaring and give you a quick burst of energy, but you'll crash fast and hard, feel fatigued and listless, and climb like a worn-out version of Rubber Band Man.

*The author takes time out for Gu. (Photo courtesy of Jay Farbman.)*

## After Your Climb

This is the easy part. Don't forget to refuel your empty glycogen stores after you exercise. You may think that once you stop working your body you can stop feeding it. Actually, it's just as important to eat post-workout as pre-workout, especially if you're planning to do anything other than lie on the couch the next day.

Joe Glickman, a veteran of multi-day mountain climbs, always marvels how, on all-male expeditions, the first or second day of conversation is filled with talk of women; but as the climb goes on, it moves to food. By the last day, the talk of food has turned into a verbal orgy of what they're going to eat first upon returning to civilization.

I, too, am usually so hungry after a climb that not eating is unthinkable. If I wait more than an hour, I've waited too long. Why? Exercise makes the cells in your muscles and liver more sensitive to insulin, which allows them to use and store glucose more efficiently. The effect wears off in a couple of hours, however. Therefore, eat within half an hour of finishing your exercise—preferably foods high in carbohydrates, not fat. (Think fruit, an energy bar, a turkey sandwich, or low-fat soup.) If you go home, shower, nap, return a phone call, and read your mail before eating, you're likely to have one depleted body in the morning.

# Driven to Drink

Okay, so you've heard about the eight-glasses-of-water-a-day rule. And maybe on a good day you swill five or six glasses. When you exercise, however, you need to do better than that. Beginners, especially, tend to overlook the importance of proper hydration to endurance. Here are a few facts that I hope will drive you to drink.

While you exercise, blood that was previously transferring oxygen to your muscles is diverted to transport excess heat from inside your body to your skin. From there your body depends primarily on the evaporation of sweat to rid itself of heat. Your heart is already pumping harder because of the competition for blood between the muscles and the skin. As you become dehydrated, you perspire less, which means your temperature rises steadily and your heart beats faster. In practical terms, your performance goes into the toilet. By not drinking enough, you risk dehydration.

You risk more than poor performance if a substantial amount of body fluids is lost and not replaced. Extreme dehydration leads to heat exhaustion—a serious condition. Be aware of the symptoms of heat exhaustion: unusual fatigue, weakness, irritability, nausea, dizziness, and "goose flesh." These are signs that you to have a tall drink right away and to lie down in a sheltered spot. If you drink religiously before, during, and after your climb, however, it shouldn't come to this. If you feel thirsty, you've waited too long.

**Finger Tips**

Bring a veggie-pasta-bean soup in a thermos to eat after your workout. It's easy to digest, nutritious, and filling.

**Hold On**

If you're feeling thirsty, overheated, and edgy, you're probably dehydrated. Dehydration is an athlete's worst enemy. Be sure to drink *before* you get thirsty.

# Quarts, Not Cups

How much do you need to drink? It depends on the weather, the altitude, and how strenuously you're working. When working hard at high altitudes, you can lose as much as five quarts a day through sweat and through evaporation of moisture through the lungs. Let's say you'll be engaging in moderate activity in a temperate climate at low altitudes. You should drink at least a quart of water every six hours. Increase the amount for heat, humidity, altitude, and the amount of strain you'll be putting on your body.

On hot days, when the air temperature exceeds your body and skin temperatures, you probably won't need to be reminded to drink; you'll be as hot and sweaty as a short-order cook. Wind cools and drys sweaty skin rapidly. Don't be fooled, however, you're still sweating and you still need to drink.

Humid days are the athlete's real nemesis. As the moisture in the air increases, the body's ability to eliminate heat through perspiration decreases—for the same reason that laundry hung out to dry on a damp day doesn't get dry. You'll still perspire, but your sweat won't evaporate quickly or cool you efficiently. Your body's only recourse is to sweat even more, which means you need to drink more.

**Finger Tips**

You'll know you're properly hydrated when your urine is clear.

**Nuts and Bolts**

**Electrolytes**, which are found in energy drinks, help the body conduct energy into muscles that are in demand during activity.

## What'll You Have?

Water or sports drinks are both appropriate. Sports drinks supply extra calories, minerals, and *electrolytes*. I've never been able to drink a quart of sports drink, however, so if I'm only carrying one bottle, I'll bring water. I like wide-mouthed polyethylene bottles; they're easy to wash and don't make water taste funny the way some cheap plastic bottles can. Carrying a pack of powdered sports drink is a good compromise, because you can mix it to taste.

Don't plan on finding water that's fit to drink along the way. If you're mountaineering on a snowy peak and are packing a stove, you can melt snow to drink. Without a stove, it is almost impossible to melt enough snow to keep properly hydrated. Hence the phrase: "Snow, snow everywhere but not a stove to drink."

### Cliff Notes

A triathlete in Boston who prefers to be known as "Psycho Fred" created the first energy drink in tablet form: Psycho Fred's Quic Discs. In the late 1990s, tired of making a mess with powders, Fred devised a pressed tablet that dissolved in water, offering athletes an easy-to-make, electrolyte-packed grape drink.

## *Java on the Rocks?*

Caffeine is a drug found in as many as 70 plants, and it also shows up in many of the foods we eat. The most concentrated sources of caffeine are coffee, tea, and soft drinks. Of these, coffee has the most caffeine—more than twice as much as tea.

Caffeine hits your bloodstream in as little as 30 minutes, and its effects may be felt for anywhere from two to ten hours. It speeds up your metabolism, heart rate, and respiration. It increases the secretion of acid in the stomach and is a diuretic (meaning you pee more). If you drink coffee before a climb, you need to counter its dehydrating effect with still more water.

I have to admit it: I love coffee. (Read: I'm an addict.) I keep a container of iced coffee in my fridge for early morning workouts and head for my French press as soon as I walk back through the door. (Did I mention I love it?) I'm sure that someday I will read one article too many about caffeine-free athletes setting world records, and will go cold turkey. For now, my system seems to tolerate coffee pretty well. If you tend to have a strong reaction to it—shaky hands or a racing heart, for example—common sense says that you shouldn't drink it before or during a climb.

### Hold On

Just say "no" to that second cup of coffee if you plan to climb in hot weather. Coffee is a diuretic, which means it dehydrates your body.

---

**The Least You Need to Know**

➤ Monitoring what to eat—and what not to eat—will keep you performing at your best.

➤ *When* you eat is nearly as important as *what* you eat.

➤ Proper hydration can make the difference between optimal performance and the big bonk—or even heat exhaustion.

➤ The amount you should drink depends on altitude, heat, the difficulty of the climb, and, especially, humidity.

➤ Coffee can get you going, but too much can wring you dry.

# Part 4
# Take It to the Mountain

*In case you missed the roughly 72 warnings I've mentioned thus far regarding the inherent dangers of rock climbing, read this: Climbing involves risk, and if you're cavalier about safety procedures, there's a good chance you will die. It sounds stark, but you need to realize the perils involved. Knowing what to expect and how to extricate yourself from tight situations will keep you safe and eager to return for more.*

*In Part 4, I spend a fair bit of time talking about the dynamics of finding a partner to go risk your neck with. This is as imprecise a science as picking a husband or wife (and perhaps a lot more risky to life and limb).*

*Crack climbing is an art unto itself. Read about this digit-abusing style of climbing before you trade in your violin for a day of "hand jams." I'll also tell you about a few other facets of climbing—"°trad" climbing vs. "sport" climbing, for example—to round out the big picture.*

*Finally, regardless how safely you climb, if you climb often enough, you're likely to find yourself in a jam. (Or is it a pickle?) Knowing what to do is a big part of turning a potential disaster into a great campfire story.*

# Safety First

In his fine book *How to Rock Climb*, John Long writes, "Risk your ass if you want to, but statistically, rock climbing is the safest of all the so-called thrill sports because it employs over a century's worth of refined technique and solid technology." He goes on to say, however, that the word "safe" should never be applied to rock climbing.

True enough. Climbing is a gear-intensive activity with its fair share of risk. Human error, technical failures, and acts of nature can strike even the most attentive climbers and turn a challenging adventure into a test of survival. (The same can be said for a drive to the supermarket, but that's a subject for another time.)

According to Long—and just about any other climber who has logged a lot of time in the mountains—you must be sure to understand the inherent risks in climbing, learn how to climb safely, and have a strategy in case you get into a jam. The gradual procedure is a time-honored tradition in virtually any outdoor sport; it's called the "learning curve." In this chapter we covers some important safety issues that go along with playing in the great outdoors, whether you're roped up or not.

# Learn to Learn

Like any good student of the martial arts, the eager beginner must (or should) honor the wiser, more experienced practitioners of the sport. Too often today it seems young climbers who cut their teeth on the plastic walls of an indoor gym think that because they can speed up a difficult route indoors, they can do the same on real rock. This is a shallow and even dangerous attitude to bring to the mountains.

Short circuiting this time-honored apprenticeship is an important point and one of the reasons why Jon Kraukeur's book *Into Thin Air* has generated so much discussion. Scores of outdoor aficionados long to climb Mt. Everest. Until you've paid your dues in the mountains, however, attempting to climb a route grander than your talent is foolish, disrespectful, and often fatal. As world-class mountaineer Alex Lowe says, "given the high cost of a mistake, a mountain apprenticeship should be long and slow, and it demands as much humility as strength and will. And acceptance, too."

*The mountain demands humility. (Photo courtesy of Nels Akerlund.)*

To climb safely, you need to be mindful of both the art and the science of this vertical game. Finding a good teacher is crucial; being a good student is more important still.

# It's the Climber, Stupid

Equipment failures in climbing have far greater consequences than in most other sporting activities. Break a ski pole mid-slope, a paddle mid-stream, or a tennis-racket string mid-serve, and you might take a tumble or have to improvise quickly; more than likely, however, you should be fine. In rock climbing, technical glitches have severe repercussions. If an anchor pops out, a rope severs, or the gate on a carabiner snaps, you're likely to fall hard, far, and fast.

Although the old climbing adage about never trusting your life to one piece of gear is good advice, it applies only to certain components of the belay. For instance, there is usually only one rope!

The part of the system that has to have at least one backup is the belay anchor. (Remember that a "belay anchor" refers to the person and equipment that will ultimately hold a fall, whereas a *running anchor* is the protection a leader places on his or her way to the next belay anchor.) Here's the twist: Running anchors are useless without a secure belay anchor.

The basics of the safety system in traditional climbing can be a bit confusing to newcomers. Here's how this stuff actually works:

**Nuts and Bolts**

A **running anchor** is the protection a leader places on his or her way to the next belay anchor.

1. On the ground, the belayer anchors himself to something big and solid that needs no backup, such as a tree.

2. The leader climbs up, placing protection in the cracks if traditional climbing, or clipping bolts if sport climbing. Each of these points is a running anchor, meaning the rope is clipped into each one.

3. The leader climbs until a secure stance is reached, then constructs a belay anchor—again, by placing gear or simply clipping bolts. Two "beefy" bolts or three bomb-proof gear placements are the minimal safety standard at this stage.

4. The leader now belays as the original belayer follows the pitch, collecting all the equipment on the way up. This is called "cleaning up."

5. The climbers reorganize their gear at the belay stance. Then, one of the climbers begins the second pitch of the climb, belaying from the same anchor point that the first climber established.

6. At the top of the climb, the two either walk down the backside of the cliff or rappel down the route. Again, a rappel anchor requires three pieces of protection or two big new bolts. Remember: More accidents happen during this stage of a climb than practically any other.

**Hold On**

As lead climber, you must place protection and running anchors carefully on your way to the belay anchor. Keep in mind, however, that all the running anchors on your rack are useless without a secure belay anchor. Always back up your belay anchor: it's the link to life that will ultimately hold a fall.

As I've said many times in this book, it's best to learn how to use your equipment from a guide or experienced climber who you trust. There is a lot of equipment for climbing and, more importantly, an infinite number of complicated and dangerous situations climbers may encounter. Learning to climb safely takes time. Climbers who have spent years or even decades in the mountains will tell you that the most important factor to climbing safely is not your gear but how well and how intelligently you use it.

# Escaping the Belay

In the majority of climbing accidents, it's the lead climber who gets injured or stuck in a hairy situation. As the belayer, you must learn to properly "escape the belay"—that is, lock off the rope so that the weight of your dangling partner is transferred to the anchor. This leaves you free to help your partner or to leave to get help. The exact procedure depends on what type of belay device you are using.

## Climbing Up

"Escaping the belay" is complicated and best left to climbers who have had hands-on instruction. The same is true for climbing the rope itself. Ascending the rope—that is, literally climbing the rope instead of the rock—isn't terribly complicated, and most beginners enjoy doing it, provided it's not in an emergency situation. Here's how it goes:

1. Wrap a Prusik cord (usually a sling, meaning it forms a loop) around both ropes. See Chapter 8 for additional Prusik information.

2. Using two opposed-gate carabiners, clip the Prusik to a half-hitched sling on your harness. When pushed up to its maximum height on the ropes, the Prusik should be at the same height on the rope as your elbow when your arm is extended. If the cord is too short, you won't get a full extension on each push. If it's too long, the weight will be on your arms rather than on your harness.

3. Wrap a second Prusik cord underneath the first knot. Similarly, use two opposed-gate carabiners that attach to a sling, which becomes your foot stirrup. (You can use the top knot as a seat and the bottom knot as a stirrup.)

4. Step forcefully on the stirrup—making it taut—while pushing the top knot up the rope.

5. Sit in your harness and take a breather.

6. While holding the rop above you for balance, loosen the bottom knot and slide it up the rope.

7. Step securely into the stirrup and loosen the top knot.

8. Push the top knot up the rope until the sling pulls on the harness.

9. Sit in the harness again and repeat loosening and moving the bottom knot. (This is a good time to recover.)

10. Repeat this process until you've reached the top.

# Staying Ice Cool

Whether you're climbing indoors in your garage or the North Face of the Eiger, managing your fear is a key part of the vertical game. However, as you venture off into more challenging and remote terrain, that little voice in your brain that often demands you find terra firma is likely to sound more often and louder. Remaining calm when you're most insecure is one of the biggest challenges in climbing. Learning to manage this unsettled feeling is an acquired skill. Climbing and communicating with a partner you trust will help you transcend that little voice. Here's a somewhat extreme example of grace under pressure.

A few years ago, Alex Lowe went ice climbing with three friends in Hyalite Canyon outside of Bozeman, Montana. When Lowe was roughly 100 feet off the ground, the entire section of ice he was climbing peeled off the rock. Hanging onto the ice like a cowboy riding a bronco bull, Lowe crashed onto a ledge 40 feet below. Though he stood up and shouted that he was fine, he was, in fact, a mess. His forehead had smashed into the *adze* of his ice axe, which nearly scalped him.

As he bled profusely, Lowe (and his partner) rappelled off the ledge, crudely taped his scalp in place, and skied back to the car. Knowing it would be a long night in the emergency room, Lowe and his partner drove to town, got some lattes at the coffee shop, and then headed to the hospital.

That's either supreme calm or one hell of a caffeine addiction.

Of course, this incident isn't just about grace under pressure; it's really about accepting the risks of climbing. No one can guarantee Alex Lowe that the next time some ice breaks his adze won't puncture his skull. He accepts the risk of climbing, knowing that his gear can't always prevent accidents, and chooses to climb anyway.

### Nuts and Bolts

The **adze**, or *hammer*, of the ice axe is used for cutting and cleaning snow from hard ice in order to insert an ice screw.

# Weathering Heights

Although weather forecasts have become increasingly sophisticated, the only thing you can really count on in the mountains is that the weather will challenge you on a regular basis. As Mark Twain said, "If you don't like the weather …, just wait a few minutes." As a rule of thumb, the bigger the mountain, the harsher and more unpredictable the weather.

### Hold On

Check the weather conditions before heading to the crag. If you're visiting a new area, talk to the locals and research unfamiliar weather patterns peculiar to that part of the country.

On shorter climbs (or while top-roping), a driving rain, hailstorm, or snow squall will usually signal the end of your climbing day. On all-day multi-pitch routes—especially in alpine climbing, where you've hiked for hours or days through the backcountry to start a climb—dealing with the wrath of Mother Nature is part of the package. In fact, coping with adverse conditions will make you a better climber.

*Always check the weather conditions before climbing. (Photo courtesy of Nels Akerlund.)*

In some ranges, afternoon showers and lightning storms are nearly as regular as Old Faithful. The Grand Teton (in Wyoming) and the Eiger (in Switzerland) are notorious for their rapid and violent weather changes. Even a modest-sized mountain like the 6,288-foot Mt. Washington in New Hampshire can produce summer storms that leave hypothermic hikers running for cover. (The highest wind speed ever recorded was 231 mph on the top of Mt. Washington. In the winter, it's not usual for temperatures to fall below minus 40 degrees Fahrenheit.)

### Hold On

Your "dexterity factor" has an inverse relationship to your "wet factor." Typically, wet equals cold equals stiff equals spastic—until even simple rope-handling tasks become challenging.

Joe Glickman, my partner on this book, speaks in awe of the violent storm he encountered on Gannett Peak, Wyoming's highest point. In July of 1997, he and two partners started the 25-mile hike to the Wind River Range at 8,500 feet in shorts and T-shirts. Five hours into the third day of climbing, they found themselves on the summit ridge, roughly 300 vertical feet from the top of Wyoming.

The weather that morning had been relatively calm, and it seemed likely they would have a window of decent weather to try for the top. Shortly after they left the protection of a *couloir* they'd been ascending, however, the wind increased and snow began to fall.

After waiting for 15 minutes, they decided to retreat. In no time, heavy snow reduced the visibility to less than 10 feet. As they headed back over the glacier to the 13,000-foot pass that separated them from their camp, the wind howled at more than 60 mph. Walking upright in the whiteout was a chore.

### Nuts and Bolts

Most climbers follow a **couloir** during an ascent. Couloirs are steep gullies on a mountain, usually filled with ice or snow, that are typically shallower and less technical than the cliffs they interrupt.

Had they continued to the top and been caught in that storm, it's very likely I would be working on this book by myself. The bottom line is that understanding the weather patterns where you climb and knowing when to back off is crucial if you want to climb there (or anywhere) again.

Of course, these are lessons learned over time. As a guide once told me, "the deadliest thing in the mountains is the ... ego." In other words, be smart and live to fight another day.

## Dress for a Mess

The topic of proper clothing is about as basic as it gets in a discussion about safety. Nevertheless, you'd be surprised how often climbers neglect or "forget" to bring the right clothing, sleeping bag, or rain gear. Perhaps the only way to really take this advice to heart is to get caught overnight in a rainstorm or shiver the night away in the wrong kind of sleeping bag. Take it from someone who's done both: Learn to carry the right stuff for the task at hand and you'll save yourself a lot of discomfort and suffering.

There's a strain of hardcore climbers who go "light and fast" and reject the thought of carrying a small shelter called a bivouac sack in the backcountry. Their logic is that if you carry something to help you weather a night outdoors, you'll use it. I disagree. Sure, it's silly to carry enough clothing to weather an Alaskan blizzard if all you're doing is a day-climb an hour from your car. (Unless, of course, you're in Alaska.) But I've endured enough radical changes in the weather to know that having a pile jacket or Gore-Tex raincoat can make the difference between relative comfort and significant suffering.

### Finger Tips

Dress in layers. You can always take off clothing, but you can't put on what you don't have. Shivering makes it hard to maneuver and kills a lot of the fun.

**Hold On**

Always bring extra clothes, including water-wicking materials for base layers, fleece for the middle layers, and wind- and water-proof materials for the outer layers—especially if you're planning an overnight trip. You'll also want an appropriately insulated sleeping bag for a night under the stars, of course. Regardless how warm it is during the day, temperatures can drop below freezing at night.

Here's a perfect example of someone taking weather conditions for granted. Last summer, a friend of mine was climbing a two-pitch climb in the High Peaks region of the Adirondacks in New York. (A *pitch* is the section of a climb between progressive belay positions. It is restricted by the length of the rope and is typically kept within shouting distance for effective communication.)

When he was halfway up the second pitch, storm clouds moved in and a bone-chilling rain showered the cliff. Although he was an experienced climber and had been there more than a few times, he left his warm gear in his pack at the base of the cliff "in case it got cold later in the day." To make a long story short, his sweaty body nearly turned to stone. His hands were so stiff that he had trouble opening the locking gate on his carabiner.

He made it down, but not without some misery and anxiety. If he had been carrying a *capeline* shirt and raincoat, he would have been none the worse for the wear.

## Electrical Storms

Lightning is one of nature's most spectacular sights. If you're caught outdoors in the middle of an electrical storm, however, the beauty quickly turns into a beast.

Because peaks and ridges produce the vertical updrafts and rain clouds that generate lightning, climbers (and golfers for some reason) must take special care to seek cover when these angry electrons start lighting up the sky.

Being meteorologically challenged, I'm not really keen on the forces that produce lightning. I do know, however, that having an effective strategy when your hair stands on end or ice ax begins to vibrate is central to any climber who hopes to spend a lot of time in the mountains.

Here's what to do when lightning threatens:

➤ If you're on a peak or ridge, get down ASAP.

➤ Avoid gullies and cracks.

➤ Don't lean against the cliff; its a potential path for electricity.

➤ Avoid water, trees, or metal objects. You're better off in a dense thicket or under a small tree or rock than under a tall powerful tree.

➤ Remain low, and sit on an insulated object such as a rope or backpack.

➤ If possible, don't hunker down under an overhang or the mouth of a cave, where a bolt of lightning could rebound from the floor to the roof. If you are on a ledge, crouch at the outer edge. And remember to tie in so that you don't fall. Even a lightning strike several feet from you can produce enough juice to send a billion electrons through your body.

➤ Remain calm and be patient. Once you've found suitable refuge, wait for the storm to pass before exposing yourself to the elements. Storms tend to move through the mountains like a freight train.

**Nuts and Bolts**

**Capeline** is a lightweight synthetic material that wicks sweat from the body and dries quickly.

**Hold On**

Each year, lightning kills more than 100 people in the United States. Climbers, who are often caught by surprise on wet rock, are in the high-risk category.

Of course, the best tip is a preventative one: Get an up-to-date weather report before you start out. In areas where afternoon electrical storms strike frequently, start early so that you can get off the mountain as early as possible.

# Emergency Essentials

Just as city slickers never leave their apartments without their keys (and an ATM card), experienced climbers have certain standard items in their pack every time they take to the hills. How much safety gear you should take is a matter of debate. Some bare-bones types argue that stuffing your pack with insurance items slows you down and hence makes it more likely that you'll get into a jam.

This, of course, is a matter of choice. I tend to be a minimalist at heart, but I've been caught high and dry enough to slowly come over to the other, more prepared, camp.

## On Topo the World

The first thing you need is a map. In Jon Kraukeur's book *Into The Wild*, the main character—a young, bold (some would say foolish) lad—walks into the Alaskan bush to live on nature's terms. After several months, he decides to return to civilization. The frozen river he had walked across in late winter, however, was now a raging river and impossible to cross. Because he didn't carry a map, he did not know that just a few miles down river was a bridge he could have crossed. Dejected, he returned to the woods, where he died a painful death from food poisoning.

**Nuts and Bolts**

Topographical (or **topo**) maps illustrate a landscape's terrain.

Of course, simply carrying a map of the climbing area isn't enough. You must know how to read it. *Topographical* (or *topo*) maps are best. I store my maps in a Ziploc baggie in case it rains or something in my pack leaks.

## Other Indispensables

Whether your climbing in the backcountry or just an hour up the trail, here's a list of items I find indispensable in the great outdoors:

➤ **Compass.** If you wander off the trail or simply get lost, a compass will get you back on track. By itself, it's a valuable asset; with a map and basic navigation skills, you won't be lost for long.

➤ **Flashlight or headlamp.** I used to carry a flashlight on overnight trips. Once I got a headlamp, however, I essentially retired my flashlight. A headlamp allows me to keep my hands free when I set up camp, get stuck on a trail after dark, or read in my tent at night.

➤ **Extra food.** Packing no-fuss, no-muss food like energy bars can make a big difference if you get lost or just bonk on the climb and need a quick pick-me-up.

**Finger Tips**

Remember to change the batteries in your headlamp or flashlight before a trip. It's also wise to pack extra batteries in a waterproof bag.

➤ **Matches** It might seem like overkill, but if you are forced to spend a night without a shelter, you'll be ecstatic you packed these ultralight items. Keep them in a waterproof container. Butane lighters work well also.

➤ **Sunscreen.** The higher the altitude, the more essential good sunscreen is. Save yourself from those UV rays and lather it on.

➤ **Bug juice.** I've been in some areas where the mosquitoes were so bad that I considered carrying a firearm. I've had reasonable success with a product called Skin So Soft, as well as with standard insect repellent. You make the call.

➤ **Pocket knife or utility tool.** I used to be a big Swiss Army Knife fan. Lately, however, I've been using a SOG tool—an all-purpose gadget with pliers, screwdrivers, and all sorts of goodies. I use it all the time, whether I'm cutting a piece of rope, fixing a camp stove, building a log cabin … well, you get the idea. Make sure the knife or tool is easily accessible.

➤ **First-aid kit.** First-aid kits come in a variety of sizes. The longer the trip, the more thorough your kit should be. Store it in a watertight container. Don't pack one, and you'll be sure to need it.

The final item required is athletic tape. Several years ago, a friend of mine was hiking on an extinct volcano in Bali. On the way down, he lost the trail and began bushwhacking. Since he was a solid climber, he decided to downclimb (sans rope) some of the vertical sections. On one sheer face, the rock crumbled, and he fell roughly 40 feet, landing feet first. Though he didn't know it at the time, he fractured both ankles. While he had the will power and fitness to get back to civilization (three days later), it was a simple roll of athletic tape that helped save his life. "Had I not taped both ankles immediately," he said, "I wouldn't have been able to hobble out."

**Hold On**

Keep your tools in working order and make sure your knives are sharp. A dull knife can be a large liability in an emergency situation. Handling a knife carelessly has led to many bloody paws, so pay attention to what you're doing.

**Finger Tips**

If you cut yourself and don't have a first-aid kit, you can substitute athletic tape for a gauze pad. To wrap a wound efficiently, fold a short length of athletic tape in two so that the sticky sides adhere to each other. This ensures that the tape's glue doesn't touch the wound. Then, using the tape as though it were a piece of gauze, wrap a second strand of tape around the "gauze" to secure the dressing.

# Emergency Medical Training

When my co-writer Joe Glickman and his climbing partner, photographer Nels Akerlund, were on the road working on their book *To The Top*—a large-format photography book about the highest peaks in each of the 50 states—Glickman was surprised to learn that Akerlund had extensive emergency medical training (EMT). Akerlund was surprised that Glickman did not.

Akerlund, who's been climbing since high school and once worked on a ski patrol in Breckenridge, Colorado, figured the training would be essential if he ever needed to perform CPR on a family member or save himself while in the wilderness far from help. Glickman, who comes from a long-line of city dwellers, figured he'd respond to an outdoor emergency like most other city folks—by dialing 911.

When you begin your climbing career, the emphasis should be on climbing. As you progress and starting thinking about climbing in remote parts of the world, it's important to know how to get yourself (and your partner) out of a tough spot. While it's clearly important to know how to get out of a tough spot at any stage of your climbing career, the further from the trail you venture the more important this becomes.

Clearly, it's beyond the scope of this book to teach you how to set a dislocated shoulder, administer CPR, or immobilize a broken leg. EMT and CPR courses are excellent skills for anyone who spends time in the wilderness. To learn the procedural side of climbing rescues, take a course with a professional guide service.

In the end, becoming proficient at extricating yourself from an emergency situations is the same as learning the X's and O's of climbing; learn to do it right and then practice, practice, practice.

**Finger Tips**

Discuss and practice rescue techniques with your partner. Challenge each other with "what if" scenarios and create contingency plans. Rehearsing a rescue strategy under controlled conditions will make it easier to execute should disaster come your way.

## The Least You Need to Know

➤ Safety starts with the climber, not with the gear.

➤ If you get in a stressful situation, stay calm.

➤ Check the local weather report before you set out.

➤ Carry essential survival clothing and gear as a matter of course.

➤ Make the time to take a course in emergency medical training.

➤ Learn how to "escape the belay" from a qualified instructor.

# Jimmy Crack Climbing

The phrase "crack climber" has a couple of meanings in the vertical community. One simply refers to a rock jock who scampers up a wall with the grace of a waterfall in reverse. As for the other—well, if you've ever seen a picture of a climber moving up a dark fissure in an otherwise smooth rock face like a spider up a drainpipe, then you've seen a crack climber.

The most visible weakness in a rock face is a fissure, or crack, stretching from the bottom to the top of the cliff. As veteran big-wall climber John Long says in his book *How To Rock Climb!*, "a prominent crack system is nature's way of telling us where to climb .... [W]hen expeditions are mounted to big, faraway cliffs, or when a beginner studies a crag for the first time, eyes naturally home in on any crack system the cliff affords."

Here's a bit of vertical irony: Although face climbing—what most of us envision when we think about climbing—is a natural movement, few face climbs follow the natural lines of the rock face. (A "line" usually refers to a possible route which climbers might take; cracks often suggest the best way up a cliff.) Since nature certainly did not sculpt either type of feature for humans to dangle off, it's a bit odd to say one is more "natural" than the other. However, cracks occur naturally and often ascending such a line is the only way up an otherwise featureless rock face (short of drilling bolts). While the debate over what's natural and what's not is best left to the pundits, climbing cracks is a game of endless body nuances that requires specific techniques. Again, Long speaks from experience: "No climber masters cracks without his share of pain and failures, and without logging many miles up cracks."

Why is crack climbing so "unnatural" compared to the contortions necessary to climb a rock face sans cracks? In general, crack climbing requires more specific and less intuitive moves than face climbing. Moreover, it's more painful than face climbing because all of that finger, hand, and foot jamming that we'll talk about hurts!

# Between a Rock and a Hard Place

Crack climbing demands subtle and arduous moves that call for the climber to either jam or torque her arms, legs, or entire body into a crack. Because the techniques are so specific to this particular discipline, becoming a competent crack climber takes countless hours of practice, regardless how strong you are on the gym wall or "regular" rock. Indeed, someone with the chops to bang out a 5.12 route indoors might struggle with a 5.9 crack climb—or vice versa. They're that different. (See Chapter 19 for an explanation of the ratings system.)

One of the biggest reasons why crack climbing and face climbing differ is that cracks can be protected with traditional gear, whereas faces often require bolt protection. Bolted cracks are very rare in the United States. So if you want to place your own gear—that is, climb in the traditional style—you have to climb cracks.

## *Why Bother?*

If crack climbing is so hard and technical, the inevitable question some beginners pose is "why bother?" If you want to climb in inspiring spots such as El Capitan in Yosemite, Joshua Tree in California, the Canyonlands in Utah, or the famed Devil's Tower in Wyoming, read on. Most of the routes on big, "classic" climbs are generally crack climbs, so it's good to know what you're up against.

Why endure the abuse that crack climbing offers? Here's a snippet from a letter a friend who had recently climbed El Capitan sent me: "El Cap offered up some of the most sustained and difficult climbing I had ever experienced. This, coupled with the extremes of weather—horizontal snow, driving rain, 90 degree heat—and the technical nature of it all, forced me to reach further into the depths of my endurance than ever before for the emotional stamina to continue. Exceedingly cathartic to say the least."

Perhaps the best reason to try crack climbing is that it requires a near-perfect balance between strength and technique. Climbing cracks enables you to experience the joy of moving on this natural line. If it sounds like heady stuff, that's because it is.

*El Capitan in Yosemite National Park, California. (Photo courtesy of Nels Akerlund.)*

## *Apples and Bananas*

Although face climbing and crack climbing are as different as apples and bananas, many of the same principles apply. You should keep your center of gravity over your feet as much as possible. On low-angled climbs your body leans away from the rock. As the angle increases, move your hips closer to the wall.

But the differences are obvious, too. Even though cracks make the proper route easy to find and follow, they frequently lack ledges to stand on or grab. If you've spent most of your time on face-climbing routes, this will feel very odd. Your holds must come from a variety of *jamming* and *finger-camming* techniques. Unfortunately, these techniques can turn your forearms to toast faster than you can say "Scar Face."

Initially, all this technical mumbo-jumbo might seem like Greek to you. With proper instruction and practice, however, crack climbing can become a rewarding experience as you work the natural features of a cliff the way a good kayaker merges with a powerful river.

## We're Jamming

Since no two climbers are the same size, keep in mind that the various techniques discussed in the following sections have nothing to do with the size of the crack, but rather with the particular move required. In other words, a climber with

### Nuts and Bolts

**Jamming** is a crack-climbing technique that requires the climber to wedge his fingers, hands, or feet into a crack for support and balance.

**Finger-camming** is a method of jamming your digits into cracks with parallel sides. In normal jams, the fingers or hands slot into constrictions. Parallel cracks require serious twisting of skin against rock to create friction. To help create torque, point your thumbs down, turn your elbows in, and draw your arms down to your body. In general, camming is a technique that enhances hand and foot jams by adding extra torque, achieved by extra twisting of the arms and legs.

small hands may use a hand jam in the same spot where a fat-fingered climber employs a two-finger stack. While there's no substitute for experience, reading the X's and O's about finger, hand, fist, and toe jams should help you as you figure this stuff out for yourself.

**Nuts and Bolts**

**Finger cracks** are thin cracks in the rock that only fingers can fit into it. **Finger jamming** is a method that requires the climber to use friction by camming her digits into a parallel sided crack. A **finger lock** is a method that allows the climber's fingers to wedge solidly into a narrow crack.

**Hold On**

Do not tuck your thumb into your clenched fist while jamming your hand into a crack. Tucked thumbs are prone to injury.

## Finger Jams

Finger-sized cracks, or *finger cracks*, can be so stingy that you'll have to fight to wedge in the tip of your pinky. On the other hand (sorry), there's ample cracks that envelop your finger beyond the second knuckle. With few exceptions, most cracks vary in thickness. As you make your way up the thin dark line, look for *constrictions* (places where the crack narrows, if only barely). Jamming the thickest part of your finger—the second knuckle—just above a constriction gives you solid purchase for a solid *finger jam*. When you bend your wrist and pull down with your arm, the knuckle becomes locked in the crack like a wedge.

To the uninitiated, this is rather hostile stuff to subject poor, unsuspecting hands to. (If you're a concert pianist, surgeon, or hand model, crack climbing might be professional suicide. Actually, it's tough on the hands even if you milk cows for a living or regularly climb cracks.)

Two friends of mine returned from a five-day, four-night climb on El Capitan in Yosemite with some of the worst dish-pan hands this side of a short-order cook. Their poor digits were so sore that they shied away from handshakes for a week.

You might not be up to a five-day slog up such a formidable big wall, but you can enjoy the same satisfaction on shorter crack climbs that are just as challenging. Regardless the size of the crack, however, there are a variety of finger techniques that will help you out of a jam.

## Hand Positioning for Finger Jamming

Although shoving your fingers into a narrow crack of course stone is like digging a hole in the ground without a shovel, take comfort; the more you crack climb, the tougher your digits will become. And as your footwork improves, the amount of pressure on your hands will lessen. (See "Taping Tips" later in the chapter for advice on how to spare your fingers from some of the inevitable abuse that comes with crack climbing.)

There are two basic ways to position the hand for the best finger jamming: thumb up or thumb down. Generally, it's best to use thumb-up jams whenever you can. Of course, there are countless exceptions and variations, but for a general discussion just know that keeping your thumbs up allows you to reach farther. In addition, since this is a more natural position, you won't have to twist a finger into the crack to get it to "stick." Simply put, the thumb-up method is less hostile to your hands.

Having said that, on steep, thin cracks, it's often better to place your hands with the thumb down. To save wear and tear on your knuckles, it's often best to shove the shank (the fleshy part of your finger between the knuckles), into the crack. Once you've jammed as many fingers into the crack as possible, pivot your wrist and pull downward. Done correctly, your finger (or fingers) acts like a camming device. In essence, instead of using a piece of pro from your rack, you're using your hand. It's sound practice to brace your thumb against your index finger to prevent your hold from slipping.

**Finger Tips**

It's better to keep your thumb up (rather than down) while finger jamming. You'll have a longer reach, and your hands will get less scraped.

Here's some key advice:

➤ Try to get as many digits as solidly possible into the crack.

➤ Once you jam your finger (or fingers) into the crack, make sure you wiggle them around to find the best fit before putting your weight on them.

➤ To enhance the jam, aggressively twist your wrist and elbow. This helps cam the fingers by adding extra torque.

## Hand Jams

*Hand jams* are often a crack climber's best friend. No stressful pinky-jamming moves are required; the cracks are wide enough so that the climber can get a secure purchase with his hands and feet. (Cracks larger than two fists stacked together require a whole slew of moves that I'll discuss later in this chapter.) Hand-sized cracks often make for quick progress because when the crack is as wide as your hand you'll be able to jam your foot in as if you were stepping up the world's skinniest ladder.

**Nuts and Bolts**

A climber uses a **hand jam** to wedge his hand into a crack for support and balance. *Fist jams* operate on the same principle.

The best analogy I've heard is that a good hand jam works like a cork in a bottle. The basic technique goes like this:

1. Insert your hand with your thumb up and your fingertips facing the heavens, and "shake hands" with the crack. (There's no need to formally introduce yourself; cracks are not easily offended.)

   Typically, the hand jam resembles a tripod, with the fingertips and base of the palm on one side of the crack, and the knuckles and back of the hand pressed against the other side.

2. Bridge your thumb against your index finger or pinky, or into your palm, depending on the width of the crack.

   There are a variety of configurations you can use. You can flex your fingers at the second or third knuckle forming two sides of a triangle in wider openings. Wedging your thumb into your palm will makes this hand jam the strongest jam of all.

3. If the crack slants aggressively, or in corners, jam your top hand thumb-down and your bottom hand thumb-up.

When you start using this technique, it's common to rotate your hand quickly as you pull up and out of the crack. Anxiety and fatigue will do that to you. Unfortunately, doing so will turn your pristine hands into a gnarly mess. Instead, rotate your wrist, not your hand, while keeping the jam as tight as possible. Your manicurist and dance partner will thank you.

## Fist Jams

When the crack is too big for a solid hand jam, make like a boxer and use your fist. Stick your hand in with no muscle tension. Once you've found a good spot, flex the muscles to apply pressure against the walls of the crack. Always look for a constriction in the crack to jam above. Here are a few ways to make this *fist jam* stick.

➤ Insert your fist straight in as though you were punching the crack (albeit very slowly).

➤ Have the palm facing out of the crack. You can wrap your thumb across the index and middle finger; or set it across the palm if the crack is tighter.

➤ If the crack is thin, release your middle and ring fingers, thereby narrowing your fist (not to mention making you look like you're saying hello to a fraternity brother).

### Cliff Notes

Near the turn of the century, climbers in Dresden, Germany, were way ahead of their time. They jammed knotted slings into cracks to ascend routes that would be considered 5.10s in today's terms—a level that wouldn't be reached in the United States until the 1960s. They still climb that way today, sometimes even barefooted.

Again, there are quite a few different angles and configurations that you can and should use. Once you learn the basics, it's up to you to find the pieces to this intricate puzzle.

## Foot Jams

The bad news is that fist jams are arduous and hostile on the mitts. The good news is that since the width of your fist and that of your foot is roughly similar, if your fist is cutting it, so will your foot.

Use the following list to decide whether to use a foot jam, and if so, how:

➤ If there's a decent foothold outside of the crack, by all means go for it. In other words, forget the foot jam and use the foothold instead.

➤ If there's no adjacent foothold, look for a constriction and place your foot just above it.

➤ If there's no constriction handy, stick your foot straight in. If there is play on either side, twist your foot laterally until it sticks.

When you use the foot jam, remember to center your weight over your feet and to avoid jamming your feet too far into the crack. Generally, any farther than the ball of the foot is overkill. Because my feet are small and narrow, my tendency is to jam them in there. I've had my feet get stuck, however, and have had to fight like mad to pull them out.

## Toe Jams

Crack climbing brings new meaning to the term *toe jam*. This is where pointy-toed rock shoes come in handy. There are countless nuances to this technique. Basically, however, you place your toes

### Nuts and Bolts

A **toe jam** is when the climber stuffs her toes into narrow cracks, bracing herself for the next move.

### Nuts and Bolts

A **chimney** is a crack in the rock wide enough for climbers to push their entire bodies through. In *chimneying*, climbers ascend a chimney by wedging their bodies into it and shimmying upward, pressing against the sides with their feet and back.

### Finger Tips

When ascending a chimney think of body as two parts: top and bottom. The bottom (legs) is the workhorse pushing you upward. The top (arms) is the stabilizer holding you in place.

### Hold On

You might consider an alternate route when faced with a chimney. They are technically demanding and therefore dangerous. Also, squeezing through an off-width chimney is exhausting work.

into the crack while turning your foot sideways, with your big toe up and your knee out. To lock your foot in, rotate your knee upward and then weight your foot. Keep your heel down. Again, practice to find the most effective position(s).

Remember to let your feet do the lion's share of the work to propel you upward. Take a brief pause on each foot jam and step as high as possible to the next move. This will keep the bulk of your weight off your arm and on your feet. No climber (short of Spiderman) is skilled or strong enough to climb a large crack without his or her feet.

# Going Up the Chimney

When you ascend a *chimney*—a crack wide enough to accommodate your entire body—you look as if you're doing an earthworm imitation. First, the upper half of your body moves. Then the lower half bunches up for the next push. (If both halves move at the same time, you'll be a dangling worm.)

Because of the great width, chimneys might seem less secure than the thinner cracks that accommodate just an arm or leg. In fact, however, they're relatively easy to negotiate. Generally, you climb narrow chimneys by pressing your hands and knees against one wall while pressing your feet and back against the other. (Kneepads are helpful.) Keep the soles of your shoes flat against the rock to increase stability. To move upward, press forward with your arms and wriggle your body toward the heavens.

In wide chimneys, extend your legs and place your feet flat against the front wall, while your back is pressed against the opposite wall. Your hands are under your butt with your palms pressed against the rear wall. To move up, press down and back with your arms (allowing your back to release from the wall) and place one foot flat against the back wall (below your hands) while sliding your body upward. Alternate legs for each move and try to let your legs do the work.

Get this technique dialed in, and you'll finally learn how Santa does it.

# Dealing with Unusual Crack Widths

"Awkward," "strenuous," and "dreaded" are some of the words used to describe *off-width cracks*—cracks that are too wide for fist jams yet too narrow for the entire body. In fact, climbing off-width cracks seems best described by the phrase "between a rock and a hard place." I like John Long's description of climbing an off-width crack that's about four inches wide (a nasty affair that requires more grunting and cursing than finesse and grace): "Repeated ad nauseam, this sequence [of moves required to climb an off-width crack] makes the Eight Labors of Hercules seem like light housework."

In the "old" days of climbing in the 1960s, off-width routes were part of the big-wall scene in Yosemite. While these routes haven't gone anywhere, not many people enjoy tackling them. In fact, 99% of climbers fear and loath off-width cracks. (Although there are a few specialists who enjoy thrashing around with "double-fist stacks," "Leavittation," "knee-locks" and "arm-bars".) Still, chances are that you'll encounter short stretches of off-width stuff, so it's good to know a few of the basic techniques:

> **Nuts and Bolts**
>
> **Off-width cracks** are cracks that are too wide for fist jams yet too narrow for the entire body.

➤ Stand sideways to the crack and figure out which side of your body to insert. You're not going to have a chance to change position once you commit to the climb.

➤ Once you pick a side, place your inside leg into the crack.

➤ Create counter-pressure on either side of the crack with your inside arm. Use your elbow and the back of your upper arm on one side and the palm of your hand on the other. You can do this by stretching out your arm or by folding it like a chicken wing.

➤ To climb, move your outside leg up to a foothold using edges around the lip for purchase. Once your foot is steady, push up on it and reset the inside leg. Grasp a secure hand position and get ready to do it again. This is rather nasty going, but it works.

I could write volumes more about the various techniques you can use, but it's best left to personal instruction and practice. Meanwhile, here are a few general tips:

➤ Try not to put too much of your body into the crack. You might feel safer if you do, but your mobility will be compromised. Stay outside of the crack as much as you can.

➤ Move as fluidly as possible; don't lunge. Generally, small movements are best. The tendency is to rush, which will trash your body quickly.

➤ Look for face holds (useable features on the surface of the rock like edges, pockets, and pinches) inside or outside the crack. Auxiliary holds use different muscles and are often easier to hold.

➤ Rest whenever possible.

➤ Remember the phrase "This too shall pass."

## Cliff Notes

Indian Creek, in Utah, is home to some of the best crack climbing in the world. It is best known for its single-pitched routes on sandstone, such as Super Crack of the Desert (5.10), Incredible Hand Crack (5.10), and The Wave (5.11). Once you've mastered these classics, have a go at Lisa Gnade's Ruby's Café—a 5.13 testpiece crack.

## Nuts and Bolts

An **arete**, from the French word for a "fish bone," is an outside corner of rock—like the corner of a house. It opposes the right angle found on the inside corner.

The **lieback** is a move used for ascending aretes and cracks in off-set walls. You use your feet to push against one surface of the rock while pulling in the opposite direction with your hands. You then walk your feet up the rock, almost alongside your hands.

# Lie Back and Enjoy the Ride

When you're climbing an *arete* (a sharp crest of rock), a crack in a right-angled corner, or a crack too narrow for jamming, the *lieback* is the only way to travel. While it can be a drag on your hands—and a fall can fire you off the rock like a watermelon seed shot out of your fingers—you can cover an amazing amount of real estate this way. This is rather heady stuff. Liebacking an arete is pretty damn tough since there is no place to oppose your hands and feet. (Try it on the corner of a house to see what I mean!) Stemming is usually preferable for inside corners, although sometimes liebacking can't be avoided.

In general, liebacking as a very natural way to climb when you have a good edge to pull on and some place to push your feet against. By pulling back on your arms and pushing with your feet, you can work in to a layback position. Shuffling hands and feet upwards allows for steady, if strenuous, gains in altitude.

One of the disadvantages of laybacking is that it is difficult to let go. If you try to remove one hand, often to place or remove protection, you risk swinging out of the equilibrium that is holding you in place. The advantage to liebacking is that it may allow you to bypass a difficult section of jamming, like those pesky off-width sections. The catch-22 with this technique is figuring out how far to lie back and gauging the distance between your hands and feet. As with all crack-climbing techniques, experience is the best teacher.

## Stemming

Should you find yourself with your arms and legs spread out on either side of a *flared chimney* or bridging the gap in a space between the walls of a wide corner, you'll be *stemming*. Unlike liebacking, while stemming you can usually free a hand to place or remove gear, without losing your position. Stemming, (sometimes called *bridging*) is an extremely cool-looking move and probably the closest you'll come to feeling like Spiderman.

In the classic stem move, your feet and the palms of your outstreched arms will (or should) be plastered on opposing walls. Staying in this position isn't really the hard part; moving is. Stemming is an advanced move that requires good flexibility, balance, and experience.

In many situations, stemming is a good alternative to liebacking. Stemming offers greater security and requires less effort. The stem position enables a lead climber to use a hand (or sometimes both) to place gear. This can be difficult (or impossible) in the lieback position.

## Taping Tips

No matter how smooth your technique, crack climbing can shred even the toughest hombre's hands. The most vulnerable areas are your knuckles and the back of your hands. This is where athletic tape comes in handy.

### Hold On

The lieback is a strenuous move that should be executed quickly. It's not the place to take a long rest.

### Nuts and Bolts

A **flared chimney** is the where a body-sized crack becomes wider.

**Stemming**, also called **bridging**, is an advanced technique used to straddle a corner or a chimney. The climber applies pressure to opposing walls with her hands and/or feet to keep from falling.

### Hold On

Keep your body facing the rock when stemming on a steep face. If your body rotates away from the rock when reaching for the next hold you'll likely fall.

**179**

**Finger Tips**

Many climbers cover the backs of their hands with cloth athletic tape to protect from abrasions.

Here are a few pointers to keep in mind:

➤ Don't wrap the tape too tightly. You'll regret it later when it's much harder to correct the problem.

➤ If your wrist or the back of your hand is hairy, shave it first. (If you have hairy palms, I suggest you consult your local witch doctor.)

➤ Tape works, but it will take a few tries to find the most comfortable tension and configuration. It's possible to remove the tape in one piece and reuse these tape "gloves" again.

## The Least You Need to Know

➤ Cracks are natural "weaknesses" or lines in the rock that present a special challenge to climbers.

➤ Finger, hand, fist, and foot jamming techniques—as well as moves for rock "chimneys"—require thick skin and a lot of practice.

➤ The stemming move is probably the closest you'll come to feeling like Spiderman.

➤ The lieback move is just what you need when you find yourself in a tight corner.

➤ You can tape your hands to avoid abrasions. (Just make sure you don't have hairy palms.)

# Sum-It Up:
# Advanced Tips

Whether you've scaled the plastic walls at your local climate-controlled gym or have top-roped at your local crag with the gang from the bar, odds are if you climb enough, you're going to want to try something more ambitious outside your area code. You could, of course, just show up at one of the well-known climbing areas around the world and hang out long enough to hook up with a solo climber looking for a mate. That happens all the time—often quite successfully—but ultimately it's a crap shoot. I've always found that it's far more satisfying to plan, travel to, and execute a climb with a partner who can share my excitement and anxiety, as well as shoulder some of the financial burden.

The $64 questions in choosing a partner are whom do you go with and how can you predict that you'll still be friends half-way up the second pitch. Mountaineering literature is filled with stories about fast friends who became nearly mortal enemies after enduring the tedium and hardship of being snowbound together in a tent.

Having said that, there are a few things you should think about to help you along in this imprecise science of picking partners. This chapter offers a potpourri of tips that should help you climb in peace…at least until that first three-day hiatus in the tent.

# Howdy, Partner

Unless you are awesomely skilled, a mad dog, or an Englishman intent on free-soloing a route (alone, without a rope), you'll need a partner. In fact, the bond you feel with another person during and after a climb is one of the profoundly satisfying aspects of this risky sport. Until you actually climb with someone, of course, you won't know what type of climber he or she is or the type of chemistry you will have.

Former U.S. Senator Bill Bradley, once a starting forward for the New York Knicks, said that when he sees someone play basketball he can tell all he needs to know about that person's character. It's my contention that you can say the same thing about someone after a day on the rocks. Is your rope mate patient or impulsive; careful or carefree; thoughtful or self-absorbed? I've seen the mellowest dudes in the parking lot turn into uptight egomaniacs once they tied into a harness.

Of course, the biggest difference between playing hoops and climbing with an unknown partner is that unless your hoops teammate is packing a firearm, it will be hard for them to kill you. In climbing, your partner literally holds your life in his or her hands (and visa versa). To state the obvious: Choosing the right partner is an important, albeit unscientific, process. Most of what follows is common sense—for example, don't climb with a convicted felon unless he has expensive gear that you don't—but it does provide a sound checklist that will help as your climbing circle expands.

**Finger Tips**

Local climbing shops or indoor climbing walls are good places to meet potential partners. They are low-pressure environments that tend to be quite social. There are often boards to post "seeking partner" notices or group activities.

**Cliff Notes**

In 1952, Dick and Nena Kelty, of Kelty Outdoor Gear, started making aluminum-framed backpacks. During World War II, Dick had become handy with aluminum while working for Lockheed. His experience paid off; the Keltys sold 29 packs their first year in business, prompting them to start a mail-order business. Today, the Kelty Outdoor Gear is one of the top outdoor companies around, offering everything from packs to tents.

# Care to Dance?

When I first started climbing, picking a partner was easy. I went with friends who had extra gear that I could borrow. Since everyone I went with knew more than I did, the selection process was rather straightforward. However, once you know the difference between a "bight of rope" and a "bite of cheese," choosing a compatible rope mate gets a bit trickier. Why? In the pub, gym, or any other place that isn't an exposed wall of rock, people have a tendency to overestimate (or overstate) their ability.

Lesson number one: The first time you climb with a new partner (even someone you know fairly well), select a route well within your respective abilities. Here's the conversation you really want to avoid halfway up the second pitch:

You: "I thought you said you could climb a 5.9 route?"

New guy: "Well, I can, or at least I did in the gym last week!"

You: "%&$@#!"

To use a dating analogy, it's best not to "go all the way" on the first date. To build a solid climbing relationship, it's usually better the first few times out to have a fine day on a challenging route than an exhilarating stress-fest on a route that pushes you to the limit.

**Finger Tips**

Get to know your partner while climbing on an easy rock route. You don't want to ruin your day—or trust your life—to someone who panics under pressure.

*Choose your partner wisely. (Photo courtesy of Mark Eller.)*

## *Friend or Foe?*

Who makes a good partner? This is sort of like asking what makes a successful marriage? Climbing with someone of equal ability might get you up and down a route in fine form, but if there's little or no joy in the process, you're climbing with the wrong mate.

Trust is crucial, and so is a melding of personality types. Two laid-back climbers might not quarrel, but if there's no pizzazz in their partnership, they might be better off with someone more ambitious. Similarly, two driven climbers could conspire to produce a formula that looks like this: 2 Type A partners = twice as many arguments.

In general, climbing relationships take time to develop. Take Ivan Greene and Vadim Vinokur, for example. Both are awesome climbers, but their styles are as different as Madonna and Mother Theresa. Ivan—who heads the indoor climbing wall at Chelsea Piers in Manhattan—is, in his own words, "a fast-and-free rock Rasta who hates indoor climbing." Vadim, also an instructor at Chelsea, is ultra-disciplined and incredibly strong but somewhat mechanical, especially outdoors. Because they worked together at Chelsea they were forced to interact.

**Finger Tips**

Just because you and your partner don't like the same movies doesn't mean you won't complement each other in the climbing game. Spend time with a potential partner to see if you share common goals and climbing methodology.

Over time this divergent duo began to rub off on each other. Ivan, a Jew from New York City who had the passion but no regular training regime, began working out indoors like Vadim, the vertical gymnast from the Ukraine who does pull-ups the way Keith Richards did cocaine. Guess what? The discipline in the gym made the free-flowing Ivan a stronger, more focused climber. Vadim, third in the world on the indoor circuit in 1998, started climbing outdoors with Ivan and became less predictable, more instinctive. He started to have fun.

While you might not find the ideal mate right away, there are a few litmus tests to determine early on if the person on the other end of your line is right for you. Consider the following:

➤ **Safety.** If you catch flak for wearing a helmet or are chided for obsessing over your anchors, you might want to re-think your choice of partners.

➤ **When to back off a climb.** The ugly three-letter word e-g-o is often operative here. Summits are great, but if one person is willing to compromise the safety of the team, you're in trouble.

➤ **Grace under pressure.** Climbing is often stressful. Fatigue, extremes in weather, and fear often push someone to the breaking point. How someone reacts in such situations can tell you a lot about your compatibility. Unfortunately, unless there's an earthquake in the parking lot, you won't know what someone is made of until the donkey dung hits the fan. As David Roberts wrote in *The Mountain of*

*My Fear*, the account of his first ascent up the east ridge on Mount Huntington in Alaska, "Courage plays a smaller part than the tension and dependence that being alone together in a dangerous place forces on men. The drama is a largely internal one, whose conflict stems from the stress between private desire and co-operative skill that climbing imposes."

➤ **Consideration.** Put another way, does your partner have your best interest in mind? The National Outdoor Leadership School (NOLS) calls this "expedition behavior." In essence, this means are you willing to do the little things that keep the ship sailing smoothly: breaking camp in the morning, coiling the rope at the end of the day, filtering water for dinner, and so forth. This sounds easy, but when you're dog-tired these small gestures—completed or ignored—have a large impact.

➤ **Goals.** Some climbers like to push the limit each time out; others, even hardcore types, like to cruise every once in a while. If you prefer to fly but your partner prefers to cruise, you've got trouble.

➤ **Beer, cheese doodles, and pizza.** Okay, let's get down to the nitty gritty. If you can't agree on a kind of beer or choice of pizza topping, some serious dissension may arise. (Anchovies? Are you nuts?) Worse, if you're partner is a macrobiotic health food devotee, you might need to retool your thoughts on pepperoni and Pringles.

**Hold On**

Don't trust your life to a stranger. Make sure you know a lot about your partner's climbing history and technical abilities before you tie in.

## Live Together First

Let's say someone seems like a good potential partner but the fear-of-commitment factor is still nagging at you. Here's a good tact to take: Romp about together in an indoor climbing gym. Sure, the difference between climbing indoors and outdoors is significant, but you can learn a lot by climbing with someone inside. Ask yourself the following questions:

➤ **How does he or she belay?** If your partner is checking out the contours of the nearby lycra shorts or appears cavalier about keeping his or her brake hand on the rope, well, you might not want to climb together.

➤ **Is he or she patient, competitive, or supportive?** Remember, how someone climbs tells a lot about him or her. If you are not with someone, you're against them—and that weakens both parties.

➤ **How does he or she react under pressure?** Casually ask him or her to recount a hair-raising jam. Such stories often reveal something significant about a potential partner.

Ultimately, regardless what you see or hear, you need to trust your gut. Again, this person holds your life in his or her hands. If you feel unsafe, you probably will be. As I said earlier, finding someone you trust and enjoy being with is a big part of what makes climbing so rewarding. Sharing an experience that's difficult to put in words creates a bond that lasts forever.

**Nuts and Bolts**

A **whiteout** is a snowstorm that reduces visibility to the tip of your nose. **Topographical (or "topos") maps** are three-dimensional illustrations of the earth's terrain (that use contour lines to represent elevations above sea level).

**Finger Tips**

Do not start your trek without setting the bearings on your compass. This is true whether you're depending on the compass to find your destination or just using it as back up.

# Where Am I?

One of the interesting and intense aspects of choosing a partner is delegating responsibility. To do this well, it's best to reach an understanding about who does what best. Some people are excellent at planning; some are excellent at navigating at night; others are terrific at finding routes. Say, for example, both of you are lost. Let the "expert" navigator call the shots. Feel free to offer constructive suggestions, but if he or she is wrong, don't become argumentative. That can only create resentment.

One of the really exciting aspects of climbing (and especially of mountaineering) is visiting new—and often remote—terrain. A map, of course, is standard fare. If you're venturing into the wilderness, however, you should know how to read a *topographical (or "topo") map* as well as to use a compass. "Hah!" you may be saying, "I have a really good sense of direction." Bully for you. In fog or a *whiteout*, however, it's ridiculously easy for even a Saint Bernard to get lost.

Just ask Joe Glickman. While on a regular training paddle in Brooklyn's Jamaica Bay, where he's gone kayaking countless times, a dense fog rolled in, and he ended up spending 16 hours in a driving rainstorm. Was he carrying a compass? No! Conversely, when he has encountered whiteout situations where he couldn't see further than his big toe, he's had a compass and made it safely back to camp. The moral of the story? Be prepared or be prepared to freeze your butt off!

Before heading into the hills, you should take a compass bearing so that you know where you and your destination are on the map. Using a compass is pretty easy but does take a bit of time and practice. Every compass I've ever purchased comes with basic instructions. Practice using it in a familiar setting to ensure that you're using it correctly.

A great way to improve your wilderness navigation is to take a course in *orienteering*. If you still can't find your way out of a paper bag, buy a *GPS (Global Positioning System)*. Although a bit pricey, they're often worth their weight in gold. It is worth noting, however, that GPS's often fritz out; compasses don't. Remember: When you're headed through a mountain range to a distant wall of rock, there aren't any service stations where you can ask directions.

**Nuts and Bolts**

**Orienteering** refers to basic navigation using a map, compass, and sometimes cutting edge technology to chart your course. **GPS (Global Positioning System)** is the most accurate navigational system currently available to the general public. Using satellites to pinpoint positioning, it will get you (on average) within 100 yards of destination.

### The Least You Need to Know

➤ Finding a suitable partner is part luck, part skill.

➤ Until you're familiar with your partner, climb routes that are well within your abilities.

➤ What really makes a good partnership? Taste in beer and pizza are just two items to consider.

➤ Before you go and climb a wind-swept ridge in Patagonia with a new mate, go to the closest indoor gym and check each other out.

➤ Finding your way in the woods requires sound map-reading skills.

# Chapter 17

# Leading the Way

---

### In This Chapter

➤ Lead climbing is real climbing

➤ Climb and protect

➤ Trad versus sport climbing

➤ Equipping your rack

➤ Falling

---

Some climbers argue that "real" climbing doesn't begin until you take the "point," or lead position. Their thinking is that until you take the "sharp" end of the rope, climbing is primarily a physical test (exhilarating as it may be) that lacks the mental challenges that make each climb so much more, well, real—no matter how awesome or difficult. This is a subject open to debate, but the point is well taken. Leading is a physical, mental, and psychological challenge wrapped in one.

As you learned in Chapter 3, lead climbing, or "leading," refers to a method of rock climbing where two or more climbers start on the ground without the aid of a top-rope and ascend a section of cliff, or even an entire rock face. Until the leader places a piece of protection in the rock, she's flying solo without a parachute. (In psychological terms, this is known as fear.)

In this chapter, I'll discuss some of the principles of safe leading on sport and trad climbs, as well as things you should note as you strive to improve as you follow the leader.

# Follow the Leader

As a good leader, you look at the world much the way a parent shepherding a youngster through city streets would. Suddenly, it's not just your life on the line when you cross the street, but the toddler's as well. The toddler, in this case, is your partner though it's not advisable to tickle them as the climb up to the belay stance.

At first, all the leading you do should be on familiar, one-pitch routes. If possible, stick to climbs you've already done on a top-rope or followed as the *second*. Another good way to start is by climbing an "easy" pre-protected sport route. This virtually eliminates the stress of route finding and allows you to get used to that shaky feeling of being above the gear. Leading under controlled circumstances like this will enable you to concentrate on the physical side of leading without having to worry about the mechanics of placing your own gear, assessing its security, and managing your rope system. (I'll get back to sport climbing at the end of the chapter.)

**Nuts and Bolts**

A **second** is the climber following the leader on a route. He typically cleans up, or removes, the protection the leader has placed while ascending.

Climbing above your protection is a large step. Once you've been accustomed to feeling the security of the rope from above, it's quite unsettling to look down and see your lifeline dangling from your harness toward a flimsy-looking carabiner well below the soles of your suddenly no-so-sticky shoes. Once you're able to function efficiently knowing that you can't sit back for a rest or shout for "Tension!" when you get spooked, you're on your way to making the transition to the sharp end of the rope.

Physically managing this new challenge before tackling the heady side of the game will make you a more confident, safer climber.

**Hold On**

Don't think about leading until you have put in the appropriate climb time. It often takes climbers years to learn the skills necessary to become the leader. Be patient and closely observe the experts.

That's why what my mother tells me about marriage is strangely true about lead climbing: "Be smart and don't rush the process." Everything you do in climbing prior to leading should be an apprenticeship. Leading should be a significant step in your climbing career, not a short-term goal. As our technical editor Mark Eller says, "Learning to lead is like driving a car. At first you feel as though you're doing pretty well—and you may be—but in retrospect you'll probably see that you were in much less control than you thought you were."

## *Leader of the Pack*

While lead climbing should be learned from an expert, you can accelerate the learning curve by reading about the do's and don'ts of this subtle art. Let's go over the basics of traditional lead climbing.

If you are going to lead traditionally, you'll be out there on natural terrain facing the uncertainty of route-finding and less-than-perfect rock, placing your own protection, setting up your own anchors, and figuring out how you're going to get down. You must be much more conservative under these conditions, because you could find yourself off-route or way out from your last good piece of protection. Such traditional leading certainly presents more hazardous variables. At the same time, however, it offers great rewards.

As you, the leader, climb, you place gear into the rock to create the protection points (or "running anchors") that you clip the rope into along the way. How frequently you place your pro is a judgment call based on the route's difficulty as well as the availability of good anchor points. If the leader takes a spill, the belayer—the person who holds the line against a fall—must lock off the rope to check the fall. Regardless how quickly the belayer reacts, the leader falls twice the distance between him and his last piece of pro, plus the distance the rope stretches. Generally, the belayer knows a fall has taken place when the leader emits a high-pitched scream that reeks of terror.

Once you find a solid ledge reachable with your remaining length of rope, you secure yourself to a series of anchor points and become the belayer for your partner below—or, in a group, for the person immediately behind you. (The last person up gathers the hardware from the rock as he climbs; more about this later.) At this point, you're acting as the top anchor in a top-rope setup.

**Finger Tips**

Pretending to lead while securely fastened to a top-rope is a great way to learn the advanced art. Tie-in as you would for a standard top-roping session and trail a rope while setting protection as you climb. It's a nice practice session with solid safety built in—especially if an experienced leader can take a look at the placements after the mock lead is over.

**Finger Tips**

As lead climber, you should always keep the rope from running behind your legs. If you fall with the rope behind you, it may flip you upside down.

## Rack 'Em

The protection lead climbers use come in many shapes and sizes—natural slings, nuts, camming devices and other types of "pro," which we'll discuss in detail later in this chapter. When a leader straps on a bunch of hardware, the whole enchilada is called a "lead rack." Cagey leaders will add or subtract gear to match the protection possibilities of a particular climb. For example, if you're going to be tackling a climb thin finger tips crack, it's wise to leave clunky pieces of protection on the ground.

On sport routes, the leader's rack might consist of a simple collection of short slings suitable for clipping into bolts. On traditional, or "trad" routes, the rack has to contain enough gear to allow the leader to protect long stretches of climbing and still have enough left over to establish a belay. The leader's rack can be carried on her harness using the gear loops or she can use a paddled sling to carry it over her shoulder like a bandoleer.

### Nuts and Bolts

**Slings,** or "runners," are loops of nylon webbing that are strong enough to hold about 4,000 pounds. Typically, they come in 1-inch width and are available at most climbing shops straight from the spool.

### Hold On

Some traditional climbers do inspect routes from above. Some, after having fallen, leave the rope clipped to the highest protection instead of pulling it back to make a pure ascent on the next try. Such "transgressions" are forever the stuff of debate.

## The Learning Curve

For some folks, lead climbing is too risky. Many people prefer to focus on the physical challenges of climbing second or on a top-rope. This is just fine and shouldn't be considered a character flaw. Leading isn't for everyone, especially considering the time it takes to become proficient.

It is interesting, however, how often climbers follow a logical progression. Initially, whether you start in the gym or outside on a top-rope, you will struggle to become competent at what seems a mysterious and dangerous endeavor.

After that, it follows that you become a sound second on a multi-pitch climb. If you're observant and curious, following a good leader should teach you a lot about gear placement and route finding. Once you've done this for a couple of seasons, it's not unusual to think about leading. Regardless which stage you reach, be patient and climb as safely and attentively as possible. The rest will take care of itself.

## Top Dog

Whether the lead climber remains the same for each pitch or members of the party take turns at the front of the rope, the following basic safety procedures should be followed on every lead:

➤ The leader's and belayer's harness buckles should be checked carefully! Are they properly doubled back? At the beginning of each pitch, the leader needs to check that he is on belay and that all knots and anchors are bombproof and appropriately connected. This is where the buddy system works best. Even the best climbers make basic mistakes, so beware.

➤ The leader must check his tie-in knot—usually a figure-8 or bowline. (The tie-in knot is fed through the harness and connects the climber to his lifeline, the rope.) Is the knot finished with a backup knot? It is also the leader's responsibility to tie in the second.

➤ The leader must check that the lead rope is correctly threaded through the belay device. He should also double check that the belayer's locking carabiner is actually locked.

➤ The leader should make sure to use established belay commands before the climb begins. This insures that all members of the team are on the same page once the climb begins.

### Cliff Notes

Joe Brown, one of the world's climbing masters, started climbing near Manchester, England, when he was 12, the same year his father died. Learning to climb on his own, by 16 he was ascending the daunting cliffs of Sheffield. By 18, he began his legendary climbing saga. Brown and his partner Don Whilans have done hundreds of routes, including the record-setting ascents of the West Face of the Dru in 1953, the Aiguille du Blatitere in 1954, and the Tower of Kakarorum in 1955.

Novice leaders often feel more intimidated the higher they get off the ground. Makes sense. However, experienced climbers know that the beginning of a climb is the most dangerous part. That's because if you fall prior to putting in the first piece of pro you'll be spanked hard. Typically, unless the terrain is easy, I climb no higher than the distance I would feel comfortable jumping to the ground. Once I get higher than that, I set pro before continuing on.

Clearly, that first piece of pro is crucial. If it fails the leader is in deep trouble. On a multi-pitch route if the leader greases off the wall he will zoom past the belay stance, a plunge that can easily wipe out the whole team.

The first piece of gear also plays another important role in the safety of the belay system. As the leader works his way higher up the pitch, any fall will cause the rope to be whipped taut. A solid first piece of gear keeps the rope close to the wall in the event of a fall, which prevents it from dislodging other pieces of pro.

## Taking Care of Second Fiddle

Once the leader reaches his stance (a safe spot to stop), creates an equalized anchor and clips himself securely in, the second can stop belaying and get ready to clean the pitch. As I stated earlier, the leader must protect the second as soundly as he would himself—and more so if the second is new to the vertical game. Rigging a bombproof anchor when belaying from above is one of the leader's most important jobs. Anything short of that is suicidal, since a faulty anchor means you may get pulled off the wall if the clean-up man falls. Here are a few hints:

➤ Always try to set up an anchor on a solid ledge.

➤ Whenever possible, rig the anchor directly above the line of ascent. If that can't be done, try rigging ap iece of protection to direct the rope over the pitch.

➤ If you're on a ledge, provide yourself with enough slack so that you can be close enough to the edge to save the taut rope from running above the edge.

➤ Not only does the leader need to be prepared to catch a fall, but he also needs to be prepared to hold his mate even when he's hanging in thin air. This means you need to be standing or sitting securely in the direction of the anticipated fall. (I suggest sitting when possible.)

➤ If your partner is a heavyweight you may consider belaying directly off the anchors so that the gear will hold your partner's full weight. That way all you have to do is control the belay line. Creating a central point in the anchor system will help. The key is to equalize all of the pieces of gear against the anticipated direction of a fall and make sure that the belay device is situated so that you can get it to lock properly. A belay plate may not work if you are positioned below it.

It may sound confusing, and perhaps it is to the novice. Equalizing an anchor is tricky business. Pick up a copy of John Long's excellent book *Climbing Anchors* which is filled with good and helpful advice. Then have an experienced climber check your work.

### Hold On

As a leader, you have to think both for yourself and for your second. You must think of the consequences of your actions for the second. A good leader will make sure that she places solid protection after each difficult move on a traverse.

➤ Assume nothing. Consider this common scenario: The leader comes to a hard move followed by an easy ledge that he will then traverse. No problem, right? He simply puts in a good piece of pro, executes the move, and walks across the ledge without putting addition pro on this "cruisey" (or easy) section. Wrong! When the second reaches this point, he has to remove the pro and then negotiate this hard move. Should he fall, the second will pendulum like an out-of-control wrecking ball. In that situation, a good leader would place another piece of pro after the hard move on a traverse. In short, the leader must always factor in what will happen to the second in the event of a fall.

# Placing Pro

When placing your protection in the rock face, an analogy to fly-fishing can be made. You might be able to catch a trout with any number of lures, but using the "right" one is a curious combination of experience and instinct. Similarly, there are scores of ways to place protection, but only time and practice will ensure the best and safest placement.

Detailing the subtle differences about how and when to use chocks, slings, and spring-loaded camming devices (SLCDs) is a skill that requires hands-on learning; however, here are several important principles that will help you learn what piece of pro goes where:

➤ Beginners almost always place more pro than seasoned leaders. That's fine. Placing solid protection at the beginning of a pitch and just before a particularly difficult section is of particular importance. This is a simple matter of physics. With less rope played out to absorb the energy of a fall, the forces on your protection are much greaterer. Higher up on the climb there's enough rope out to help dissipate the energy of a fall. There's also more protection between the airborne leader and the ground.

➤ Anticipate the crux (the most difficult part of a climb or pitch) and place your pro when you can. Assuming there is a better placement just above such a hard move can lead to serious airtime.

➤ For an experienced climber on a moderate climb, moving 10 to 15 feet between pieces of protection should be fine. That's roughly eight placements for a 135-foot pitch. However, take notice of ledges or trees that you may encounter should you fall. Beginning leaders should probably strive for solid gear placements every body length or so, roughly 6 to 8 feet between pieces.

➤ Remember that the protection for a lead climb is called a *belay system*. A system uses several parts that function as a whole. Poised before a difficult-looking section of climbing above, you may want to take the time to set several closely spaced pieces of gear. You'll climb more confidently knowing that if one piece fails there is another close by to stop the fall.

### Hold On

Meticulously place your SLCDs in cracks and check that all four cams are touching the rock. A weighted SLCD with only two or three cams in use has a high chance of failure.

### Finger Tips

Typically, you'll use wedge-shaped chocks in narrow cracks and hexes and camming units in wider cracks.

**195**

➤ Learning to anticipate is key. Beware of "running it out" (running out of rope before you find a secure belay stance) on easier sections of climbing. Also consider the implication of a hold breaking when you are a long way above your past piece of pro.

➤ Learn to make use of long slings to keep the rope running in a straight line. Too many serpentine twists creates "rope-drag"—a problem that can bring the leader to a grinding halt.

# From Soup To Nuts

Okay, so now you have at least a basic understanding of the mind-set of the leader—when to place pro and the importance of looking rather than leaping ahead. What follows are some solid guidelines of how to utilize the array of protection sold in climbing shops. Remember, the most expensive piece of pro isn't always the best.

## *Go Nuts*

The wedged-shaped stopped nut is usually the best tool for narrow cracks. Nuts work great when the crack offers well-defined constrictions. Such cracks cause a leader's eyes to light up: All the leader has to do is drop in the appropriate-sized nut, sit it with a sharp tug, and clip on a short sling or quickdraw. Once the nut has been attached to the rope via the sling the leader moves up again.

Life gets a bit more complicated when the crack and the nut don't match up just right. Sometimes the fit can be secured by turning the nut on its end and fitting it lengthwise. (This is particularly helpful if the back of the crack won't allow the whole nut inside.) Also, beware of placements that don't swallow the whole chock; you want it securely back in there where it can't be easily dislodged by the rope. Here's the catch-22, if you place the wedge too far back, you might hear a lot of bellyaching from your second whose job it is to pry it out of the rock.

Larger chocks often have more exotic geometry than the simple wedge design of smaller nuts. One of the most versatile designs is the six-sided hexcentric shape that Yvon Chouinard and Tom Frost first introduced. The protection possibilities of the faithful hex have been time-tested over three decades and it's still one of the best choices for larger sized crack protection. Although it's worth noting that Metolius has come out with a new twist on the old design by introducing their curve-sided Hex-2000, a slight improvement on this well-proven tool.

## *Spring to Safety*

Spring-loaded camming devices (SLCDs) are cool looking pieces of pro that have revolutionized lead climbing. They are especially prized when the crack you want to climb refuses to offer up nice bottleneck constrictions to drop chocks neatly into. Camming units can even effectively protect parallel-sided cracks. Here are some helpful hints about handing SLCDs:

➤ Check the rock for quality. A well-positioned camming device in "bad" rock is like tying a horse to a lily.

➤ Pull back the trigger device to retract the cams and securely place the device inside a crack.

➤ Position the stem of the device in line with the anticipated direction of a fall.

➤ Release the cams. All the cams should make contact with the rock surface. Ideally, all the cams should be equally extended.

➤ Resist the urge to push the cam too far back into the crack; it may become impossibly stuck.

➤ Set the cam with a sharp tug, in line with the anticipated direction of a fall.

➤ Cams can be placed in horizontal cracks but beware when the stem extends out of the crack. If the stem is a rigid design, a hard fall might break the camming. To avoid this unpleasant scenario, try pushing it deeper into the crack or use one with a flexible shaft.

## Sling Time

In an era when climbers are often infatuated with shiny, high-tech gizmos like $60 SLCD's that sparkle in climbing shop display cases, the sling remains one of the cheapest and most effective pieces of pro in a leader's arsenal. Don't make the mistake made by many beginning leaders and ignore this extremely versatile tool.

Long slings can be hitched around natural chockstones or knobs, tied-off over rock flakes, even threaded through a hole in the rock itself. The beauty of such placements is that they're real secure and easily removed by the second. For traditional leading I always carry at least five pre-sewn loops of webbing which can be hitch together to make a long sling.

# Cleaning Up

If the lead climber is the captain of the ship, the second (or last) person up is the steward. As a result, the *clean-up climber* serves a very important function.

Here's what you should know:

➤ Once the leader has yelled "On belay!" and you're ready to climb, the clean-up climber needs to gather, or clean up, the pieces of pro that the leader has set in stone. When I first started climbing, I tried to rack the gear in an organized manner. By the time I reached the leader, however, I often ended up looking

**Nuts and Bolts**

The **clean-up climber** is the second of two climbers, or the last of a group of climbers. She removes and racks the gear as she follows the leader up a route.

**Nuts and Bolts**

A **quickdraw** is a short sling that joins two carabiners, which are then used to clip into pre-drilled anchor bolts.

**Hold On**

A sloppy or slow second puts himself and the leader in danger. The second's hands and feet can get tangled in hanging gear, interfering with moves and belaying.

*A full gear rack. (Photo courtesy of Mark Eller.)*

like a Christmas tree decorated by a drunk; slings, quickdraws, and chocks hung off me every which way.

➤ Take your time racking the gear. Being sloppy not only slows you down but can be dangerous. It's easy to drop equipment when it's all tangled up like fishing line. Place your quick-draws and chocks racked on the gear loops on your harness and wear your sling bandoleer style across the shoulder.

➤ Once you reach the belay site, tie in to the anchor that the leader has set up. Good leaders will instruct you where to go and how to tie in. Once you're safely tied in, it's time to return all the leader's goodies.

➤ Removing pro can be either incredibly easy or comparably unnerving. Usually, removing a chock is as difficult as pulling a knife from a wheel of cheese; just tug on it in the opposite direction in which it was placed. If it was slotted down and behind a constriction, remove it by pushing back and up. However, sometimes 20 drawn horsemen can't yank these suckers out of a slot. Typically, the best tactic is to take the loss and leave the little bugger behind.

When Joe Glickman and Nels Akerlund were climbing Granite Peak in Montana for their book *To the Top*, Nels was the clean-up man behind the third member of their party, a terrific climber named Ryan Hokanson. On the way out, they had to walk across a steep snow bridge that dropped off several thousand feet on each side. Halfway across this precariously pitched piece of real estate, Nels stopped to clean up a spring-loaded camming device placed in a crack up above the snow bridge.

After several minutes, he shouted that he couldn't get it out. The ever mellow, unflappable Ryan told him to keep trying. Several anxious minutes later, Nels remained stymied. Ryan said he really needed it. All the while the three of them were standing on what amounted to the side of a snow-covered A-frame house 2,000 feet above terra firma. Finally, Nels, who had by that time invented new combinations of vulgarities in a variety of languages, told him he'd pay Ryan $10 if he could move on. Ryan relented only after Nels promised to buy him the largest hamburger in the Big Sky state.

The lesson here is to carry (1) a *chock pick* to prod stubborn placements and (2) enough pro to be able to absorb the loss of pieces that you can't shake loose.

**Nuts and Bolts**

A **chock pick**, also known as a *nut tool*, is a metal device with a pointy tip to pry protection from the rock. Be careful not to damage the wires of smaller nuts with this tool.

## When Is Enough, Enough?

When you're in a popular climbing area, knowing how much gear to take is pretty easy. You can either ask someone who's just done the climb or better yet look in a guidebook to get the facts.

When you're in a remote area, the leader will have to make a judgment call. Take too much gear, and the climbing can be slow going; take too little, and you might have to climb with far less protection that you'd like.

**Hold On**

If you take too much gear, you have to carry the extra weight and equipment, taking away some pleasure from your climb. If you take too little gear, however, you may put yourself in danger by having to climb above the protection.

While there's an amazing variety of good pro out there, this stuff is expensive. (And many of the serious climbers I know are poor.) As a result, many climbers own a modest amount of protection. Pooling gear among teammates is standard practice so that the team has a complete *rack*.

Regardless of the size of your pocketbook, you'll need a variety of chocks, carabiners, and runners, as well as a belay device and a chock pick. (To brush up on these device names, see Chapter 4, "Gearhead 101.") Once you've climbed for a while, you'll learn

**Nuts and Bolts**

A **rack** is all the gear a lead climber takes along with him for his team.

### Finger Tips

Although most of your carabiners will be non-locking, be sure to include locking biners for situations where the gate may be jarred open in a fall. Always bring extra carabiners as a back up. The main function of locking biners is to create bombproof belay stances.

### Hold On

Meticulously place your SLCDs in cracks and check that all four cams are touching the rock. A weighted SLCD with only two or three cams in use has a high chance of failure.

### Finger Tips

Novices should beware of climbing beyond your ability. Always think ahead. When choosing between two routes on a multi-pitch, select the one that will set up the next route that fits your skill level. You may have scouted the way up the wall, but do you know where the rappel route is that can get you safety back down?

what will work on 80 to 90 percent of the climbs you'll do. In general, taking more gear than you need is better that carrying too little—for obvious reasons.

As we mentioned earlier, there are two basic ways to carry this hardware: on a sling worn over your shoulder or on the loops on the side of your harness. What you do is often a matter of personal preference. On very steep or overhanging routes, however, the gear on a shoulder strap may shift around your back. This makes access difficult and puts more stress on your hands.

Gear worn on a harness is better for weight distribution. If you're making your way up a wide crack, however, you may get hung up. So there are pluses and minuses to each method. Unfortunately (or fortunately?), learning through trial and error is the only way to figure out a system that works for you.

Regardless which way you carry the load, it's important to rack your gear in a manner that will allow you to quickly locate what you want when you want it. Racking things according to size—small stuff up front, progressively larger gear as you go back—works well. Whatever you do, however, do it the same way so that you've got it down pat.

## Which Way Up?

Learning to select the best route to the top in traditional rock climbing is a little like teaching someone the best way to play poker. You can show them the X's and O's, but the nuances of these pursuits is more art than science. In short, finding the line of least resistance requires spending time in the hills—preferably with more experienced hands.

The best way to combat the uncertainties early in your leading career is to consult a recent guidebook and read the description of a route carefully before leaving the ground. Do not try a route that is not clearly described in a climbing guide.

If you decide to lead on an unfamiliar route, keep the following tips in mind:

➤ Study the route from below. Experienced climbers check out a wall for the first time the way a surfer eyes the ocean when the surf is big: scrupulously.

➤ Learn to spot significant features that the prospective line of ascent may travel: large cracks, a chimney, or prominent ledges.

➤ Look for small trees, which often indicate belay ledges.

➤ Be wary of an "easy" line that leads to an overhang or blank wall. A dead end 400 feet off the ground is a serious obstacle.

➤ Be prepared to change your plan once you take to the rock. Often, sidestepping around the corner will reveal a better line that you didn't see from below. In other words, plan ahead and be flexible.

➤ If you've strayed from a well-traveled route, study the rock for signs of wear and tear to get you back on track. Very often the color and even the texture of the wall is smoother and lighter after countless hands and feet have pawed their way to the top.

**Hold On**

Traditional leading is serious stuff. Gym experience alone will not prepare you to be a competent leader. Do not fool yourself into thinking otherwise. Your life (and your partner's) depends on it.

# Sporty Leading

Where traditional climbing requires all of the protection-placing savvy and route-finding instincts outlined above, there is another way to lead that requires less skill in these areas—sport climbing! On sport routes the protection is fixed and "all" the climber has to do is hang a quickdraw and snap in the rope. Without having to pause in the middle of hard moves, sport climbers have been able to raise the proverbial bar of what was previously thought possible. For many climbers—new leaders and veterans alike—the security that reliable fixed gear offers is also appealing, since few climbers have the skill and confidence to place removable protection and climb at their physical potential.

Sport climbing offers some practical advantages. Because it requires less gear, it's cheaper to start than traditional climbing. Sport cliffs often feature roadside access. With a short approach and the protection already in place, you can do many pitches in a day. In addition, climbing rope-lengths at a time on easier routes should improve your endurance. After a season of clipping bolts, you might even find that the increased stamina and power that you've gained on sport routes will help you when you lead traditional routes.

It's worth noting that sport and traditional climbers (often referred to as "rad" and "trad") don't always see eye to eye. As we've said, sport climbing requires that the pro be permanently fixed into the rock, usually in the form of bolts (drilled metal studs with brackets mounted flush to the rock). While a bolt with a carabiner-accepting "hanger" is hardly visible from the ground, many "trad" climbers detest the thought of

**201**

altering the natural landscape in any way. Furthermore, trad climbers often argue that climbing on fixed protection eliminates the adventure and risk of climbing.

### Cliff Notes

In September 1997, there was a ban on the use of belay and rappel anchors on multi-pitch traditional routes in Idaho's Sawtooth Range. Boasting more than 40 peaks over 10,000 feet, the Sawtooth area has attracted climbers from around the world since the 1950s.

One word to the wise: Sport climbing is far from risk free. Be careful to follow the same pre-climb inspection of your gear and belay just as you would do for a traditional lead. Because sport climbing allows the leader to push their physical limits, plan on falling more frequently than you would at a traditional area. Of course, logging air-time is always hazardous so make sure you know how to fall.

### Hold On

Sport climbing refers to lead climbing done with the security of pre-placed protection anchors (usually bolts). The concentration is on sheer gymnastic movement, often pushing the limits of what's physically possible and doing so without big risk. To a sport climber, the physical climbing moves are the goals themselves, and the route might be achieved only after having its harder sections practiced on a top-rope. The achievement comes when, after all of the falling and hanging and inspecting, the climber makes it to the top in a single push from the ground without a fall, making what is known as a "redpoint" of the route.

## Logging Airtime

"Airing it out," "logging airtime," and "hang time" are all climbing terms for falling. Before braided nylon ropes, falling was anathema to climbers since the ropes often snapped. Today, many lead climbers consider falling a standard part of the sport—especially when leading sport routes. To get the most out of sport climbing, you must learn how to act decisively on the lead. When you are starting out, it can be especially hard not to freeze or back down from a situation where you might take a fall. If you have a hard time committing, bolster your confidence by taking short practice falls backed up by a top-rope; or by falling from progressively higher points above a bolt; or by climbing in a gym (where bolts are often only a few feet apart). Once you learn to go for it, you will find that trying moves that might cause you to fall is a lot more fun than sticking to ones you are sure you can do.

### *Gravity's Rainbow*

The beginning lead climber on a traditional route should strenuously avoid falling. As stated earlier, the emphasis at first should be on learning to place protection and on route finding, not on pushing the physical envelope. Again, climbing and protecting your butt are separate facets of lead climbing.

Regardless of how carefully you climb or how "easy" the route is, of course, the possibility exists that you will fall. This means that your protection must be perfect. Even if the climbing is easy, make sure that your protection is strong enough to hold a grand piano.

**Finger Tips**

Always make sure that your protection is fail-safe—even on easy climbs.

## How to Fall

It sounds odd, but good climbers usually fall gracefully. You won't want to practice this on rock, but you can take a few controlled tumbles indoors at a gym. Try to maintain body control on the way down, keep facing the rock, and avoid the dreaded tumble.

*Lead climbing indoors at Chelsea Piers, Manhattan. (Photo courtesy of Mark Eller.)*

### Hold On

Falling is part of the sport. You should trust the equipment and setup. If you've taken the necessary precautions, all you can do when you fall is to keep your feet out in front of you to prevent a "face plant," and try to relax.

### Nuts and Bolts

A **pendulum fall** is when a climber loses contact with the rock and swings wildly back and forth across the face of the rock, and sometimes into the rock.

Regardless the type of rock you're on, the best tactic is to act like a cat: neither freeze nor make like a rag doll. Keep a few things in mind if and when you do take a plunge:

➤ If you're on a slab, try to slide down on your feet while pressing both hands on the rock. Keep your chest as far away from the rock as possible. Done correctly, this steep-angled slide might mean death to your rock shoes, but you should be fine. If you freeze, you're likely to tumble and get hurt.

➤ On vertical rock, you won't slide, you'll fall fast—at roughly 32 feet per second. Don't flail; you're likely to bang your hands. Try to extend your legs a bit and bend your knees to absorb the shock. Keep your arms and legs clear of the rope. Stay as relaxed as possible.

➤ On *pendulum falls*—which are often the most dangerous since you'll be swinging into the rock—the cat stance is your best bet. Mentally rehearsing what to do will help you to react if a pendulum fall does occur.

➤ It's not uncommon when your strength starts to wane on a particularly difficult move to anticipate a fall before you peel off. If you know you are going to fall, warn your belayer.

---

### The Least You Need to Know

➤ Leading is a thinking person's game.

➤ The lead climber needs to use sound judgment when selecting gear, finding routes, and placing protection.

➤ Taking the "sharp" end of the rope on a sport route will get you used to the unnerving feeling of being above your last piece of gear.

➤ Buying, arranging, and caring for your rack are important factors for climbing well and safely.

➤ Falling is an art. Make like a cat, and relax.

# Double Trouble

If I haven't yet convinced you of the importance of climbing conservatively, this chapter ought to do it. The element of risk in climbing is both the best and worst aspect of the sport. It gives you a rare opportunity to directly confront and overcome fear, and it plunges you into a state of mindfulness like nothing else. But when risk comes home to roost, the combination of injury, isolation, and hostile terrain can make for truly nightmarish situations. I find that the more I learn about how to respond to a climbing accident or emergency, the more determined I am never to experience one.

That said, you need to approach every climb with the conviction that this time, something bad could happen. This will force you to be prepared and will greatly facilitate whatever response is required of you. Follow the commando's credo: Expect the unexpected. Mother Nature offers incredible treats to those who come prepared.

Emergency situations are always unique, requiring a good deal of improvisation and a cool head. But the more you know, the more you'll be able to draw parallels between your own experience and the new situation you find yourself in. Start with some basic skills, which I'll talk about here. Whatever you do, always think through the specific risks of each climb beforehand. Remember to notify someone about where you are climbing and when you expect to return. This can really help rescuers trying to track you down!

# Get Defensive

The most fundamental safety technique is to approach all climbing defensively. Set up your ropes and anchor systems with the conviction that if something can fail, it probably will! Integrate back-ups into your system to cover such a mishap (to do this, you must understand your equipment; beginners should make this a priority). On any climb where there is even a slim chance of being caught in bad weather or being forced to spend the night, carry a minimum of gear to protect yourself. (See Chapter 14 to get the skinny on what you'll need.)

*Feeling under the weather? Be prepared. (Photo courtesy of Nels Akerlund.)*

### Finger Tips

Work with an experienced climber to create a checklist of things to bring. Don't leave your house without filling your bag with all the necessities. Many climbers get into trouble with an "I-won't-need-this" attitude.

Beware of letting down your guard too soon. If you are in hazardous terrain, stay tied in! Far too many accidents occur as people walk in or around climbing areas. It's sort of like the saying that most car accidents happen in the parking lot. Don't let your vigilance go off-duty just because you're not actually climbing; you might still be exposed to rockfall from above or in danger of a slip. In fact, some of the most tragic and preventable of all mishaps occur on major climbing exhibitions when climbers—unroped and without crampons—puttering around their tents at the end of the day slip and slide to their deaths.

View other climbers as potentially dangerous. Don't linger beneath groups on top of a cliff; think rockfall,

rockfall, rockfall. On Granite Peak in Montana, I heard of a climber killed by a rock that was apparently thrown by a climber up above. Whether it was intentional or accidental, the result was the same: a dead climber.

When you're climbing in a crowded area—or simply within earshot of other climbers—be sure to address the members of your party by name when calling out instructions or otherwise communicating (you don't want anyone to mistake your cry of "On belay!" for that of their own partner.) And be alert for carelessness in other climbers. Your safety consciousness cannot compensate for another's lack of it. Don't be afraid to speak up if you feel another climber is putting you at risk.

# Injured Climbers

Let's say you've done everything right, and something still happens. The lead climber breaks a leg in a fall. Someone dislocates a shoulder or gets hit by falling rock. These things can and do occur, and when they do, the climbing partners need to respond quickly and effectively.

The first decision is whether to descend on your own or to seek help. Of course, before you begin any climb, you should know what your rescue options are. Whatever your opinion of cell phones ringing in restaurants or theaters, in an emergency situation, they can cut hours off rescue time.

Consider what happened to Joe Glickman's wife Beth, who was bouldering up a dry streambed in a deserted canyon in Santa Barbara with her sister Amy and friend Craig. Two hours into the climb, her sister fell five feet flat on her back and went into a severe back spasm. Craig took off back down the mountain for the nearest pay phone while Beth waited for hours with her sister as twilight fell and the temperature dropped. It was impossible not to imagine that Craig, who was running like a mountain goat fleeing from a burning building, had also fallen on the way down. In fact, Craig probably set a record for the descent; it just took the rescuers a long time to reach them toting their equipment. A cell phone would have allayed a lot of anxiety.

## Hold On

Prepare for the worst. Bring back up equipment, bad-weather gear, and warm clothing. A planned three-hour climb can turn into an overnighter.

## Finger Tips

Keep a first-aid kit in your pack at the base of the top-roping area. When you're heading for the multipitched terrain, bring an all-purpose tool and roll of athletic tape for unforeseen emergencies.

## Finger Tips

Get help. Some climbing areas have organized groups of professional rescue agencies or knowledgeable volunteers ready to assist climbers in need.

**207**

### Hold On

Unless breathing is being cut off, don't move an injured climber if you suspect back, neck, internal, or head injuries. If the head has to be moved to open the airway, a chance of paralysis is better than certain suffocation. Of course, the specifics of how to perform CPR and other emergency medication procedures need to be learned in a class.

### Hold On

If you're rappelling with a second person or heavy bag, you'll probably need to increase the friction you get from a standard rappel device to compensate for the extra weight. Use a Prusik (as discussed in Chapter 8) for a safety back-up.

## What Next?

What happens after a climber is injured is a serious subject that's largely outside the scope of a beginner's guide. As I've previously mentioned, however, the leader of any climb—long or short—should articulate a plan to the rest of the party should injury strike any member.

There are as many ways to extricate an injured climber as there are ways to get injured. Clearly, any injury that occurs in the backcountry—and especially on technical terrain—is serious. A large, well-equipped rescue party has a lot of options for a safe rescue. A small party, depending on the situation, will have to do whatever it takes to comfort and evacuate the victim. Climbers in small parties should carry a variety of emergency gear that includes extra slings and biners. Again, if you're going to venture far from the beaten trail, you'd better know basic first aid or be prepared to pay the consequences.

## Lowering

Depending on where you are and the extent of the injury, there are several options you can exercise to get you or your fallen comrade off the mountain:

1. Downclimbing: If the injury is too serious to continue but not serious enough to impair motor function, a person can downclimb with the aid of a tight belay.

2. Rappelling: This also falls under the not-too-seriously-injured category. There are many ways to set up the rappel, so you'll need to have learned the ins and outs of this climbing skill beforehand.

3. Often the best solution is to do just what the heading implies: lower the injured climber down. To lower off, the healthy climbers belay the hurt person to the ground, using a belay system rather than rappels. This is almost always the best thing to do if the team is within a rope's length of the ground.

4. Back-carry: This works only if the victim has a lower body injury and the rescuer is as strong as a lumberjack. Nevertheless, I've seen this technique of carrying someone over your shoulder like a sack of potatoes used in the mountains, and it works as long as you don't have multiple carriers or don't have to travel a great distance.

208

# Chopper!

While the helicopter has forever changed mountain rescue, many people think it's made some climbers careless, thinking any bonehead move they make will be remedied by the big bird in the sky that will pluck them out of the abyss and back to safety. This, of course, is both an arrogant and potentially fatal way of thinking. I've read a fair bit about helicopter rescue in the Alps, on Denali in Alaska, and in the Himalayas. And believe me, you don't want to be in the position to need one.

### Finger Tips

Going down is typically easier than going up. Consider a rescue action that takes you to the base, rather than to the top, of a route.

### Cliff Notes

A dramatic helicopter rescue can be seen in the IMAX film "Everest." Beck Weathers, a climber who'd been left for dead after spending the night out exposed above 26,000 feet, somehow struggled on his own back to camp. After he was escorted down by other climbers, the pilot who airlifted him out performed the highest-altitude air rescue ever, landing between two gaping crevasses at 19,860 feet.

Hopefully you'll never need to know about the wonders of a high-speed rescue. A chopper can take a passenger by landing or by hovering and lowering a sling or stretcher on a cable that is operated by a power winch. The biggest X factors are stabilizing the victim and making sure the pilot can clearly locate you if you're in dense brush or under heavy cloud cover.

# Self-Rescue on Snow

The higher you go in the mountains, the more you'll find solitude, beauty, and snow—no matter what the season. Often, beginning climbers get into climbing after reading about the exploits of high altitude mountaineers like Reinhold Messner or Greg Childs, or more recently by reading Jon Kraukeur's *Into Thin Air*. These tales of risk and

### Hold On

Do not rush and make mistakes. "Clear thinking" are the key words. Repeat them. Know them. Make them your mantra. Your priority is to carefully check your gear, work pragmatically, and get to safety.

daring often draw armchair adventurers to safer forms of climbing—until they are ready to attempt a technical route on a glaciated mountain such as Washington's Mt. Rainier, Mt. Hood in Oregon, Mt. McKinley in Alaska, or some other remote back-country piece of real estate.

Here's an obvious caveat that is violated all the time: Don't attempt to climb a major mountain until you have mastered a variety of mountaineering skills. When Joe Glickman climbed Mt. Rainier, he saw people heading up the glaciated slopes with only one crampon or with an axe designed for ice climbing instead of mountaineering. These basic mistakes are an invitation to disaster. If you aren't experienced, go with an established guide. The first thing he will show you is fundamental crampon and ice axe techniques.

# Self-Arrest

Writing about mountaineering for the "Weekend Warrior" column in *The New York Times*, Jerry Beilinson had a great line about *self-arrest*: "A self-arrest may sound like what happens when a crooked police officer is overcome with guilt, but in the real world it's a term for how to stop when you fall on an icy slope and start to slide out of control."

**Nuts and Bolts**

**Self-arrest** involves digging the pick of your mountaineering axe into a snowy slope to halt a fall before the climber starts to slide out of control.

**Hold On**

Approach self-arrest like an actor does her performance. Do several dress rehearsals with fully loaded gear under safe, simulated conditions.

Actually, it's ideally done *before* you start to slide out of control. In either case, self-arrest is a technique using an ice axe that alpine climbers need to know if they expect to spend a lot of time on big snowy mountains like the Rockies and Alps.

How important is this skill? Many climbers think it's the most important snow-climbing skill—one you need to be proficient at until it is as automatic as picking up a dollar bill that you drop on the ground. Not only is the skill essential if you expect to stop a dangerous slide, but it also helps brace you in the snow if you have to hold a rope mate who has fallen.

The technique isn't terribly difficult, but there are a few keys you need to do to make it work. Since one can fall in any number of positions, listing the ways you need to contort your body to dig the pick of your ice axe into the snow would take up too much space. Basically it would be like describing how to slide into second base; the act isn't that complicated but the execution is all in the doing. It is best to have an experienced mountaineer show you the X's and O's of this invaluable skill that requires you to dig the pick of your axe into the snow and weight it with your upper body ASAP. If you can't—or won't—take a class, study a book that illustrates how and practice on a short, modest slope until you're confident you could arrest a fall on a steep icy slope. The odds are that you'll be performing a self-arrest while wearing a full pack, so after learning sans gear, work on it while loaded down. Learning in combat conditions is a good way to get hurt.

*Learn self-arrest techniques before you tackle snow and ice. (Photo courtesy of Nels Akerlund.)*

If I'm on a steep or technical slope, I often rehearse in my mind what I need to do in the event of a fall. This is different than thinking, "I hope I don't hit the deck." Rather, it reminds me to focus on proper placement of my feet and hands. If I do fall, I know I'll automatically do what I need to do to stop the slide.

## Crevasse Management

Falling into a crevasse is every alpine climber's worst nightmare. These often-immense fissures in a glacier invite the curious with their hauntingly beautiful icy blue walls and punish the unsuspecting with their dead-end depths that seem to run straight to Hades.

There are many ways to extricate a climber out of a crevasse, and all of them begin with a well-executed self-arrest. As soon as one member of a roped team falls into a crevasse (usually by stepping through a crumbly snow-bridge), everyone else on the chain needs to hit the deck and lean on the pick of their ice axe as hard and fast as humanly possible. After that, the number of possible rescue methods are too numerous and complex to list here. These are skills you need to learn from the pros, so if you're going to climb mountains with crevasses, take a class in winter mountaineering.

# First Class First Aid

In Chapter 14, I touched on the importance of carrying an adequate first-aid kit. This would include carrying medicine if you or someone in your party is allergic to bee stings or a snakebite kit if you're going to be climbing in rattler country. Commercial first-aid kits are often good, but you'll want one that is compact and sturdy because it will be jammed into a pack and take a fair bit of pounding.

### Finger Tips

When wrapping a wound with athletic tape, try folding the athletic tape in two so that the sticky sides are touching each other. Use this as a bandage so that the tape glue doesn't touch the wound, and then wrap the tape "bandage" with another strand of tape to secure the dressing.

### Nuts and Bolts

**Hyphothermia** is when the body's temperature falls too far below 98.6 degrees Fahrenheit, limiting blood flow to extremities and vital organs.

It sounds rather trite when contrasted to a serious injury like a broken bone, but treating blisters early on can make the difference between a sore spot and raging infection. Knowing how to prevent (and, if it's unavoidable, dress) blisters will save you a lot of pain and suffering. The same applies to using sunscreen. A nasty sunburn early in a climb can cause many a sleepless night, and a tired climber makes more mistakes. Take care of the "simple" things, and you'll be safer.

Perhaps the best item you can store in your kit is the name and number of the closest emergency services in the area of your climb. Few climbers I know take the time to do this small bit of research, but if you ever do need to know, you'll be eternally grateful you decided to be safe and not sorry.

# Hypothermia

*Hyphothermia* occurs when the body's temperature falls too far below normal, causing limited blood flow to extremities and vital organs. It is often the result of inadequate covering in frigid air or water.

Signs of hypothermia include the following:

➤ Shivering, goose pimples, and pale, numb skin

➤ Disorientation, amnesia, belligerence, or irrational behavior

➤ Lethargy

➤ Losing and regaining consciousness

## *How to Get It*

Hypothermia is a subject Joe Glickman, the more adventurous (and less intelligent) member of your writing team, has more experience with. Avoiding what Joe has done over the years is a great primer in Hypothermia 101.

The night before a snowshoe marathon in 1989 in the Adirondack Mountains in upstate New York, Joe and his younger brother Marshall decided to make like mountain men and sleep outside. They walked through thigh-deep snow and set up camp in the woods on a clear, cold February day. That night the temperature dropped 30 degrees to a balmy –5 degrees Fahrenheit. Nothing unusual in the High Peaks, but when your sleeping bag is rated to 32 degrees Fahrenheit you might as well try napping in a meat locker in your underwear.

Flash forward to 1995, when Joe, an avid kayaker, paddled the length of the 2,600-mile Missouri River by himself. Again, he brought lots of warm clothing and sturdy gear that was adequate for nighttime temperatures in the low teens. (This was early April in Montana.) However, he wasn't prepared for the semi-freak blizzard in a desolate stretch of the river that dropped 12 inches of snow and sent temperatures plummeting to –15 degrees Fahrenheit. Jogging all night in an abandoned 19th-century log cabin kept him alive.

### Hold On

If you're visiting an unfamiliar area, listen to the local weather forecast. Also, talk to the locals in the area because they're usually up on weather patterns unique to their area. Weather can be localized in specific areas or it can move quickly, changing in the blink of an eye.

### Cliff Notes

Rainbows usually indicate good weather. They are the result of sunlight shining through droplets of water vapor that act like a prism in the air following a rainstorm. The prism effect actually splits the light of the sun into its component colors.

Finally, there was the late October night when Joe got lost in the fog in Jamaica Bay in Brooklyn and paddled around for 15 consecutive hours in a driving rainstorm—not a pretty sight since he was wearing only shorts and a T-shirt.

## How to Avoid It

All three incidents offer prime examples of what fine mess inexperience, naïveté, or bullheadedness (or all three) can get you into. Always be prepared for a wide range of weather possibilities. In the mountains, the difference between day and nighttime temperatures is dramatic. I've headed up Mt. Washington in New Hampshire in July in shorts and a T-shirt and encountered hail three hours up the trail. With the proper clothing, this is no big deal. Without it, your sweaty body can turn to stone quickly.

Here are a few tips to help you avoid hyphothermia:

➤ Always have enough food and water in case you get lost or your core body temperature drops. Eating energy-rich foods and drinking warm liquids before hypothermia sets in is an excellent way to keep the shivers and shakes at bay.

➤ If you can't get or stay warm in your sleeping bag, you might have to do what Joe did in Montana: Keep moving. Jogging in place, doing pushups, and the like can bring your body temperature back to normal and warm your frigid hands and feet.

➤ If you're with a partner and can't get warm on your own, have your mate crawl into your bag and snuggle. You'll be surprised by the amount of body heat generated.

➤ Carry waterproof matches on day hikes and a stove anytime you hit the backcountry for an overnight. If there's nothing to burn, warm your hands over a pot of hot water and drink, drink, drink hot liquids until you can drink no more.

➤ Line your pack with a heavy plastic bag. If you drop it in a stream or find yourself in a drenching rain, you'll have warm clothes to change into. Lying around in soggy clothes is a sure ticket to freezing your bunions off.

### Hold On

If someone you're with is suffering from hypothermia, you want to warm him immediately. Wrap him with a warm blanket or jacket, then cover the first layer with plastic or insulating foil. Feed them hot beverages high in sugar to replenish their energy.

### Nuts and Bolts

**Giardia** is a painful stomach virus caused by *giardia lamblia*, a type of bacteria found in the intestines of humans and animals. Giardia is curable with antibiotics.

# Bad Water

As a kid, I remember happy campers drinking from the streams in the backcountry. Today, however, it's hard to find a place where the water is safe to drink. I know many campers and climbers who are "too thirsty" to purify the water and who pay the price later. Most of the contaminated water is due to *giardia*, a violent stomach virus. There are a myriad of other animal and human contaminants, however, which make iodine pills and water filters invaluable on any trip into the woods.

Tiny iodine tablets are easy to use on any trip. They come in small glass vials that can be purchased at most outdoor stores and kill most bacteria. You add pills to the water and wait 20 minutes to let them take affect.

Unfortunately, iodine tastes nasty and turns your container a dingy pink. It sure can be a lifesaver, however.

On the fourth day of the Raid I discussed earlier, my teammates and I trekked from 11,000 to 14,600 feet. We were completely out of water and dehydrated when we reached the top. We were excited to see a lake in the distance but crushed when we realized our only water source was a brown, lumpy lake. But you know what they say, "When in Rome…." We had no choice. We gritted our teeth and poured the brown muck into our *Camelback* bladders. We tossed in extra iodine pills to (hopefully) kill everything. Not only did I live to tell the tale, I didn't get ill.

Some outdoor enthusiasts prefer filters as an antibacterial weapon because they removes more microbes. But they are bulky and can take up a lot of space in a pack. If you're in the market for a filter, following are a few things to keep in mind. (For more information on filters, see Appendix F.)

➤ How much water does it handle and how long will it take to purify a quart?

➤ How easy is it to clean the filter?

➤ How porous is the filter or membrane in the purifier? Don't skimp; get a filter that removes all but the tiniest microbes.

### Nuts and Bolts

A **Camelback** is a hydration system that athletes wear on their back. It is a small backpack-like bag that holds a plastic bladder (with hose) which releases liquid when you make like a baby by biting the nipple and sucking.

### Hold On

If the water looks or smells *really* bad, don't use it. Iodine and filters won't remove some strains of bacteria. Consult your local expert and discover which type of purifier best suit your needs.

### The Least You Need to Know

➤ Climb boldly but wisely. Risk is ever present in the mountains—even if you do everything right.

➤ To avoid falling rocks in a crowded area, communicate clearly and stay clear of the parties above you.

➤ Reacting quickly and calmly to minimize further injury.

➤ Climbing on snow requires its own set of safety techniques.

➤ Be sure to bone up on preventing and treating hypothermia.

➤ Use filters or iodine tablets to purify water you find on the trail.

# Part 5
# The View from the Top

*Climbers climb because they love to climb, but they also do so because they love rock and love to travel. In fact, climbing taps into that most primal of human needs: exploration and the lust for adventure. You might not care whether you're climbing granite, limestone, or styrofoam, but knowing a little about each will help you when you're on these respective surfaces.*

*My loves of climbing and traveling are so intertwined that I can't separate the two. When I study a map of New Hampshire, New Mexico, or Papa New Guinea, I inevitably check out the mountainous areas and contemplate what kind of climbing is there.*

*In Part 5, I provide a subjective guide to some of my favorite spots as well as a concrete guide to rating the routes you'll find yourself on—at home and abroad. And if you're thinking about ice climbing or scaling big snowy mountains, I offer some advice on those subjects as well.*

*I've always found that regardless of what type of sport I do, I enjoy it more if I'm not sucking wind and counting the minutes until it's over. Simply put, the fitter your body, the happier your mind. I'll provide a lot of valuable information to get you stronger, more flexible, and more fired up. The mind/body relationship is one of the coolest things about climbing. The fitter you are, the more you want to climb; the more you climb, the fitter you get. If this seems baffling, read on.*

# How You Rate

Long ago in the Far East, students of the martial arts studied and studied. After 10 years or more, the sage teacher would award a black belt that confirmed expert status. When martial arts came to the United States, the belt system came with it.

In a sense, today's systems for rating mountain climbing routes are the equivalent of martial arts belts. When climbers first started climbing, there was no ratings system, just climbers climbing to climb. (Don't try that sentence at home.) Over the years, however, climbing organizations in various countries established ratings systems, and today, most of the routes you attempt will already have been rated for difficulty. As a result, climbers have come to consider the higher-rated routes as feathers in their caps—an attitude of dubious merit in a sport where ego can easily get in the way of safety.

Of course, the ratings systems established in different countries around the world can be extremely helpful—especially if you travel to a new climbing area. Unfortunately, no worldwide standards have yet been ironed out, leaving climbers to figure out relative standards from country to country. This chapter will help put them in perspective as well as give you a sense of the wide ranges of challenges that await you.

# The Problem with Ratings Systems

A *ratings system* is a valuable tool to help climbers gauge what they're up against. However, there are at least two dangers with any "scoring" system, and both of them start with E-G-O. Since the advent of official ratings, many climbers have been preoccupied with mustering the highest rating they possibly can in order to convince themselves (and anyone who will listen) that they're hot stuff. Beware of this kind of climber when you're looking for a new route. Selecting a partner based on his or her own self-assessment can be risky because there are a lot of indoor climbers able to scamper up a tough route in the gym who lack the experience and moxie to climb well and safely on a comparably rated route outdoors. As world-class climber John Long said: "The difference between top-roping a difficult climb in an indoor climbing gym and leading a long, complex free route in the mountains is the difference between a match stick and a blow torch."

**Nuts and Bolts**

A **ratings system** is a commonly agreed upon method for assessing the relative difficulty of a climbing route.

While Long's statement is true, there are a few things that need to be said to round out the discussion. First, climbing a "long, complex free route" is outside the scope of even a bold and talented beginner. Second, top-roping a 5.9 route in the gym is a legitimate, even noble, aim.

The bottom line is that chasing the ratings is a legitimate goal for some climbers—not to prove to others how hot they are, but as a measure of how they're climbing. Ratings matter a lot to climbers who are interested in seeing how hard they can climb.

Rating climbs is a confusing topic for neophytes, but they invariably will want to know how hard they are climbing and what all these difficulty ratings mean. It is just human nature to want to know how we are doing. The thing most people ask at the top of their first climb is "how hard was that?" Only after that do they want to know how to get down!

**Nuts and Bolts**

Not to confuse you, but you should know a bit about the topic of **sub-grades**, which are given in letters or with the "+" or "- " symbol. A "5.7+" is a hard 5.7, but should be easier than a 5.8 or even a 5.8-.

Ultimately, the type of climbing one does—sport, traditional, indoors, or expeditions on remote mountains—has more to do with an individual's preference than the intensity of the challenge. In other words, a week-long adventure race might be analogous to a long free climb, whereas a five-mile road race is comparable to a sport route by the side of the road. The point is that it is just as possible to push your limits on the shorter, safer, route as it is on the more exposed, longer one.

Ratings—including sub-grades—also differ from area to area. Although a route in the low-lying Shawangunks of New York should ideally be just as difficult as a similarly rated route in the towering Tetons of Wyoming, this is often more theory than fact. (And, in fact, the route in the Gunks is probably harder.) Actually, it's best to assume that ratings are uniform only within a specific area.

*Be careful. Difficulty ratings may vary from area to area. (Photo courtesy of Mark Eller.)*

While ratings do vary, they are much more consistent than the ratings used in, say, white water paddling, since the holds on the rock don't change much. When a climb is first established, the rating is often not very accurate, but after a consensus has been reached in the local climbing community, perhaps after a dozen ascents, it is rare for a rating to change much at all. So while the climber who makes the first ascent of a climb gets the honor of grading and naming their route, the grade is not confirmed until the route has been repeated several times.

The other reason there can be a discrepancy from one area to the next is the phenomenon of *sand-bagging*—a nasty climber's habit of deliberately underestimating the difficulty of a particular route. Essentially, this comes down to arrogance, since it's meant to make outsiders look bad when they climb in a new area. This isn't very common, however, so fret not.

**Nuts and Bolts**

**Sandbagging** is when a climber deliberately underestimates the difficulty of a particular route.

**Finger Tips**

Even if you're a skilled climber, it's a good idea when visiting someplace for the first time to start out on a climb well within your capacity in order to see whether your interpretation of the grade jives with theirs.

It's generally true that older, more established climbing areas adhere to a more conservative grade. So, for example, a 5.5 route in the Shawangunks, a place that has been visited by virtually every climbing legend, might be rated 5.5+ or 5.6 at the New River Gorge in West Virginia.

Such variances can be confusing, but as climbing continues to grow in popularity, the routes will likely be graded on a more consistent basis. Until that time, the ratings debate gives us climbers something to talk about when the weather gets cold.

Now let's get down to the nitty-gritty of the ratings systems.

# Just the Facts, Ma'am

While the origins of the rating systems is an esoteric subject, it's worth noting that in the 1920s, a chap named Willo Welzenbach came up with the first rating system by using a combination of Roman numerals and adjectives borrowed from the British system to compare and contrast the routes he was scaling in the Alps. Welzenbach's methodology is the basis of the UIAA ratings system (which I'll explain later on). The system used in the United States is the Yosemite Decimal System, or YDS ratings. Let's take a look at the general classifications used in North America as well as the major systems of ratings rock routes used around the world.

# The Class System

In America, we break the basic difficulty of a climb into a numerical "class" from one to six. Here's what it all means.

➤ **Class 1: Walking**  I've never met a Class 1 route I couldn't handle, even in heels after a solid evening of imbibing. If you need to use your hands on a Class 1 climb, you've had far too much booze to drink.

➤ **Class 2: Hiking**  This pertains to walking on an established trail or picking your way along a streambed. Usually the trickiest thing to negotiate are rocks and roots; however, I have been on various trails that were sound under foot but very exposed and hence required supreme concentration.

➤ **Class 3: Scrambling**  This involves hiking over terrain that's steep or unstable enough to require climbers to use their hands. While climbing high points out West, Joe Glickman did a lot of Class 3 stuff on Boundary Peak in Nevada, King's Peak in Utah, Granite Peak in Montana, and Borah Peak in Idaho. Rarely is a rope needed unless you're too shaky to move without one.

➤ **Class 4: A route sketchy enough so that a fall could kill you**   While a rope isn't always needed, it's essential that you carry one. If you're on rock, you'll need your hands; on snow or ice, you'll need an ice ax and crampons. Depending on your skill level, the weather, the terrain below, and your level of fatigue, it's often advisable to place protection in the rock.

## Cliff Notes

An example of a Class 4 climb is a route Joe recently climbed called the "Trap Dike" on Mt. Colden in the Adirondacks. Most of the climb is just a hard (and beautiful) hike; however, high above the valley floor is a frozen waterfall. The crux is a 50-foot section that is steep enough to require an ice axe (or two) and crampons. It's not technically demanding, but if you fall, your climbing career might come to a dramatic end.

Joe and his mates took the time to rope up and enjoyed the section rather than fret about getting through it.

➤ **Class 5: Free climbing**   Free climbing is technical climbing and the subject of most of this book. While there are intense experts (as well as intense lunatics) who climb sustained Class 5 routes alone and without a rope (a.k.a. "free soloing"), with few exceptions, free climbing usually involves a rope and specialized equipment for protection such as chocks and camming devices. (The YDS grades are themselves really subgrades. So a "5.11 c" is a fifth class route, has a difficulty of YDS ".11," and is subgraded "c.")

➤ **Class 6: Direct aid or aid climbing**   *Direct aid* (or *aid climbing*) is when the rock you're on is so sheer or devoid of holds that it's impossible to climb without using artificial means, such as a platform or collapsible

## Nuts and Bolts

**Free climbing** is ascending a route without the aid of gear. Upward movement relies solely on the climber's hands and feet over natural holds. The rope is used only for safety.

**Direct aid**, also known as **aid climbing**, refers to ascents that rely on gear—rope, nuts, bolts and SLCDs—to climb otherwise "unclimbable" sections of a route.

ladder. This is climbing big-wall style and requires a lot of technical expertise. Aid climbs are noted by the letter *A* followed by a number from 0 to 6 to rate the difficulty.

Here's the skinny on aid ratings:

➤ **A0**  Solid, often pre-existing placements like a bolt ladder for aiding on.

➤ **A1**  Easy, solid placements. All of the aid placements are sufficient to hold a leader fall.

➤ **A2**  More difficult placements, utilizing special aid gear like knifeblade pitons or aid-only nuts. A few of these placements would fail if the leader were to fall.

➤ **A3**  Sustained difficult aid placements, many of which would not hold a leader fall, but with occasional solid placements on larger gear. Hook placements are often necessary.

➤ **A4**  Few placements would hold a fall. Advanced tricks are needed, including extensive hook placements. (You might live: akin to defusing a bomb.)

➤ **A5**  No placements would hold a fall. A faulty piece will "zipper" the whole pitch down to the belay. (You could, possibly, live, but don't bet on it.)

➤ **A6**  The belay itself is not capable of holding a fall; one faulty placement and the whole team goes to the bottom. Not a good time. (If you fall, you and everyone tied to you dies.)

# Class 5 Refined: The Yosemite Decimal System

In the 1930s, the Rock Climbing Section of the Sierra Club modified Willo Welzenbach's ratings system. Twenty years later, Jim Bridwell, one of the legends of the vertical game who did many first ascents on the awesome walls in Yosemite Valley, CA, invented the *Yosemite Decimal System* (YDS).

Originally, the YDS broke Class 5 climbs into decimal points from 5.0 to 5.9. (At the time, anything above 5.9 was thought to be impossible.) Even though Yosemite legends like Bridwell, Royal Robbins, Yvon Chouinard, and Warren Harding (the first person to climb El Capitan) kept "upping the bar" by climbing more and more difficult lines, all the hardest routes were tagged 5.9, and then 5.9+ for the really outrageous stuff.

**Nuts and Bolts**

The **Yosemite Decimal System** (YDS) used in North America is a method of categorizing terrain according to the technique and equipment needed to traverse it.

Finally, in the 1970s, the ceiling was lifted on the grading system on unaided rock routes. To date, the hardest routes climbed are rated 5.14+. Above 5.10, to further define the difficulty of these impossibly hard routes, the letters *a* through *d* were added.

Typically, the rating of any particular climb refers to the hardest individual move on the route. So, for example, on a two-pitch climb rated 5.9, you might find one or two moves of 5.9 and two dozen 5.6-ish moves. Again, this is why when you're climbing a new area, you should have a thorough guidebook to tell you what lies ahead or select your routes conservatively.

Here's a general look at what you can expect on fifth-class climbs based on the Yosemite Decimal System (YDS).

**Finger Tips**

Three decades ago, 5.10 was considered the end of the rating scale. All the climbs established in this era had to fit into the scale between 5.0 and 5.10. A lot of climbs were stuffed into grades between 5.6 and 5.9 to make room for the "ultimate" standard of 5.10. Today, with 5.14 well established (and 5.15 knocking at the door) there is a lot more room in the difficulty scale. It is rare to find truly sandbagged ratings on climbs established in the last decade or so, although there are still some significant regional differences.

## Easy as 5.0 to 5.4

These routes have holds as pronounced as the rungs on a ladder. Although they definitely warrant a rope, they're not steep enough to present a problem to even the most humble beginner wearing running shoes—provided the person's physically fit and not paralyzed by a fear of heights. In fact, for people who enroll in climbing courses specifically to overcome this fear, these are the routes to climb.

## Cruisin' at 5.5 to 5.8

This is the domain of advanced beginners and intermediates. At the upper end of this realm, it's highly advisable to wear rock shoes and have adequate instruction. The first time I ever climbed on a top-rope outdoors, I scratched and clawed my way up a 5.7 route. Not only was it a demonstration of Terrible Technique 101, but I expended so much energy, I was virtually shot after three trips to the top. Climbing at the lower end of this scale is ideal to work on your technique and experience the pure joy of scaling vertical rock.

## Look, Ma! 5.9 to 5.10

Climbers who can lead routes of this difficulty are the real deal. Remember, just two decades ago, 5.9 was thought to be the end of the line. Unless you are a well-trained gymnast or complete freak, this is the province of seasoned climbers with solid technique and strong hands and fingers. (Again, at 5.10, it is common to switch to letter subgrades. A grade of "5.10a" is easier than "5.10b," or "5.10c." At the letter grade of "d," the number grade is on the margin of changing, so the next step after "5.10d" is "5.11a.")

# Holy Cowabunga: 5.11 to 5.14+

This is reserved for superheroes, squirrels, and Sly Stallone. Generally, the 5.11 to 5.12 range is considered expert climbing, and the really, really hard stuff, 5.13 to 5.14, is considered elite-level climbing. Maybe 8 percent to 15 percent of climbers fit into the expert level, and about 2 percent to 6 percent climb solidly in the elite class. It's a similar gap as that between sub-2:40 and sub-2:20 marathoners.

Until a 16-year-old wonderboy named Chris Sharma *put up a climb* called Necessary Evil in the Virgin River Gorge in 1997, there was only one 5.14c climb that had ever been done in this country. One of the most amusing things about these greased-pole-hard sport routes is their names—part homage, part gallows humor: Surf Safari, Heart Full of Ghosts, Ice Cream (sounds like "I scream"), and Super Tweak, first climbed and named by Boone Speed, a climber with a cool name of his own.

**Nuts and Bolts**

To **put up a climb** means to pioneer and name a climb.

It's thought that someone sometime soon will climb a 5.15 route. If so, I'd love to be there and see it. Odds are I won't have to wait long. Just before the publication of this book, Katie Brown did a 5.13d at the Motherload in Kentucky on her first try—the first time a woman has ever climbed at that level without extensive rehearsal on the route. That is an elite-level effort for sure. (Mark Eller, our tech editor, who is also a fine photographer, was there climbing and didn't have his camera. Nice going Mark!)

**Cliff Notes**

With over 30 wins under her harness, Lynn Hill was the first woman to dominate competitive climbing and has set many records and broken many barriers during her almost two decades of climbing. In 1979, she became the first woman to complete a 5.12d. In 1986, she shifted to competitive climbing and won world championships several years in a row. In 1990 and 1992, she was the first woman to complete a 5.14a and to "on-sight" a 5.13b, accordingly. ("On-sight" means the climber leads the route on the first try without prior inspection.) Lynn made sure to break the barrier on one of Jibe' Tribout's routes – a famous French climber who once proclaimed that no woman would ever climb a 5.14. In 1993, she became the first to free-ascend the Nose on El Capitan.

## By the Book

If you don't consult a good guidebook (or talk to climbers who are familiar with it), you won't know much about the route's overall characteristics: its exposure, opportunities to place protection, and more. Luckily, most guidebooks offer two ratings for a route: the general difficulty and the toughest move. This quality rating, which sounds like a sex and violence guide for movies, was devised by James Erickson in 1980 to give climbers an indication of how funky each climb really is. It should be noted that although the "movie guides" are catching on, they're not commonly used in many guidebooks:

➤ **G** Ample places to place pro. If done correctly, the climber is not likely to fall too far.

➤ **PG-13** Poor gear placements for at least part of the climb with enough protection in the crucial sections.

➤ **R** Not many places to place solid protection—even the crux moves may not be well protected. Hence it's possible that the climber could take a long fall on sound protection or a short one onto poor pro, which may result in it getting yanked from the rock.

➤ **X** Precious view the opportunities to use gear on the route. Generally, a long fall will be your last. To use the movie analogy, this is no place for a Pee-Wee Herman to expose himself.

# 'Round the World

As I said earlier, there are several systems for rating rock climbs, depending on what part of the world you find yourself in. While climbers doing their thing in North America will learn the nuances of the YDS rather quickly, if you travel abroad, you'll need to understand the rating system used in that particular country. The following table gives you an idea of their relative difficulty.

## Rock-Climbing Rating Systems Worldwide

| UIAA | USA (YDS) | FRANCE | BRITAIN (technical) | BRITAIN (severity) | AUSTRALIA | GERMANY |
|------|-----------|--------|---------------------|--------------------|-----------|---------|
| I | 5.2 | 1 | | moderate | 9 | I |
| II | 5.3 | 2 | | difficult | 10 | II |
| III | 5.4 | 3 | | very difficult | 11 | III |
| IV | 5.5 | 4 | 4a | severe | 12 | IV |
| V- | | | | | 13 | V |
| V | 5.6 | | 4b | very severe | 14 | VI |

*continues*

# Rock-Climbing Rating Systems Worldwide  Continued

| UIAA | USA (YDS) | FRANCE | BRITAIN (technical) | BRITAIN (severity) | AUSTRALIA | GERMANY |
|------|-----------|--------|---------------------|--------------------|-----------|---------|
| V+ | 5.7 | 5 | 4c | | 15 | VIIa |
| VI- | 5.8 | | 5a | hard very severe | 16/17 | VIIb |
| VI | 5.9 | 6a | | E1* | 18 | |
| VI+ | 5.10a/b | 6a+ | 5b | | 19 | VIIc |
| VII- | 5.10c/d | 6b | | E2 | 20 | VIIIa |
| VII | 5.11a | 6b+ | 5c | | 21 | VIIIb |
| VII+ | 5.11b | 6c | | E3 | 22 | VIIIc |
| VIII- | 5.11c | 6c+ | 6a | | 23 | IXa |
| VIII | 5.11d | 7a/7a+ | | E4 | 25 | IXb |
| VIII+ | 5.12a/b | 7b | 6b | | 26 | IXc |
| IX- | 5.12c | 7b+/7c | | E5 | 27 | Xa |
| IX | 5.12d | 7c+ | | | 28 | Xb |
| IX+ | 5.13a | 8a | 6c | | 29 | Xc |
| X- | 5.13b | | | E6 | 30 | |
| X | 5.13c/d | 8b | 7a | | 31 | |
| X+ | 5.14a | 8b+ | | E7 | 32 | |
| XI- | 5.14b | 8c | 7b | | 33 | |
| XI | 5.14c | 8c+ | 7c | E8/9 | 34 | |

*All gradings are subjective.*

*\*E = Extremely severe*

## Give Me a U

The UIAA (Union Internationale des Associations d'Alpinisme), the governing body of mountaineering, uses Roman numerals to rate the difficulty of a climb. (Check the preceding chart to see the relative scale.) However, their rating does not tell you any other vital information like length or danger of the climb.

The French Grades are by far the most common for the majority of climbing done in Europe, including France, Italy, and Spain, where the important cliffs are located. These are predominantly sport-equipped routes.

## Tally Ho

Probably because I don't climb in England, I've always found the British system befuddling because it combines descriptions of the overall difficulty with an adjective and a numerical grade that tells you how tough the toughest move is. Although that sounds rather straightforward, the descriptions of the climb are often subdivided. (Hard Very Severe is HVS, whereas Extremely Severe, the toughest, is just E and then subdivided from E1 to E9. Just writing about it makes me think of an Abbott and Costello routine. And then for no reason that I can tell, the grade starts at 4a with the hardest current climb being a whopping 7b. Even though it's British, it's all Greek to me. Tech editor Mark Eller said it best: "Nobody understands the English grades, not even the Brits!"

**Finger Tips**

The approach and remoteness of an area will affect the grade of the actual climb. This will be noted in regional guidebooks.

## Australia and South Africa

Compared to the British system, that of the Aussies and South Africans is logical to the extreme. (Or is it logical to the "severe extreme"?) It starts at 1 and currently climbs up to 34. What a relief!

## May We

Since the French are such sport climbing fanatics (their best rock jocks are celebrities), their ratings system is often used on sport climbing around the world. It runs from 1 to 9 and is broken down into a, b, and c.

In the Alps, arguably still the mecca of alpine and ice climbing in the world, there is the International French Adjectival System (IFAS), a catchy phrase if ever there was one. This system is quite thorough, revealing just about every variable you could care to know. It has six categories. Basically, all you need to know right now is that *facile* is easy; *tres difficile* is difficult with a capital D; and *abo* is "abominable," as in: "Make sure you have an excellent life insurance plan."

# Bouldering

Bouldering—climbing without a rope and usually no more than 6 to 10 feet off the ground—has its own ratings system. Actually, it has two systems: the "V" system used in the United States, invented by boulder maven John "Vermin" Sherman, and the one used in France, the Fontainebleau scale, which resembles the French sport grades. (Fontainebleau, the bouldering capital just outside of Paris, has a cool color-coded system that you can follow all through the forest.) Here's how the "V" system works:

V0    Interesting climbing, about equivalent difficulty to climbing the crux moves on a 5.9

V1    Equivalent difficulty to climbing the crux moves of a 5.10

V2    Equivalent difficulty to climbing the crux moves of a 5.11

V3    Equivalent difficulty to climbing the crux moves of a 5.11+

V4    Equivalent difficulty to climbing the crux moves of a 5.12

| V5 | Equivalent difficulty to climbing the crux moves of a 5.12 |
| V6 | Equivalent difficulty to climbing the crux moves of a 5.12+ |
| V7 | Equivalent difficulty to climbing the crux moves of a 5.13 |
| V8 | Equivalent difficulty to climbing the crux moves of a 5.13 |
| V9 and above | As hard (or harder) than the crux sections on the most difficult roped climbs |

*Bouldering in Fountainebleau, France. (Photo courtesy of Mark Eller.)*

### Hold On

Ratings are subjective to the terrain you're climbing. If you're smaller than your climbing partner is, you might find a V4 to be more like a V8, whereas your partner may find it a true V4.

Again, the same rules of subjectivity apply. The good thing about boulder ratings, however, is that you know almost immediately how difficult something is after you try the first few moves.

# Snow and Ice

Rating ice climbs is difficult given the variable conditions that change the same route from year to year (and even week-to-week). I know some ice climbers who scaled a 250-foot frozen waterfall in the Adirondacks on Saturday; when they returned on Sunday to climb another line, it was gone. (The ice, that is.) To compare this to the rock-climbing world, it is as if a climb can be a 5.10 one week and 5.6 the next.

## Cliff Notes

On May 16, 1975, Junko Tabei, founder of the Ladies Climbing Club, became the first woman to summit Mt. Everest. At 4-foot-11, this 35-year-old mother of three raised $5,000 for the expedition by giving piano lessons.

There are three ratings systems in North America, but the New England Ice System (NEI), adapted from the Scottish system, is the only one to concern yourself with for your first season or two. The range is from NEI 1, which is easy, low-angled ice; and NEI 5, which describes multiple-pitch routes with sections of vertical ice longer than 50 feet. (A plus or minus sign may be added for further delineation.)

# Inside

Some gyms use the YDS; others have their own systems. Plastic climbs can simulate the difficulty of outdoor sport routes almost exactly. Of course, traditional climbing is not easily replicated in the gym, because the challenge is less about the moves and more about climbing while placing gear.

When you do take your indoor act outside, start slowly and remember that to climb with grace and style, not to hack your way up the toughest grade you can.

## The Least You Need to Know

➤ A ratings system is a tool that helps you pick a route that's within your abilities.

➤ There are five classes of backcountry travel; Class 5 provides the best view.

➤ The Yosemite Decimal System (YDS) runs from 5.0 to 5.14d.

➤ Different countries have different codes for rating climbs.

➤ Bouldering and ice climbing have different ratings systems.

# Chapter 20

# Want to Play in My Rock Garden?

## In This Chapter

➤ To know your rock is to love it

➤ Granite, Sandstone, Limestone & Co.

➤ Pack it in, pack it out

➤ Let sleeping rocks lie

➤ The Sawtooth controversy

Sebastian Junger's *The Perfect Storm* is a moving account of a once-in-a-century storm in 1991 that killed the six-man crew of a fishing boat in the North Atlantic. What I found so impressive about the book is the way Junger clearly, even clinically, describes the forces of nature that produced 100-foot waves.

I've always been intrigued by the person or forces that shape a work, event, or place. While I'm not a geologist, I am curious about the forces of nature that shaped the rocks I climb. Whether I'm in Arches or Canyonlands National Park in Utah, Needles in South Dakota, Yosemite in California, or the Rockies in Colorado, I want to know more and why and how.

It might sound too obvious to be true, but I think one of the reasons climbers climb is that they love rock almost as much as they enjoy climbing. Perhaps the Buddhist monk Thich Nhat Hahn was speaking about rocks and climbing when he said, "Understanding and love are not two things, but just one."

Even if you have little or no interest in the difference between igneous versus sedimentary rock, the type of surface you're on plays a significant part in how you climb. It's my contention that the more you know about the rock itself, the more in tune you'll be with it while you're climbing.

What follows are some basics about most of the rock types you're likely to find yourself playing on, as well as some specific information about the techniques you'll need to make it work.

*Mt. Whitney, California. (Photo courtesy of Nels Akerlund.)*

# Rock Types

Whether I'm climbing quartz, granite, or the side of a building, I try to practice one basic principle—to be mindful and try to see all that the rock has to offer. By that I mean to use your senses and feel the incline and to scan the rock for foot and handholds. Not only will this make you more proficient technically, it will help you relax. Constantly evaluating yourself ("How am I doing now?") insures a compromised performance. The more you flow with the natural lines of the rock, the less your need to try to conquer it with sheer willpower.

This might sound rather esoteric, but once you begin to climb a lot, you'll see what I'm taking about. As climber Steve Ilg says in his book *The Winter Athlete*, "Ridding ourselves of differentiation and separateness while being our movement is where genuine sport performance begins." In other words, see, feel, and learn from the rock, and you will be a more effective climber.

### Hold On

Always focus on your footwork, regardless of the type of rock you're climbing. Constantly search for edges and pockets to place your feet—especially on a steep face.

# Granite, Damn It!

A photo in John Long's *How To Rock Climb* shows a climber placing a piece of protection along a thin crack 2,500 feet above the treetops on the Shield Route on El Capitan in Yosemite. Since these precariously-placed climbers are neither "standing" on land nor floating in air, you can understand why Long calls such big wall fiends "granite astronauts."

What you'll notice from the photo (or from a trip to Yosemite) is that the granite surface seems as smooth as a polished table. Step closer and you'll see crystals and cracks and a whole slew of rocky wrinkles that can usher you higher if you know how to use them.

The high-tech astronauts who venture ever upward, adhering to these towering walls like so many flies on sticky paper, are following in the footsteps of pioneers who understood that the climber's job is to look, listen, and learn as he treads lightly in one of the world's greatest rock gardens.

If form and content are one and the same, then it stands to reason that content influences form. (If that makes no sense, fret not, just read on.) Whether you climb in Yosemite or on any other granite wall, it's helpful to know that granite is an igneous rock, which means it was formed from molten rock. As this volcanic mess cooled, it crystallized. The slower the cooling, the larger the crystals. The larger the crystals, the better the friction for the climber.

Granite comes in a wide variety of shapes and textures. Granite Peak, the highest point in Montana, for example, is about as smooth as an enormous pile of blocks just spilled out of a bag. Then there's the slick big-walls in Yosemite and the coarse, much more crystalline stuff at Joshua Tree National Monument in southern California or Needles in South Dakota that offer traditional face-climbing routes.

*Granite Peak, Montana. (Photo courtesy of Nels Akerlund.)*

**Hold On**

Granite often has a slick and featureless surface. There is not much to hold on to, forcing climbers to ascend via cracks. Of course, today's elite climbers don't need more than a few wrinkles to get up a "featureless" wall.

In general, however, climbing granite means negotiating cracks or trying to make like a spider on smooth, often featureless, slabs. If you're used to "normal" climbing routes, you're likely to think that there's nothing to grab and no place to step.

As you might recall from Chapter 15, granite climbers become proverbial "crack heads" who travel by the hand jam, lieback, and other chimney maneuvers. Climbing cracks can be (and often is) an arduous and painful way to go. The good granite climber is continually scanning the smooth surface below for any bump, blimp, or dip that will hold a rubber sole to rock.

Whether you're climbing a thin crack in Yosemite or a friction route like Sliding Board in New Hampshire, know that this surface requires endurance, patience, and know-how.

## Sandstone: Life's a Beach

Almost any generalization you make about sandstone (other than "it was formed by intense pressure under the sea") can be quickly contradicted.

When most people think of sandstone, they think of crumbly, soft, fine-grained rock in the Southwest that you can scratch with a fingernail. However, go climb at New River Gorge in West Virginia, Eldorado Canyon outside Boulder, Colorado, or the Shawangunks in New York; the sandstone is as hard and compacted as the densest granite.

Along with granite, sandstone is the most prevalent type of rock. Although it has as many diverse textures as Liberace had candelabras, sandstone generally offers fairly good friction and frequently has distinct crack lines that offer good spots to place protection.

**Cliff Notes**

In 1979, Ray Jardine invented the Friend, a device that vastly improved the safety of placing protection in parallel sandstone cracks. He successfully used it on Yosemite granite, and soon, sandstone climbers were convinced.

From a geological perspective, I find it interesting that sandstone was formed in the sea as layer after layer of sediment settled to the bottom. As weight, time, and heat worked their magic, these individual grains formed solid rock.

Two key ingredients are factored into the make-up of sedimentary rock: the size and kind of sand grain, and the glue that joins them. If the sea was wild during the sedimentation, then the individual grains in any one layer are likely to be large.

Take the Gunks in New York. That they are basically made up of pebble-sized "sand" suggests the shallow sea in which the sediment was deposited was agitated, to say the least. Similarly, Puddingstone rock, a popular climbing spot near Boston, has grit the size of baseballs. The conditions that move boulders the way a washing machine tosses socks are something the climber-turned-geologist might enjoy pondering.

The most magnificent sandstone climbers had to be the ancient cliff-dwelling Native-Americans in Colorado and Arizona. When I visited Mesa Verde National Park in Colorado and Canyon de Chelly in Arizona, I was blown away that the populations of entire villages—young, old, and the infirmed—lived hundreds of feet off the ground in sophisticated structures constructed in the side of a cliff. Until you stand in one of these cliff dwellings and look out over an expanse of red stone that was once the bottom on an ocean, you can't appreciate the basic reason why climbers climb.

Although you might be too absorbed in the process of moving from one hold to the next, when you're poised on a ledge, think about the fact that you are climbing a vertical cross-section of the bottom of an ancient sea. This geological fact means that your time on the rock is more like a day at the beach than you previously imagined.

**Finger Tips**

An easy sandstone route is a good place for beginners because of its obvious (flat but sharp) handholds.

**Cliff Notes**

Many old cowboy movies and car commercials have been filmed in the American Southwest. It seems Hollywood is as drawn to red sandstone as climbers are.

## Lovely Limestone

Like sandstone, limestone was formed in water many moons ago. Instead of compressed grains of sand, however, limestone is made of the shells of sea-faring critters. Whereas sandstone cliffs are vertical beaches, limestone walls are one big fossil.

*Climbing limestone in Italy. (Photo courtesy of Mark Eller.)*

Again, maybe it's just me, but I get a kick out of thinking of all those little calcareous little guys joined at the bivalve in one massive prehistoric pile, towering above the sea to form the white limestone cliffs that climbers love so.

### Finger Tips

Natural protection is hard to come by on limestone because it doesn't crack into patterns like most other forms of rock. Therefore, most limestone routes are bolt-protected.

### Nuts and Bolts

**Solution pockets** are the indentations on limestone walls that climbers use to ascend a route.

In France, where climbers are treated like rock stars, limestone climbing is considered the "bee's knees" of sport climbing. Since limestone doesn't crack into patterns like most other types of rock, solid places to put protection are lacking. As a result, most limestone routes are bolt-protected (meaning they're pre-drilled.) To show how ingrained the climbing culture is in France, the small towns near these cliffs consider bolting almost as a civic duty. Hardware stores in southern France advertise deals on power drills for the wall the way ours promote sales on linoleum.

Typically, limestone is pocked with holes called *solution pockets*. These are often big, hand-sized buckets; more often they are shell-sized depressions that can accommodate one or two fingers. As a result, pocketed limestone is brutal on the finger tendons. Limestone climbers must beware and train their fingers well. (Many tape each finger by wrapping a figure-8 band piece of athletic tape to bolster the tendon around the joints.) Whether you tape or not, using an open grip is the ticket to maintaining sound digits.

Locating good footholds on limestone can be like finding a parking spot in Manhattan. The slick wall might afford finger-sized holds, but these are generally too small for your five toes. And the good footholds that do exist often get slick with repeated use. As a result, limestone climbers wear rock shoes that are so pliable that they can stick a pointed toe into shallow holds almost as if they were climbing barefoot.

## The Best of the Rest

If you're not stepping on a vertical dance floor made of granite, sandstone, or limestone, you will no doubt find yourself on one of the following. Here's a quick review of the best of the rest:

➤ **Volcanic rock**   Smith Rock in Oregon and Devil's Tower in Wyoming are both volcanic but are as different as soup and nuts. Smith Rock has an endless supply of tiny edges and pockets that has tempted some of the world's best climbers onto its bedeviling surface, which initially appears as blank as a Valley Girl's face. The legendary Devil's Tower, on the other hand, that massive tree stump soaring 800 feet above the ground, is a plug left over from an eroded volcano. To scale this monolith, you must do a million stem moves between the giant columns that run up this magnificent tower still considered sacred to Native-Americans.

**Hold On**

Finding a good foothold on the smooth limestone surface is often difficult. Stepping on a slick foothold has intimidated more than a few climbers.

**Finger Tips**

Smith Rock in Oregon is noted for its bolted-sport climbing routes that draw many of the world's best climbers.

➤ **Dolomite**   This rock is less dense than limestone and tends to layer and "chunk," which provides climbers more cracks and fissures to use for protection. For a crash course in this great rock, take a trip to the Dolomites in northern Italy.

➤ **Slate**   I tried to climb slate once and will probably not try again. Because slate is so smooth and crumbly, it's a constant exercise in nerve management. There's little to stand or hold on to, and placing pro is funky at best. Even bolts are shaky since slate peels off like the skin of an onion, taking protection and climbers with it. If you are still inclined to check it out, head to the quarries of Wales, which are the true testing grounds for "slateheads."

➤ **Quartzite**   This rock, which is common on the East Coast of the United States, is a more solid form of sandstone. One of the properties of quartzite is very irregular and difficult to find good places to set gear. However, this rock is primo for finding big hand and foot holds.

## 239

# Treading Lightly

It's worth noting one of the controversies in climbing circles concerning the "improvement" of certain rock routes. By this I mean chipping holds in otherwise blank sections of rock or adding on pieces of stone (or even man-made grips) to make a sport route possible. Of course, climbers are always improving the rock by cleaning away flaky rock from ledges, but alteration by addition is another matter entirely.

This, of course, shouldn't concern the beginning climber, but it is worth stating that bolting, drilling, and/or changing the rock in any other way is severely frowned upon in most circles. The only thing one can be certain about is that this will remain a hot topic of debate for many years to come.

## *Access Issues*

As climbing becomes more popular, the impact on both public and private climbing areas is becoming more of an issue. To state the obvious, it's crucial to respect these areas so that they can be used and enjoyed by everyone. In his book *How To Rock Climb*, John Long eloquently states: "Part of the allure of rock climbing is that it is more than just a physical exercise; we are intrinsically bound to features that nature has provided us. The environment is fragile, and the promise to maintain it is an integral part of our outdoor experience."

Here are some suggestions:

➤ Don't litter. The litter problem is most glaring on big mountains like Mt. McKinley in Alaska and in the Himalayas. It isn't always easy, but try to live by the credo: If you pack it in, pack it out!

➤ Be humble enough to pick up trash left by others.

➤ Use established trails. Mountains are rugged, but the ecology that surrounds them is often fragile. Plant and animal populations are delicately balanced, and small changes in the soil or plant life can have significant consequences. This might sound silly, but if you check out the deeply eroded paths at popular crags like the Gunks in New York or Ceuse in France, you'll see what I mean. Entire areas have been stripped of their vegetation.

➤ Don't alter the rock with hammers or drills.

➤ Use chalk judiciously.

➤ When climbing on private property, request permission from the landowners and respect "No Trespassing" signs.

**Finger Tips**

Use a color of chalk that blends in with the rock. White chalk on rock is an eyesore.

The bottom line is that you need to take care of the environment or you're likely to lose access.

# The Access Fund

One of the salient issues that climbers face is gaining access to the rock. In the '60s, when climbing was an esoteric activity pursued by a select band of mostly "out there" guys, such a topic seemed ridiculous to discuss. As we move toward the next century, however, the loss of excellent climbing spots is an issue that affects every climber. Enter the Access Fund. The American Alpine Club formed the Access Fund in 1989. The following year, the Access Fund became an independent organization that focused solely on domestic climbing problems in the United States.

Today, the Access Fund's involvement at hundreds of climbing areas around the United States shows the pressing problems in this once esoteric sport. Consider that the Access Fund has done the following:

➤ Worked to reverse or prevent closures of climbing areas

➤ Rebuilt old trails and built many new ones

### Cliff Notes

John Muir, who founded the Sierra Club with his supporters in 1892, is credited with the establishment of Yosemite and Sequoia National Parks and convincing President Theodore Roosevelt to conserve 150 million acres of forestland. Muir, born in Scotland in 1834 and raised in the United States, was a writer and an adventurer who traveled to Europe, Asia, Africa, and Alaska. He was also a terrific climber who scampered up many killer routes in Yosemite. He published more than 300 articles and 10 books on his journeys and theories.

➤ Funded climber education projects

➤ Filed lawsuits against the National Park Service to protect Yosemite's Camp 4, the non-motorized campground that has been home to some of the world's greatest climbers

➤ Worked to acquire or preserve threatened land at Castle Rock Ranch (ID), Self Road (CO), and the New River Gorge (WV).

In short, if you love to climb and love the wilderness, feel free to support the Access Fund. (For contact information, see Appendix E.)

# The Sawtooth Range Story

The 40 jagged peaks of the Sawtooth Range in southern Idaho tower 10,000 feet above the spruces, lodgepoles, and pines that surround them like the world's largest welcome mat. These rugged mountains (sometimes referred to as the "gem of Idaho") challenged climbers from all over the world—until the proverbial dung hit the bureaucratic fan.

In 1997, Bill LeVere, the supervisor of the Sawtooth, recommended a plan that sought a ban on the use of fixed climbing anchors, pitons, and slings on all new climbing routes. His thinking was that such "installations" were "permanent improvements" and therefore violated the 1964 Wilderness Act. (Of course, he neglected to note that National Park road, hotels, and logging concessions were often granted exemptions from these wilderness restrictions.)

Only six months later, LeVere's plan had become national policy and the screaming started in earnest. Some, like Lloyd Athern of the American Alpine Club, called the ban the biggest threat to climbing in the last 20 years. The back-and-forth battle is too complex for this book, but suffice it to say that the debate was heated.

The Wilderness Watch, a rather reactionary environmental organization in Montana loathed by practically every climber I know, said the ban needed to go further, that all existing anchors should be removed. The Access Fund claimed LeVere's decision was way out of line, since he had misread the Wilderness Act. No matter. When the decision to back LeVere's plan was handed down, the protesters went bonkers.

### Cliff Notes

In 1980, President Jimmy Carter authorized the protection of 56 million acres of prime Alaskan territory, more than doubling the size of the wilderness system. The same legislation created the Glacier Bay, Lake Clark, and Katmai National Parks.

The controversy became a national debate that ended up on the desk of the Forest Service headquarters in Washington, D.C. The big wigs in D.C. said that none of the removed bolts could be replaced. The fixed-anchor ban became national policy that applied to all Forest Service wilderness areas. As a result, some of the country's best climbing—such as Tahquitz Rock in California, the Cirque of the Towers in Wyoming, and Mount Stuart in Washington—were effectively shut down. In my opinion, this was a highly stupid policy decision that throws the baby out with the bath water.

In the "old" days of climbing, such a brouhaha was unimaginable. There simply weren't enough climbers for anyone to notice. The climbers who were hammering pitons into the rock were basically doing what climbers did in those days. Today, with wildernesses threatened by industry and developers, with more climbers taking up more space, the various forces out there are more likely to bang heads. As climbers, all we can do is hope that the rocks we love so much are left open and accessible for anyone who treats the area respectfully. Climbing responsibly and supporting environmental organizations—like the Access Fund—that are fighting the good fight is our civic and moral responsibility. If this sounds too heavy, you've got your head in the sand.

---

### The Least You Need to Know

➤ Be alert and notice all that the rock surface has to offer.

➤ Different types of rock require different techniques.

➤ Respect the wilderness ethics of the areas where you climb.

➤ Leave your power drills and bolts at home.

➤ The controversy in Idaho's Sawtooth Range has swept the country.

# Rock My World

Even if you live in the most urban of urban areas, a good place to climb is rarely too far from home. Typically, climbers from the Big Apple drive 90 miles north to the renowned Shawangunks. If I'm pressed for time and don't feel like climbing indoors, I can always do a bit of bouldering on Rat, Cat, or Chess Rock in Central Park—smack in the middle of one of the busiest cities in the world. The bike ride from my apartment takes about six minutes.

The bottom line is that if you want to climb, you'll find a place to climb. When Steve Ilg couldn't get to the San Juan Mountains surrounding his home in southwestern Colorado, he practiced buildering (climbing on buildings) on an ancient rock wall near an abandoned courtyard. As he wrote in *The Winter Athlete*, "Climbing on this dilapidated wall held an athletic mysticism that was as beautiful a feeling as the one I receive in the high mountains. Upon this grizzled wall, which would hold no normal person's interest whatsoever, I found bliss." In other words, if you don't have a view of the Rockies in your rear window, fret not; and even if you do, improvising on an old neglected sandstone wall can refine your climbing skills.

# America the Beautiful

Toss a pebble on a map of the United States and a first-rate climbing facility won't be far away. Anyone who has done a bit of traveling in the United States knows that the geological diversity is nothing short of spectacular. Variations in climate, rock type, and difficulty allow rock jocks to cruise from warm-weather site to warm-weather site 365 days a year. (Okay, let's make that 363 days a year; you might want to take a weekend off.)

I know one climbing devotee who spent a summer living in a cave in Yosemite (to save on park fees). When it got too cold, he headed home to Seattle to earn a few dollars, working as a window washer. (No fear of heights there.) From there, he hit Hueco Tanks in Texas. When he ran out of money, he washed a few more windows and headed to the next cool (warm) spot to do what he loved best—climb. Now that I think about it, he might have been the most motivated window man in the state of Washington; the more he worked, the sooner he could go visit another wonderful climbing area.

### Cliff Notes

Established on March 1, 1872, Yellowstone was the first national park in the United States. Egyptian pharaohs are said to have had wildlife sanctuaries there 4,500 years ago.

I love to look at maps and think about where I'll go next. Look at any state park in any of the 50 states, and I bet you find some good climbing spots. Of course, you can climb on the big stuff, such as the High Sierras of California, the Tetons and Wind River Range of Wyoming, or the Rocky Mountain National Park of Colorado. There are more moderate yet still challenging climbs in the southeast, such as Stone Mountain in North Carolina. The East has plenty of great spots. Head to the old, weathered rock around North Conway, New Hampshire (the site of great winter ice climbing), the Adirondacks in upstate New York, or any one of the 10,000 places in between. You'll be "At Play in the Fields of the Lord"—to borrow from Peter Mattiessen's novel—in such a variety of inspiring places that you'll wish there were two of you.

Here are thumbnail sketches of some of the best fields to play in. Even if you're not in the mood to climb, just hanging out in these beautiful areas will keep you off the psychiatrist's couch.

# Go West

Listing the best climbing spots in the West is like counting the pizza parlors in Manhattan: nearly impossible. In California alone there are more terrific spots than there are swimming pools in Los Angeles.

Yosemite National Park tops my subjective list of "don't miss" spots. I waxed poetic earlier in this book about the awesome climbing there for good reason. It boggles the mind. Joe Glickman, who first visited Yosemite in 1988 while cycling across the United States, speaks incessantly about the lightening storm that lit up the dark, menacing sky, casting brilliant flashes of light on the towering walls of this otherworldly valley. What Joe didn't know then (but knows now) is that these "freak" occurrences are commonplace in Yosemite.

Anyone who is anyone has climbed here—from John Muir to Royal Robbins to Lynn Hill to the next hotshot trying to cut his or her teeth on the most beautiful concentration of vertical rock I've ever seen. Ansel Adams' breathtaking shots of Half Dome and El Capitan and Tuolumne Meadows have always moved me. When I stood in the valley for the first time, the sheer volume of the rock dwarfed my expectations. I couldn't wait to come back, and I hadn't even left yet.

That Yosemite has drawn the best climbers from around the world doesn't mean it's off limits to mere mortals like you and me. Yosemite offers many short and easy routes, quite accessible to beginners. Countless guidebooks and guide services are available in the park, so check 'em out.

Joshua Tree National Park in southern California is a prime spot, especially if you're looking for perfect weather in a gorgeous locale with a variety of routes. The best times to visit this high desert are October through December and March through April. Although it's known primarily for its lead climbing, I've browsed through guidebooks that list more routes than any five climbers could do in a lifetime. The same can be said of climbing in the Sierras.

In addition to Yosemite and Joshua Tree National Parks, check out the following:

➤ **New River Gorge National River, West Virginia.** This sandstone mecca offers over 1,400 established climbs ranging from 30 to 120 feet. Although there are some beginner climbs, most of the routes are geared toward advanced and expert climbers (5.9 to 5.12).

**Finger Tips**

The Yosemite Mountaineering School offers rock-climbing classes at Tuolumne Meadow during the summer months. You can sign up for a one-day course (starting at $45) or go for the more advanced three-day package (starting at $140).

**Finger Tips**

Although there are some sport routes in Joshua Tree, it is known primarily as a traditional lead-climbing and bouldering area. The weather there is best from October to December and from March to April.

➤ **The Seven Devils Mountains along the Idaho-Oregon Border.** Bound by the Snake, Salmon and Little Salmon Rivers, the spectacular mountain range spans from the base of the Snake River at 1,000 feet all the way up to the 9,393 summit of He Devil.

➤ **The Shawangunks, New Palz, New York.** Ninety miles from Manhattan, the "Gunks" offers a thousand packed sandstone routes for all climbing abilitlies.

➤ **Lolo Pass area in Montana.** Just 40 miles southwest of Missoula, the jagged granite domes offer fabulous 40- to 300-foot friction climbs, packed with awesome edges, pockets, and cracks.

➤ **The Wasatch Range in the Salt Lake area.** Big and Little Cottonwood Canyons offer grand granite routes as do the lovely limestone sport routes in the American Fork canyon.

*American Fork, Utah. (Photo courtesy of Mark Eller.)*

➤ **Devil's Tower in Wyoming.** Climbing on the bizarre volcanic columns is truly a close encounter of the third kind. The easiest route to the top is rated at 5.6. (Note that climbing on Devil's Tower is subject to severe restrictions due to its importance to Native-Americans.)

➤ **Boulder, Colorado.** There is so much great climbing around this sports-obsessed city that you could fill a bookshelf with all the guidebooks written on the cool climbs there. Check out the sandstone of the Flatirons, the granite of Boulder Canyon, and the steep walls of Eldorado Canyon, and you'll begin to understand why climbing is nearly a religion in this lofty playground. (And if you like gourmet coffee like me, Boulder is the place to be.)

➤ **Smith Rock, Oregon.** Beautiful volcanic rock called welded tuff, and fully bolted sports climbs entice climbers of varying abilities.

**Cliff Notes**

In 1911, John Otto was arguably the first to climb the 500-foot Independence Monument that borders Utah and Colorado. The route Otto fashioned is still in use today.

## East at Least

The Shawangunks, where I've climbed more than in any other area, is the Yosemite of the East—not for the similarity in geology, but because of the number of climbing luminaries who have negotiated the thousand-plus routes made famous by their horizontal holds and overhanging roofs. Climb the "Gunks" in autumn if you can; the crowds are smaller, and the views more spectacular.

I'm amazed how rarely I hear people mention the wild and unspoiled beauty of West Virginia. (Perhaps the state needs a catchy PR campaign.) The New River Gorge offers a recreational orgy. Not only is the climbing great—the Endless Wall is a classic—but you can go berserk hiking, mountain biking, river rafting, or kayaking. Seneca Rocks, not far to the north, is another wonderful area, with a variety of routes and plenty of exposure. While you're there, you can take a quick hike to the highest point in the state, 4861-foot Spruce Knob.

## O! Canada

Picking the best climbing spots in a country as large as Canada is impossible at best. While the Canadian Rockies are stunning, just west are the spectacular Bugaboos—granite spires sprouting from an ice field in the Purcell Range. These rugged mountains provide some of the best alpine-style climbing in North America.

Vancouver, British Columbia is one of the most livable large cities I've ever seen. And one of the most beautiful drives I've taken heads north from Vancouver to the Whistler Ski Area. Along the way is the town of Squamish (not to be confused with

**Hold On**

Beware of routes that seem simple at first glance. Many of the routes in the Canadian Rockies require you to rappel to an exposed hanging belay area.

**249**

"squeamish"), a launching point for some really great climbing. There are the short top-rope routes of Lighthouse Park and the towering walls of The Chief, which loom above the town. This is crack climbing country, so "lie back" and enjoy the view. (If you don't get it, read Chapter 15.

# Europe

The glaciers and sheer rock faces of the Alps were the birthplace of alpine mountaineering. In the past few decades the area has become the center for sport climbing as well. Although *bolt protection* has created a bit of controversy in the United States (see Chapter 20), it is accepted in Europe, enabling the best sport climbers in the world to tackle climbs that were previously thought impossible. The top European climbers, particularly alpinists and competition climbers, enjoy widespread popularity and are treated like national treasures.

**Nuts and Bolts**

**Bolt protection** is the permanent placement of bolts in a rock with a drill.

Unlike in the United States, where you often have to travel great distances to get from one cool spot to the other, the concentration of first-rate rock in a relatively condensed area makes the Alps a prime spot for the vacationing climber with ample ambition but not a lot of time. And, of course, when you're not getting vertical, sit down and consume the best food and drink in the western world.

## *Parlez-Vous Climbing?*

The French are known for being arrogant about their food, wine, painters, philosophers, and, well, the list goes on. You might as well also include rock climbing and mountaineering. Jon Krakauer tells an amusing anecdote about a conversation he had in a bar in Chamonix, a climbing mecca eight miles from the point where Italy, Switzerland, and France share a common border. (It's not far from Mount Blanc, which, at 15,771 feet, is the highest point in western Europe.)

**Nuts and Bolts**

To **paraglide** is to ride the air currents in a parachute-like contraption. Paragliders jump off mountains and float down to the ground. (For the record: This is a spectacular way to get killed.)

Krakauer told his French counterpart that he had climbed an "improbably steep spire" called the Grand Capucin. The Frenchman, who had also climbed the route, was impressed until he learned that Krakauer didn't *paraglide* down from the summit or free-solo the route (alone and without a rope). Incredulously, he asked Krakauer, "Did you not find the experience a little—how you say in English—'banal'?"

Then again, perhaps the French are arrogant since they know that they have some of the best climbing (and climbers) in the world. You name it, and they have it in glorious abundance.

Here are a few sites that should make you a bit "haughtier:"

If you're in Paris, check out Fontainebleau, a pristine forest that features the best bouldering in the world. Bouldering fanatic Ivan Greene, author of *Bouldering in the Shawangunks*, goes there often and always returns pumped out of his mind. Check out the area in Fontainebleau called L'Elephant, which has more than 400 problems!

The region of southern France called "Provence" boasts the most celebrated sport climbing in Europe. The city of Buoux features hundreds of famous sport climbs on heavily pocketed, mostly overhanging rock. Even more impressive than Buoux, the Verdon Gorge rises out of nearby Lake St. Croix. Bullet-hard limestone and routes nearly a thousand feet long make this spectacular gorge one of Europe's most inspiring places to climb and afterwards to eat.

Just north of the Provence region, a recently discovered cliff called Cëúse has eclipsed even Buoux and the Verdon Gorge with the number of extreme routes it offers. If cutting-edge sport routes don't fit your ability level, try Orpierre, a nearby village that features hundreds of well-protected climbs at more moderate grades.

### Hold On

If you're climbing the classic Petit Dru, beware of the intense after-noon sun, which can burn your skin. Also be mindful of the petty criminals, who can burn your wallet. In other words, don't leave valuables in your car.

### Finger Tips

Spring and fall are the best times to climb in Fountainebleau; *par contre,* the period from November to March tends to see a lot of rain.

## The Spanish Fly

It's only fitting that Spain, the birthplace of the tacky rubber used for the soles of rock-climbing shoes, features world-class climbing in a variety of forms. Here are three suggestions:

➤ Outside Madrid is the Regional Park of Cuenta Alta of Manzanares. You can scamper up the huge, pink granite slabs of El Yelmo or climb the bolted sport routes in a place known as Rompeolas.

➤ The jewel of Spain is the long narrow chain of the Pyrenees. These sharp, highly dramatic mountains aren't particularly tall (only three summits reach 11,000 feet) but there are more than 50 over 10,000 feet. The climbing there would leave a poet speechless. High waterfalls, scores of caves, and glaciers make the Pyrenees a paradise for both alpine climbers and hikers alike. And if you if tire of camping, there are more than 60 climbing huts that you can stay in.

➤ The Balearic island of Mallorca is another Spanish hotspot, home of some of Europe's best sport routes.

## Ciao Bella

The Italians have turned both carbohydrates and climbing into art forms. Alpine climbing, skiing, and hiking are nearly sacred pastimes in the Italian Alps. Guidebooks detail just about every route in these rugged mountains. After all, climbers have been coming here for centuries. The fabled Dolomites are certainly one of Europe's most extensive ranges for adventurous rock and alpine climbing.

If you're interested in accessible sport climbing, check out a few of the spots near the town of Arco in northern Italy. After climbing, you'll have the painful decision of which excellent restaurant to dine in. One of my friends prefers the routes and chow in Finale Ligura on the Italian Riveria. These are the decisions that try a climber's soul.

*Climbing near Arco, Italy. (Photo courtesy of Mark Eller.)*

## Wolfgang Who?

The Frankenjura region, located in central Germany near the city of Nürnberg, features an extensive range of cliffs. The climbing in Frankenjura is extremely diverse, with plentiful moderate as well as dicey one-finger moves on radically steep stone. Though most of the routes are short, some of the climbs here are among the most difficult in the world. This is where German rock legend Wolfgang Gullich established an insanely difficult route called "Action Direct," one of the most revered accomplishments in sport climbing history. The best time to visit is during the summer months.

## Going Nor Way?

Norway is the most beautiful of all the Scandinavian countries. The Lofoten Islands, 120 miles north of the Arctic Circle, are considered among the most beautiful parts of Norway. No wonder it's referred to as "the Magic Island." The traditional routes on the granite here are ideal for climbers eager for a true adventure. June through August is prime climbing time. Bring your woolies and sunglasses, however; nights are always chilly, and it never really gets dark in the summer.

# The United Kingdom

I've always been intrigued how the geography of a place affects the inhabitants. Does the land shape the people, or the people the land? The tales of daring and boozing among the climbers in England, Scotland, and Wales are the stuff of legend. Feel free to climb hard with these guys, but don't compete with the blokes in the bar. If you want to see a prime example of the expression "mad dogs and Englishmen," check out a video titled "True Grit." It's distributed in the U.S. through Rock and Ice magazine. Simply put: Those guys are nuts!

## England

Your best bet when in the Northwest part of England is to head to Manchester or Sheffield, pick up a guidebook that lists the dozen or more major crags located within an hour's drive, and climb to your heart's content. More than 10,000 routes are documented, many of which are on steep, slippery limestone. These routes are home to England's famous (or infamously scary) Gritstone routes and boulders. The limestone is very difficult indeed. For more moderate limestone, check out Portsmouth, south of London.

## Scotland

The Scots are some of the hardiest climbers and outdoor types you'll ever want to meet. Indeed, you'll need a robust attitude when a lovely ("lufflee") July day in the Highlands features just two hours of sun.

Ben Nevis, Scotland's tallest mountain, is world famous for its hiking and "full" conditions during the winter. (Picture of rain, sleet, hail and snow all

**Finger Tips**

Insects swarm en masse during the rainy season in Scotland. It's best to hit the rocks in Scotland (or Scotch on the rocks, if you prefer) in the spring and summer, when the typically arid weather keeps the biting inhabitants at bay.

at once and you'll understand the meaning of "full" conditions.) A route called Minus One Direct on Ben Nevis is rated at 5.7. There is plenty of big-time exposure—even on the easy routes—so make sure you climb with experienced hands.

## Wales

The majority of good climbing in Wales is within an hour's drive of the village of Llanberis located in the Northwest. Here you'll find the tallest rock in Britain, Clogwyn du'r Arddu ("Cloggy" to you and me.) There is a wealth of limestone sea-cliff climbing in this area. Again, pick up a guidebook and make sure you find out where the castles are. The weather usually stinks, so you'll want to do some indoor exploring. You can always scale the castle wall, of course, but beware of the armed knights. If you're in the South of Wales, check out Pembroke's wealth of bolted sport climbs. We're happy to report that both sport and traditional styles coexist peacefully in this country (as well as in many other places in Europe).

# Spanning the Globe

Seneca, a Native-American, wasn't talking about climbing when he said "I am not born for one corner; the whole world is my native land." Nonetheless, his sage words apply. Another great quote I like, by that wild Spanish dreamer Cervantes, applies here as well: "Journey over all the universe in a map without the expense and fatigue of traveling, without suffering the inconveniences of heat, cold, hunger, and thirst."

Here's a quickie guide to the some of the best of the rest. It's a subjective and random sample of places I've been and/or hope to go.

### Cliff Notes

After watching David Lean's *Lawrence of Arabia*, Tony Howard became obsessed with exploring and climbing Jordan's magnificent Wadi Rum—a white and pink sandstone mountain. After begging and pleading with the Jordanian government, he was allowed to visit Jordan as a climbing scout. In the fall of 1984, Howard and his climbing buddies discovered and made the first ascent of Jebel Kharazeh.

## Australia

Here are three excellent places to climb if you find yourself in the Land Down Under:

➤ Mount Arapiles in Victoria has more than 2,000 routes, mostly of the traditional lead variety. There are plenty of moderate routes on this hard sandstone, as well as some severe lines to keep you honest.

➤ West of Sydney are the Blue Mountains. Here you'll find scores of bolted routes on rough sandstone. The weather is great, the camping is located close to the climbing areas, and the towns around the rock are heaps of fun to check out.

➤ Tasmania, an island south of Melbourne, has some intriguing climbing. Hobart, the capital, has a long band of brown limestone called Organ Pipes, as well as several quarries that feature bolted sport routes.

# Nepal

Of all the places in the world that I haven't been to and long to go, Nepal is at the top of the list. Nepal is virtually synonymous with towering mountains. There are roughly 50 summits higher than 24,000 feet and hundreds more higher than 20,000. (The tallest mountain in North America, Denali, in Alaska, is just a shade over 20,000 feet.) Nepal is the home of Everest, the Mother Goddess (29,028 feet); K2 (28,169 feet), the second-highest mountain on earth; and Lhotse (27,940 feet).

### Cliff Notes

A Himalayan potato farmer shattered the Mount Everest speed-ascent record in October 1998. Breaking his own record by almost two hours, 33-year-old Kazi Sherpa "raced" from base camp at 17,600 feet to the 29,028-foot summit in a remarkable 20 hours and 24 minutes.

Whether you trek to Everest base camp, around Annapurna, or to the top of the 22,494-foot Ama Dablam, this mecca of lofty places should be high on your list.

# Patagonia

If Nepal is number one on my wish list, Patagonia is number two. The weather in Argentina is wet, windy, and capricious, but the compact chain of jagged granite spires and sheer rock walls that rises from the 200-mile long icecap is as grand a landscape as the earth has to offer.

Surrounding the icecap is a forested valley filled with flowery meadows. Paine Grande, the highest summit at 10,000 feet, is a snow and ice peak that requires significant alpine skills. Cerro Almirante

### Finger Tips

The weather in Patagonia is best suited for climbing from December to early March.

Nieto is considered the only major peak that should be attempted by relatively inexperienced alpinists. One of the classic trekking routes is to circumnavigate the entire massif, a hike that can be completed in seven or fewer days.

**Cliff Notes**

Although discovered in 1870s, the Paine Grande was not declared a national park until 1959. The Paine sits on the southern tip of the Patagonian icecap Hielo Sur, spreading over 200 miles of the Andean crest.

## South Africa

Table Mountain, which was first climbed in 1503 by Antonio de Salanha, an Admiral in the Portuguese navy, dominates the lovely city of Cape Town. By the turn of the twentieth century, there were 50 different routes up this powerful flat-topped peak. Today, you can climb to the top and take a cable car down.

**Cliff Notes**

By the mid-1600s, it was common for Dutch sailors docked in South Africa to climb Table Mountain. In the late 1880s, 19-year-old Gustav Nefdt turned the climbing world around with his solo ascent of Toverkop in Cape Province.

Because South Africa was banned from the sporting arena for so many years, few climbers thought it a viable place to visit. In the past five years, however, there has been a mini-boom in sport climbing over there. In fact, this wide-open country offers just about anything a jock could want: biking, hiking, running, paddling, and more.

## The Least You Need to Know

➤ From California to Maine, the United States has a vast array of vertical places in which to play.

➤ If you can't find at least a handful of exciting climbs in the Canadian Rockies, you can always check out the Bugaboos.

➤ For centuries the French, Italians, and Spaniards have been arguing about who has the best climbing. Why not trek over to Europe and decide for yourself?

➤ Climb in England, Scotland, or Wales, and you'll tap into a rich history of hardened climbers.

➤ If you've exhausted the United States, Canada, and Europe, there's always the rest of the world.

# Mountaineering: Don't Try This at Home

*Climbing* is as broad a term as, say, *traveling*. There's indoor, outdoor, rock, ice, and mixed-route (a combination of rock and ice) climbing; there's also bouldering, buildering, and mountaineering. They all fall under the "climbing" umbrella, however. All are related and many of the skills and principles apply to them all. For example, although rock and ice climbers use dramatically different techniques, the rope work and protection systems are quite similar.

At the upper end of the risk-and-reward spectrum is mountaineering. While I'm more of a warm-weather rock jock than a snow bunny, many of my friends who are keen on mountaineering insist that there's nothing quite as satisfying as a technical climb on a beautiful mountain. Having climbed Cotapoxi, a 19,000-footer in Ecuador, I can begin to appreciate the challenge and intensity of multi-day climbs on imposing mountains like Denali in Alaska, Kilimanjaro in Tanzania, Aconcagua in Argentina, or any of the towering giants in the Himalayas.

Again, every mountain is different; virtually all the biggies have multiple routes to the top. Some offer pure rock routes; others require ice- and snow-climbing skills. Some demand all three. And they all require ample fitness and, perhaps more importantly, determination.

While being familiar with basic rock-climbing techniques is an asset in the mountaineering world, a new set of rules reign. In this chapter, I offer some insights and anecdotes that will familiarize you with the equipment you'll need, how to use it, and what to expect in a unique world where each step leads to thinner air.

# Snow, Snow, Snow

Early on in their recent bid to climb the highest peaks in each of the 50 states, Nels Akerlund and Joe Glickman were driving to Humphreys Peak (12,633 feet) outside Flagstaff, Arizona. As they cruised past the sun-drenched hills dotted with evergreens, they wondered if a modest-sized mountain like Humphreys would have any snow on it in late April.

Suddenly, as if on cue, they topped out over a ridge at roughly 8,000 feet and BOOM!—the imposing peak leapt into the blue sky as white as a priest's collar. Later they learned that 44 inches of snow had fallen just days earlier. Even so, there were several feet of the white stuff covering all but the lower third of the mountain.

**Finger Tips**

Before you start on your mountaineering adventures, hook up with a guide service to learn you the basics, like self-arrest and trekking with crampons.

What Nels and Joe quickly learned is what any experienced alpine climber knows: Snow is a standard part of mountaineering. If you're not fond of the fluffy stuff, you're in the wrong line of play, even if you climb during the hottest part of the summer. In fact, in July 1998, when Nels and Joe climbed Gannett Peak in Wyoming, they got hammered by a blizzard that dumped a foot of snow high on the 13,804-foot mountain in a matter of hours. And while it's unusual, it's not unheard of for a "small" mountain like New York's Mt. Marcey (5,344 feet) to see snow in June.

*Snow climbing, Mt. Marcey, NY. (Photo courtesy of Nels Akerlund.)*

Of course, there's snow and then there's ice. Ice climbing is its own animal. It's dangerous and thrilling and an awesome physical and mental challenge. The specialized nature of climbing vertical ice—via the aid of two ice axes, rigid crampons, and tubular ice screws—is different enough that before you gear up and tackle a frozen waterfall, you should seek expert instruction.

## Axe Me

There are two basic types of axes used in high places: "The so-called "tools" used for climbing frozen waterfalls and other vertical walls of ice, and the mountaineering axe used to ascend less technical routes on snow and ice. Ice climbers use two short axes, one in each hand. Mountaineers use one axe, which is longer and has a less pronounced curve on the pick side.

Ice climbing was revolutionized in the mid-1970s when ice climbing equipment and techniques evolved to allow climbers to ascend vertical and overhanging ice. The ice axe was central to the revolution. Shorter axes with sharp, curved picks allowed climbers to hang from minimal rock and protection. Wrist loops connected tools and climber, making it possible for climbers to hang from their wrists rather than having to grip the shaft. These sharp tools are remarkably efficient and extremely satisfying to swing into soft ice.

If you're going to find yourself hiking on snow and ice, you'll need a mountaineer's axe. Here's a small example that illustrates its importance. On Humphreys Peak, the dynamic duo of Nels and Joe had just one ice axe between them. Most of the climb required nothing more than strong legs and lungs. On one particularly steep, snowy slope, however, "Axeless Joe" virtually had to get down on all fours to avoid sliding down the slope while Nels trudged confidently to the top.

In short, without a good ice axe (and the skill to use it), safe alpine travel is next to impossible. If your axe handle is long enough, you can use it below the *snow line* like a cane as you hike up (or down) a rocky bit of trail. Its primary purpose, however, is to help you negotiate steep, icy slopes (usually while wearing crampons) and to stop a fall before you slide wildly out of control. It can also serve as a brake as you *glissade* (slide down a slope on the seat of your pants). In addition, this versatile tool can double as a heavy-duty tent stake and is invaluable in crevasse rescues.

### Nuts and Bolts

The **snow line** is the point where the snow and rock meet. To **glissade** is to slide down a slope on the seat of your pants.

### Finger Tips

Ice axes with a moderate hooking angle (65 to 70 degrees from the shaft) are good for general mountaineering uses. Axes with sharper angles (55 to 60 degrees) are recommended for technical ice climbing.

Early on, mountaineers used long wooden staffs with metal points. As steeper and steeper slopes were attempted, climbers turned to shorter and shorter axes. Generally, the more alpine climbing you do, the shorter your axe is likely to be. Joe Glickman, who is 6'4", started climbing with an 80-cm axe, which is long. On low-angled slopes, it worked well, but on the steeper stuff, it was a liability because it was more cumbersome to maneuver. After a season of climbing out west, he trimmed 10 cm from the shaft—ouch!—and found it much easier to negotiate the steeper slopes.

## Anatomy of an Ice Axe

When you take a course in winter mountaineering, one of the first things the instructor will do is review the components of your axe. Here's what you need to know:

➤ **The top**  Also called the "head" of the axe, the top is made of steel and has three separate features: the pick, adze, and a hole in the head through which you can thread a wrist leash.

➤ **The pick**  Yvon Chouinard, the founder of the outdoor gear company, Patagonia, and perhaps the best ice climber of the 1960s, had been climbing some of the great ice faces of the Mont Blanc massif but felt that the straight picks that were aligned perpendicular to their handles could be improved. So, in 1966, this self-taught blacksmith and his climbing partner (an aeronautical engineer appropriately named Tom Frost) designed an ice axe with a *pick* with teeth that hooked downward in a gentle curve. It was a stroke of genius. For the first time, technical ice climbers could ascend vertical (and even overhanging) ice faces. Although the technical ice tool is shorter and the curve is sharper than the mountaineering axe, the innovation loomed large for mountaineers because the hooking action allows the axe to dig in faster when one attempts to stop a fall during a self-arrest. The teeth on the under side of the pick provide the bite.

➤ **The adze**  Think of the top of the axe as a combination of a pick axe and garden hoe. Opposite the pick is the *adze*. This wide, sharp side of the axe is an all-purpose cutting and digging tool (which is, regrettably, often ignored by beginners.)

➤ **The shaft**  When I was first shopping for an ice axe, the clerk showed me an axe with a straight-grained hickory handle. It was so aesthetically pleasing I felt like buying it and hanging in on my wall next to a classic pair of wooden snowshoes. Although wood-handled axes are obviously still available, I recommend getting one made out of either titanium, Kevlar, fiberglass, aluminum, or

**Finger Tips**

The adze is ideal if you're breaking up snow and ice to dig a tent platform or need to chop away at an icy slope. And when you can't find an ice scraper when you return to you car after the climb, it's an effective tool to clean your windows.

some combination thereof. Regardless of the material, however, the important thing is to get the right size. Consult with an expert but make sure they know what they're talking about. When Joe Glickman was shopping for one in an outdoor shop in New York City, he was picking the salesperson's brain on which type he preferred. During the conversation, he told the guy that he was going to climb Denali in Alaska. The salesperson asked, "That's about 40,000 feet isn't it?" Joe replied, "Yeah, they recently discovered it's 11,000 feet taller than Everest." While most of the sales people you'll encounter in a quality outdoor store do know what they're talking about, if you have any doubts about their recommendations, ask someone else.

➤ **The spike**  At the bottom of the shaft is a triangular-shaped metal *spike*. It's important that this remain sharp in order to punch through dense snow and ice. If you'll be using your axe for balance—say, when you're moving through a rocky section on an alpine climb—be careful not to dull the point.

**Nuts and Bolts**

The **pick** is on the head of an ice axe, opposite the adze. It is usually curved, providing secure hooking action in snow or ice.

The **adze** is the head of an ice axe opposite the pick. Typically made of steel, this wider, sharp side of the axe is an all-purpose cutting and digging tool for snow and ice climbing.

The **shaft** is the handle of the ice axe. It's typically made of aluminum, titanium, or a composite, such as fiberglass, Kevlar, or carbon filament.

The **spike** is the metal tip at the bottom of the shaft.

## You and Your Axe

An ice axe is an extremely useful tool, but it's also a potentially hazardous piece of equipment if not handled and stored properly. First off, remember to carry the axe carefully. Don't just toss it down when you take a break. If you do, the odds are that someone in your party will step, sit, or in some other creative way, impale him- or herself on it. Just as bad—or perhaps worse—it's likely to slide down the slope to parts unknown. (This is the mountaineer's version of heading upstream without a paddle.)

Because of the axe's penchant for creating mayhem, it's best when you're not using the sharp and pokey sucker to slip it through the ice-axe loop on your pack and strap it down. Placing a rubber or leather guard over the pick and adze is a safe way to travel and store your axe, especially if you need to stuff it in your pack for storage on an airplane.

**Hold On**

The top and bottom of an ice axe can be very sharp. Be careful when handling it. You should purchase a rubber or leather guard to protect the adze and spike.

There are a few things to keep in mind when you're holding your axe on a steep incline. I was taught to hold the top as though I were walking with a cane with the adze forward. Later, an instructor taught me a valuable little trick: Instead of flipping the pick forward to perform a self-arrest, climb with the pick facing forward. Unless you wrap enough duct tape around the head to create a pad, however, this feels quite uncomfortable. But once you do, it's easier to perform a self-arrest.

**Hold On**

Some backpackers use tiny instep crampons with four or six points for crossing short snow fields. These crampons do not have points at the heel or toe and are by no means suitable for mountaineering.

# Foot Fangs

In the late 1800s, climbers who wore hobnailed boots were able to ascend ice faces as steep as 40 or 50 degrees by hacking steps and handholds up the slopes with crude, heavy ice axes. In 1908, an English climber invented a crampon with ten downward-pointing spikes. Roughly 25 years later, two more forward-slanting spikes protruding horizontally from the toe were added. These 12-point models enabled climbers to "front-point" up a slope and eliminated the odious task of chopping steps. While 12-point models remain the standard for mountaineering, the mono-point crampon—one single spike protruding from the toe—has become popular among ice climbers.

## *Rigid or Hinged?*

The first time you don a pair of crampons, you will feel a bit like a medieval knight. These menacing 12-point weapons come in two basic varieties: rigid or hinged. Hinged is the choice for mountaineers because it gives when you walk. Rigid is preferable for technical climbing when you're front-pointing up vertical ice.

For crampons to fit your boots, they need to be "crampon" compatible. This means that your boots must have grooves in the front and back that allow the crampons to fit snugly. (Plastic boots are warmer and dryer and hence preferable on "colder" mountains. All plastic boots are crampon-compatible.) If you do a lot of hiking but plan on climbing steep, snowy mountains, you should consider a pair of boots that are light and comfortable enough for the trail, yet rigid and strong enough to support steel spikes.

**Finger Tips**

Rigid crampons are better than hinged crampons when you climb steep ice because they're designed for front-pointing up technical ice. Their stiffness enables you to keep your heel lower, making front-pointing less tiring.

Joe Glickman once met two guys in the Wind River Range who were attempting to climb Gannett Peak (a glaciated mountain with extremely steep slopes and sketchy summit ridge) with crampons they had attached to their running shoes. While I generally endorse the expression "If the shoe fits, wear it," it's foolish to rig such a flimsy setup.

## *Fit*

Find the person who has ever had a crampon work loose in the middle of an icy slope (in the dark while half-asleep) who didn't panic, curse a blue streak, or invoke the name of God—and you've found one cool cucumber. Thankfully, it's never happened to me. When Joe was climbing Mt. Rainier via the Kautz Route, however, he looked down the middle of a slope that bottomed out hundreds of feet below and saw his crampon dragging alongside his boot like a cheap roller skate that had come dislodged. One of the guys he was with, a climber with years of experience, said that when that happened to him, he would retire those crampons even if there was nothing wrong with them. "It's just bad luck," he said.

If this ever happens to you, look around to see whether there's a decent spot nearby to stop. If so, slowly make your way there, sit down, and fix it ASAP. If not, plant your ice axe as deep as you can into the snow and tie yourself off so that you don't go anywhere if you slip. Then, sit down and put it back on pronto.

Here's some additional advice: Not only do you need to make sure that the crampons you buy fit snugly on the boots you own, you should put them on several times before heading out to make sure you can do it in your sleep—and certainly in the dark. In other words, don't try them on for the first time when it's dark and you're about to head up a slope that would thrill an Olympic bobsledder.

I can't stress this point enough. In the middle of a blizzard on Gannett Peak in Wyoming, Joe and Nels had to put on their crampons as quickly and efficiently as possible. (Strapping them on without gloves turned their hands numb in minutes.) If that had been the first time they had strapped them on, they would have been in deep doo-doo.

There are two basic ways of attaching your crampons: with buckled straps or with the newer step-in/clamp-on variety. Each has its merits, but if you do buy the strap-on kind, the neoprene-coated nylon ones are the best. They're strong, won't absorb water, and don't stretch. The same can't be said of leather or straps made of nylon or fabric webbing.

Finally, remember this: Wearing crampons around camp is like handing a two-year old a martini—a disaster waiting to happen. Inevitably, you will step on your tent, the rope, or a five-pound bag of oatmeal—anything and everything that you don't want to puncture. Unless you're camped on a dangerous incline, take them off as soon as possible and make them the last piece of gear you put on before heading out.

**Finger Tips**

The best strap-on crampons are made with neoprene-coated nylon. They're strong, water-proof, and don't stretch.

**Hold On**

Although leather crampon straps are less expensive than synthetic straps, they stretch when wet and can easily rot and break. Fabric webbing, not recommended either, readily accumulates snow and often freezes to the buckle.

# Glacier Trekking

If you're wielding an ice axe and wearing crampons, odds are you're trekking on a glacier. I've never seen or been on a glacier that didn't take my breath away. These imperceptibly slow-moving beasts are profound places of peace and stillness—until enormous chunks come cascading down the mountain like the world's most violent ice machine.

## *Beauty and the Beast*

Perhaps it's the contrast between the beauty and harshness that makes glacier travel so intense. When Joe climbed Mt. Rainier, he was continually amazed by the multiple personalities displayed by the heavily crevassed mountain.

*Ice climbing in a crevasse on Mt. Rainier. (Photo courtesy of Nels Akerlund.)*

For the first two days of his climb, the upper-third of the mountain was covered by a mushroom-shaped cap known as a "lenticular cloud," which looks like a UFO and is formed when the warm, moist air from the Pacific Ocean collides with the cold air over the mountain. On the morning of the third day, it was gone, providing climbers with the most dramatic unveiling they could ever have hoped for.

The beauty seemed more delicate when he realized that the mountain could squash him like a bug. At Camp Hazard (11,600 feet), a wall of ice as big as a 10-story building peeled off the cliffs directly above where Joe was camped and hurtled south with a sickening roar. Reasonably sure that he'd be buried alive, he assumed a karate stance and froze like a proverbial deer in the headlights as ice particles showered him. Standing nearby was Kurt Wedberg, who has ascended the mountain more than 85 times and seen similar wrecks countless times. "Cool!" he said, as if watching fireworks from a distance. "That was a big one."

### Finger Tips

Survival, not speed, defines success in alpine climbing. Ascending depends on solid ice or snow conditions and good weather. Patience and tenacity are essential.

### Cliff Notes

Utah boasts some of the top ice climbing in the United States. Routes in the Wasatch Range offer various types of ice falls. Conditions are usually solid from late November through early March. Provo Canyon is a "hot" cold spot, offering classic routes, such as the 1,000-foot Stairway to Heaven, the Finger of Fate, and the Fang.

## Rope-a-Dope

Roping up on a glacier is like using your seat belt each time you drive; most of the time you don't need to, but when you do, it will save your life. Writing about Mt. McKinley in Alaska, the highest mountain in North America, John Krakauer said, "…even the flattest, most benign-looking terrain can be riddled with hidden crevasses, many of which are big enough to swallow a Greyhound bus, no problem."

But, as he goes on to point out, a crevasse doesn't have to be huge to be fatal. In 1984, Naomi Uemura—Japan's legendary mountaineer and polar explorer—vanished after returning from the summit of Mt. McKinley, making it the first solo winter ascent on this incredibly cold mountain. It is generally believed that he fell into one of the relatively small crevasses on the lower regions of the mountain. The point remains: If crevasses litter a mountain, rope up whether you're a world-class climber or a regular Joe.

### Hold On

Regardless of your familiarity with the glacier, always rope up!

Typically, rope teams of three or four are best. This allows climbers to be sufficiently far apart to give the rest of the team enough slack in case they need to arrest a fall.

Tying into the rope is simple. The front and rear climbers usually tie a figure-8 knot into their harness while the middle climber(s) clips into an overhand or figure-8 on a bight. (See Chapter 8 for a refresher course on knots.) The tricky part, however, is knowing how to negotiate a glacier. Avoiding large, gaping crevasses is easy; it's the hidden ones that usually claim novices. Until you know how to read a mountain, stick to an established trail and go with a guide or experienced mountaineer.

## The Rest Step

Novice climbers who lack the patience or experience to understand how draining it can be to hike for long periods of time in the thin air often start too fast and pay a steep price later. Here's where the *rest step* comes in.

What's the rest step?

### Nuts and Bolts

The **rest step** is a slow but efficient style of walking uphill that helps you maintain a steady pace.

It's a methodical yet highly efficient style of walking that helps you maintain a steady pace. Basically, after each forward step, you pause momentarily on your rear leg, which you lock at the knee so that skeleton, not muscle, bears the load. When you synchronize your breathing with each step, you'll find that you can click into a rhythm that helps you move steadily upward and onward.

In fact, virtually all the guides who work for Rainier Mountaineering Inc. (RMI), the largest guide service on Mt. Rainier, are so accustomed to using the rest step that they use it walking up the stairs at sea level.

# Head in the Clouds, Feet on the Ground

Clearly, high places have fascinated mankind throughout history. Every once in a while, however, a spectacular event occurs that refocuses the public's interest in mountain climbing.

### Hold On

Crevasses, avalanches, and other unpredictable weather conditions make alpine mountaineering a lot riskier than sport climbing at your local crag. It's essential to learn mountaineering skills from knowledgeable experts and to ascend with qualified guides.

In 1953 Sir Edmund Hillary and Tenzing Norgay captured the world's attention with their historic climb of Mt. Everest. More recently, books and films have achieved the same effect. One such example is *Seven Summits*, a book about two multi-millionaires who raced to become the first men to climb the highest peaks on each of the seven continents. Other examples include

John Krakauer's tale of disaster *Into Thin Air*, and the IMAX film *Everest*. These have inspired scores of neophytes to attempt these lofty peaks before they had the chops to do so.

## Cliff Notes

Catherine Destivelle, born in Algeria in 1960, is regarded as one of the world's top alpine climbers. Her accomplishments include climbing the Nameless Tower in the Karakorum and the Bonatti route on the North Face of the Matterhorn, plus solo ascents of the North Face of the Eiger (in winter, in just 15 hours) and the Bonatti Pillar on the Dru.

Admiring these places is noble, and dreaming about climbing them is inspirational. But venturing up their grand slopes before you've paid your dues in the hills is fool-hardy and, worse, dangerous to you and the pros who will try to rescue you.

## The Least You Need to Know

➤ The bigger the mountain, the more snow and ice you'll get—and the more you'll need to know.

➤ The ice axe is one of the most versatile and important tools an alpine climber can own.

➤ Crampons are to the feet what the ice axe is to the hands.

➤ Trekking on a glacier requires experience, fitness, and patience.

➤ Before you start climbing "trophy" peaks, make sure you learn the ropes.

# Chapter 23

# Basic Training Boot Camp

## In This Chapter

➤ Train to reduce strain

➤ Stretch or bust

➤ Nice abs

➤ Climbing drills

➤ Attitude is everything

I'm not sure if I love to compete because I love to train, or if I train because I love to compete. Probably a bit of both. When I raced bicycles full-time, it seemed I spent more time in the saddle than out. After three seasons of fighting injuries and fatigue, the training became more of a chore than a joy, and I knew it was time to try something else. I enjoyed doing triathlons (swim/bike/run) but, once again, to compete at the national level, the sacrifices become quite steep.

Climbing unites the physical intensity and mental challenge that I love about sports, but with little of the performance angst. Whereas climbing outdoors in a beautiful setting is always gratifying, I've done races that felt like total disasters. For most of us, climbing isn't about winning and losing. (Like the "house" in a Las Vegas casino, the mountain never loses.) Rather, it's about interacting with the environment to meet a formidable task that is honest and without hype.

Whether I'm trekking up a 19,000-foot mountain or climbing a 150-foot route in the Shawangunks, I enjoy the visceral sensation of moving on the rock, I enjoy the problem solving, and I love seeing how I will react in a tight situation. And since I'm a fitness freak, I love knowing that how I perform has a lot to do with how I train.

Whether I'm striving to scratch my way up a route that has defeated me or trying to climb a familiar route with less strain, the essence of this pure challenge elicits my competitive spirit in a way that energizes and inspires me. After years of the ultra competitive world of professional bike racing, climbing has made me realize that competition is a wonderful and healthy thing, a very natural impulse. The way to find the balance we call "healthy competition" is not to deny that we are interested in performing well but to strive for our best performances without focusing exclusively on out-performing someone else.

# Better to Train Than to Suffer

In the early days of climbing, training wasn't much of an issue. In fact, some of Britain's top mountaineers—men who shouldered huge packs in the thin Himalayan air—smoked cigarettes and subsisted on a diet most experts would consider perfect for cardiac arrest. After the climb, cross-training consisted of hoisting beer mugs until their arms were tired.

These days, climbers are doing what was once thought impossible: climbing outrageous sport routes, solving previously unsolvable boulder problems, and racing up the highest peaks in the world without supplemental oxygen. Much of this has to do with the modern strength- and cardio-training regimes world-class climbers adhere to. Take incredibly fit climbers and have them train like Trojans in the gym, and they return to the hills fitter than ever.

But even if you're not going to scamper up some ridiculously difficult route, getting fitter will make you a better and safer climber. Not only will you be able to take on bigger challenges, training intelligently will give you the physical reserves that allow your mental faculties to function at their best.

Let's take a typical beginning lead climber. She hires a guide, learns how to place protection, and after practicing on a top-rope begins leading her own climbs. Her technical skills are adequate, but while leading a climb she gets extremely fatigued and puts in several pieces of suspect gear. When she pops off the rock, some of the pieces of gear fail and she takes a long and frightening whipper. Not good. However, after a month of bouldering and doing laps at the gym, she returns to the pitch with the guns to lead it comfortably, making sound gear placements all the way to the belay ledge. In this case, our hero did not need to improve her knowledge of protection skills to lead the climb safely—she just had to improve her fitness!

## *Everest, Ho!*

In the IMAX film *Everest*, Ed Viesturs, America's best high-altitude mountaineer, is shown riding his mountain bike in the backcountry of Utah like a man late to his last meal. Over this magnificent footage, his wife says something like, "For most people, a five-hour bike ride is a full day's work; for Ed, it's a warm-up."

Part of his prowess in the rarefied air is a genetic gift, but much of his success is how often and how hard he trains down on the ground. I've shouldered a pack above

19,000-feet, and so watching Viesturs function so efficiently on the upper reaches of Everest blew my mind. On summit day, the film shows the former Mt. Rainier guide heading alone into the frigid darkness at 11 P.M., breaking trail in thigh-deep snow. It sounds corny (or maybe I'm a sucker for outdoor action heroes) but this feat of strength and courage made me cry.

### Cliff Notes

In the world of endurance athletes, Helen Klein is the champion of resiliency. The 75-year old has completed over 50 marathons, 100 ultra-marathons, including the Marathon des Sable (seven days, 142 miles in the Sahara Desert), as well as the Ironman Triathlon in Hawaii and the Eco-Challenge race in Utah—a nine day, 370-mile adventure race. The kicker is that she didn't start running or competing until she was 53 years old.

While climbing Everest should be the province of experts, seeing how this film moved so many people says to me that humans need to dream and to strive. In my mind, everyone who is able should try to push themselves into an extraordinary situation so that they can be inspired by their own performance rather than someone else's. Whether the challenge is large or small, there is something worthwhile out there for all of us. It could be scrambling up an intimidating route at your local crag, climbing a mountain that you've long dreamed about, or just learning to overcome your fear of heights.

An excellent way to realize these desires is to get out on the rock and in the gym (or hopefully both) and train. Being fit will make you feel better, climb more fluidly, and get hurt less often. (Again, fitness often equals safety.) Heck, if you get fit, you might become inspired to trek to Everest base camp and check out the high-altitude junkies through the binoculars.

### Hold On

Being out of shape not only limits your ability on the rock, it ups the odds of getting injured. Climbers use endurance and weight training to strengthen the heart and other muscles in the body.

## It Pays to Be in Shape

A while back, Joe Glickman was hiking on Mt. Marcey, the highest point in New York. On the way down, he came upon a stumbling, cursing, almost hysterical woman who was repeatedly hurling her huge backpack down the trail. Just before Joe approached her, she threw the pack into a stream and began jumping up and down on it like the chimpanzee in the Samsonite suitcase commercial. When Joe asked if he could help, she ran ahead without her gear. Joe shouldered her pack and followed.

At the trailhead, he learned that she and her fiancé, a dentist who had run off ahead of her, were on a weekend hike. She was a novice backpacker, slim but out of shape. After reaching the summit, she and her fiancé had a dispute. She was so exhausted that she had a conniption.

While the story is rather ridiculous, it illustrates my point: To truly delight in climbing, hiking, or just about any other pursuit in the great outdoors, it pays to be in shape. Clearly, it's not necessary to be fanatical about training to enjoy a hike or mellow climb, but I've always found that I enjoyed being in the mountains more when I struggled less.

### Finger Tips

Climbing stairs with a loaded pack is a great way to train for slogging up a mountain.

The second (and perhaps less obvious) moral of the story is this: Never go camping with a dentist—and certainly don't marry one until you've successfully summited a mountain together.

*Greater fitness = more fun. (Photo courtesy of Mark Eller.)*

## Total Training

I'm continually amazed by how specific muscles adapt to a particular task. I regularly cycle, run, swim, kayak, climb, and lift weights, but when I took a two-week Navy Seal training course in Central Park, I was so stiff the first week that I felt like a creaky old door—until my muscles warmed to the task. Even today the mere mention of the word that starts with "push" and ends with "up" gives me flashbacks. The saying "use it or lose it" really does apply.

Rock climbing is a pulling/pushing activity. While the upper body pulls, the lower body pushes. Not only are the large muscles in your back and arms called upon, but the forearm, wrist, and finger joints are taxed as well. The same is true of the lower body. The hips and hamstrings do most of the work, but the calves and ankles need to be strengthened as well. What I've seen time and time again is that if one part of your body is substantially weaker than the other, odds are that you'll get injured or at least suffer nagging pain.

For this reason, climbers need to follow a training program that builds overall body strength, as well as one that serves their specific aims. Think of your training as a wheel with at least three spokes: strength, flexibility, and endurance. Each spoke is important, and any two without the third will make your ride bumpy.

### Finger Tips

It's common for beginning climbers to grasp rocks with a white-knuckled death grip. Relax and don't forget to breathe. Throughout the day, drop your shoulders, loosen your grip, and take a few deep breaths.

## Breathing

Breathing is one of the most neglected (and important) facets of training. Whether you're on an overhanging ledge or strength training in the gym, practice breathing from your belly. Dubious? Try it right now: Breath as rapidly as you can but don't take deep breaths. What happens? You start panting and tire quickly. Now breathe deeply from your abdomen. Inhale through your nose and forcefully exhale through your mouth, expanding your belly as you release your breath. The difference is significant. You'll have more energy, be more focused, and stay more relaxed when the going gets tough.

Work on your breathing while lifting in the gym or walking up a flight of stairs. Work on it when you're sitting in traffic. Try it now. Don't scoff; your climbing (and life) will improve.

## Center Yourself

In my dictionary, *balance* is defined as "a stability produced by even distribution of weight on each side of the vertical axis; a physical equilibrium; mental and emotional steadiness."

Balance is fairly easy to define but rather difficult to train. It's crucial in order to be more graceful in a sport known as "the vertical dance." (It's no coincidence that gymnasts and dancers make good climbers.)

The more you climb, the better your balance will become, as you learn to adapt to this foreign environment. Being mindful of what works and what doesn't will speed the process. Pay attention to your technique (weight over your feet, hips leaning away from the rock, and so on), breathe from your belly, and concentrate on staying centered. The more intensely you interact with the rock, the easier it is to execute effective, fluid movements.

Here's a good way to prove my point: Try traversing an easy section of rock just a few feet off the ground. Concentrate on your breathing and feel the rock under your hands and feet. After each "lap," relax the tension in your hands. Once you are very comfortable on a section of rock, try it again, using one hand this time. Then try it again without using your hands. The biggest difference is being relaxed and mindful. When you can do the same line without using your feet, you're really onto something.

### Hold On

Many new climbers learn the ropes at a local climbing area. This is good for your social life but tough on your concentration. Try to block out distracting noises and movements when you're working the rock. Focus on the task at hand. You'll have plenty of time to schmooze at the end of the day.

The mental side of balance has always intrigued me. If you take to the rock feeling hostile toward your boyfriend or the motorist who cut you off a mile up the road, odds are you'll climb with inferior balance. Before you take to the rock, spend a few moments calming your mind. Deep breathing works for me. Don't dismiss this as New Age mumbo jumbo. The Tibetan translation of the word *meditation* means "training the mind." Not enough climbers or athletes realize that a steady mind and an emotional stability are powerful fitness tools. As fitness guru and rock and ice climber Steve Ilg says, "We should not 'Just Do It,' we should 'Just Be It.'"

# Try Softer

Most motivated athletes don't have to worry about trying too hard; that's the way they're programmed. What we do need to do is to try softer. Most of us spend 99 percent of our time on strength and cardiovascular training but virtually no time on flexibility or mental training. While strength and endurance are crucial, if you're not flexible, each will be compromised. Worse, if you're like me, you'll break down.

Paradoxically, flexibility is not a skill that allows you to gain something per se; instead, as Steve Ilg says, "it enables you to *release* something that is already within you." I can't stress this point enough. After years of suffering from injuries, I realized that stretching was no longer an option but a necessity if I was to continue training with any intensity. During an injury timeout, I promised myself that I would stretch for at least 15 minutes after every workout. That was seven years ago. I've missed only a handful of workouts since.

Initially, stretching is tough going. It can be painful and frustrating. Once you limber up, however, your body will thank you. The exciting thing about improving your flexibility is that it not only helps keep you off the DL (disabled list), it makes climbing easier. Handholds that once seemed just out of reach are now there for the taking. Flexible hamstrings enable you to stretch for ledges that you might normally only stare at, wishing you were six inches taller.

The best route to take if you haven't stretched before is to take a yoga class. If you don't have the time to pick up a book or video on the subject and learn a few of the poses. Short of that, there are countless books and videos on stretching. And any decent personal trainer at your gym can show you the basics. Here are a few guidelines to get you started:

➤ Begin with a brief (5–10 minute) warm-up.

➤ Ease into the stretches. Don't bounce.

➤ Stretch until you feel "mild" discomfort. Over-stretching does more harm than good. Remember, this isn't a test to see how far you can bend. Try softer, not harder.

➤ Always breathe from your belly. Breathe into the muscle(s) that you are stretching and relax any auxiliary muscles that you may have contracted involuntarily.

➤ Hold a stretch for 10 to 30 seconds. Instead of keeping track of time, I concentrate on my breathing. Typically I hold a stretch for 10 deep belly breaths.

### Hold On

Each time you train doesn't need to be an all-out, go-for-the-gold effort. Instead, vary your workouts. Label some days "technique and finesse days" and others "moderate-to-intense efforts." Your workouts will not only be more interesting, but your body will respond better. Working a muscle breaks it down. The muscle grows when it has a chance to rest.

### Finger Tips

Stretch your fingers, wrists, and forearms before each climbing session. Do wrist-rolls and try squeezing an old tennis ball to warm your finger muscles.

## Head to Toe

Here are some basic stretches to lead you down the path of least resistance:

➤ **Neck:** With you back straight and feet shoulder width apart, lean your head forward until your chin touches your chest. Gently roll your head from your left shoulder to the starting position and then to your right shoulder. Repeat several times. This is a great tension tamer.

➤ **Shoulders:** Rotate your outstretched arms to get the blood flowing to your shoulders. Next, raise one arm above your head and let your hand drop behind your head. Grab your elbow with the other hand and gently pull it toward your ear. Switch arms and repeat.

### Hold On

Move your head subtly during neck rolls; don't jerk it all the way back. The muscles in your neck are sensitive and can strain easily.

### Finger Tips

Use a towel or webbing for assistance if you're not flexible enough to grab your feet during hamstring stretches. Wrap the towel or webbing around the ball of your foot, hold on to both ends, and slowly pull your foot toward your head, holding for 20 seconds. This helps stretch your calves as well.

➤ **Back:** With your fingers interlocked, reach to the sky as high as you can and extend the stretch until you feel a gentle pull in your lower back. This is where learning a few yoga stretches will reap huge rewards.

➤ **Hips:** While standing, place your hands on your hips and make full circles in one direction, and then in the opposite direction. I enjoy using a hoola-hoop, though I do draw a few stares— usually of envy.

➤ **Hamstrings:** Tight "hammys" are the leading cause of back problems. There are countless stretches to limber this chronically tight area. Lie on your back, clutch your left knee with your fingers interlocked, and gently pull your knee to your chest. Then do the right leg. Another of my favorites is to sit with one leg outstretched and the other foot flat against my inner thigh. Bending at the waist, I lean forward until I feel a gentle pull in my hamstring. When I first began, I could barely touch my toes; now I can put my forehead on my knee. In that gap is the difference between chronic tension and a far greater ease of movement.

➤ **Groin:** Sit on the ground and bring your feet to your groin so that your knees look like the wings of a butterfly. Put your forearms on your knees and gradually push down.

➤ **Calves:** Stand on the edge of a curb or step on the balls of your feet and let your heels ease to the ground.

➤ **Forearms:** Place your hands on the ground and gradually lean forward to stretch your inner forearm. Rotate your hands at the wrist to get the blood flowing.

➤ **Hands:** Carry climbing putty—blue goo—to squeeze while driving to a climb. It will calm your nerves and get your hands limber. Also, make like a pianist and wriggle and scrunch your fingers around until the kinks are gone.

# Pump It Up

Good climbers don't necessarily need to be able to do push-ups and pull-ups like a Navy Seal, but it certainly helps. Vadim Vinokur, one of the best sport climbers in America, does hours of pull-up exercises every day. (I've heard that he can do 10 consecutive one-armed pull-ups. Just for the record: doing one is next to impossible.)

*Pull-ups are a great way to get in shape for climbing. (Photo courtesy of Mark Eller.)*

Although proper technique will always win out over brute strength, the climber who has both is armed and extremely dangerous. World-class climber Alex Lowe has tremendous technique but he's also a pull-up fanatic who reportedly does 300 a day. (Think about that!) Most of us would be lucky to do that many in a week. The point remains, however: Strength training can make an average climber good and a good climber excellent. (If for some odd reason your climbing doesn't improve, at least you'll look great at the beach.)

## *Lats, Pecs, and Delts*

There are countless strength-training regimes you can follow to build upper-body strength, most of which are also sound for building overall strength and endurance. I try to train my upper body two to three times a week and my lower body once or twice. I've found that two to three sets per exercise works best for me.

### Nuts and Bolts

**Momentary failure** is the point at which you no longer can lift the weight without "cheating" or losing technique.

The key to maximizing your time in the gym is to limit your rest between sets—anywhere from 30 to 60 seconds. (More than that and you lose the training benefit.) Experiment to find a weight that allows you to reach *momentary failure* somewhere between the 8th and 12th repetitions. Remember, isolating the specific muscle is the key, not pushing as much weight as possible.

It's wise to do strength training in phrases. The type of high-volume lifting recommend here, using very little rest, is effective for building muscular endurance. This is a great strategy if a climber needs to improve fitness, but it is not as efficient for the climber who wants to increase power. Let's say that you're a climber who can pull several small overhanging moves without fatiguing, but you come up short when there is a single powerful roof move to pull through. Your muscular endurance is fine, but you need to improve power. The right training strategy in this case is to do short, intense boulder problems or weight training movements, keeping the reps low and the rest periods long. This will make for the best gains in explosive strength, or power.

Let me give you a basic idea of what I do on upper-body days. If the following exercises mystify you, hire a personal trainer or read a book on strength training.

➤ **Back:** Lat pull-downs, bent-over rows, pull-ups.

➤ **Chest:** Inclined dumbbell presses, dips, flat bench presses.

➤ **Shoulders:** Seated military presses, lateral raises, and upright rows.

➤ **Arms:** Bicep curls and tricep extensions.

➤ **Forearms:** Forward and reverse wrist curls. Squeezing putty while on the telephone is also a good way to strengthen your hands and forearms. Steve Carlton, a Hall of Fame baseball pitcher known for his fanatical (and innovative) training methods, used to immerse his hand in a pot of uncooked rice and wriggle his fingers around. (Try brown rice; it's healthier.)

## Gluts, Quads, and Hams

As I've said numerous times in this book, good climbers climb with their legs as much as possible and use their upper body for balance. This is why climbers who can't do more than two consecutive pull-ups can climb exceedingly hard routes. If you're interested in moutaineering, strong legs are a must. Rock jocks don't need to train their lower body as often or intensely as they do their upper torso, but having strong, flexible legs will only help your climbing.

Here are a few exercises to build legs that will get you to the top:

➤ **Squats:** These are perhaps the best lower-body exercise you can do. They work your butt, quads, hips, and spinal muscles. Since they require excellent form and concentration, they work your mind as well. If you've never squatted with free weights, learn how from someone who has, or stick to a squat machine that restricts your movement.

➤ **Squat jumps:** You can do squat jumps instead of squatting with a barbell, or, if you're really looking for a burn, right after. (A note of caution: Warm up before doing either of these exercises.) Here's what you do: With your hands behind your head, squat down with your thighs parallel to the ground and jump as high as you can, thrusting your hips forward. Land, squat, and jump explosively again. Two to three sets of 8–10 reps will leave your quads burning and lungs longing for air.

➤ **Legs curls:** This excellent exercise works your hamstrings, the long muscles in the back of your legs. The basic technique is simple once you've found a leg curl machine. Simply lie on your stomach and pull the weight toward your butt with your heels. Again, stretch well before doing this.

➤ **Calf raises:** Seated or standing calf raises on a specifically designed calf machine will do the trick. If you don't have access to this equipment, stand on a firm step on the balls of your toes and raise up as far as you can go. Do three to five sets of 15 for a good burn.

## Abs

The stomach is one of the few body parts that you can train every time you hit the gym. It's also one of the most neglected. A strong upper and lower body is great, but if your mid-section isn't strong, you won't be able to utilize your strength as efficiently.

There are countless exercises for your abdominal muscles (or "abs"). Sit-ups and crunches give upper abs the washboard look. Leg raises and inverse crunches are great for the lower area. As one of my climbing friends likes to say, "Strong stomach, strong mind."

**Finger Tips**

Use the ab-crunch and lateral-twist machines at the gym to build your stomach muscles. Unlike sit-ups and crunches, these machines allow you to add weight and, thus, build muscle faster.

## Climb, Baby, Climb

As I said earlier, the best way to improve your climbing strength is to climb. There are several drills you can do indoors or while bouldering, however, that will help you when you hit the real rock. Here's a profile of three different facets of your climbing that you can target:

➤ **Power:** Perform a sequence of four to six difficult moves, rest for three to five minutes, and repeat until you can't do it anymore. This is a tremendous exercise that requires concentration and supreme effort. The best way to do this drill is unroped on a small boulder or bouldering wall at a gym.

### Finger Tips

How long does it take you to stop gasping for air after running up a flight of stairs? Recovery after exertion is a true test of fitness. Interval training is the key to quick recovery. Whether you're biking, swimming, or running, go hard for one minute, then bring the pace down for two minutes to catch your breath. Repeat this sequence three to five times. As you get fitter, adjust the amount of effort, time, and recovery. And always make sure you warm up first.

➤ **Endurance:** Pick a route that you've got dialed in and do "laps" on it without stopping. Climb continuously for five minutes, building up to 15 or 20. You'll be sucking goose eggs quickly. Remember: form, form, form.

➤ **Technique:** Pick a sequence of moves (easy to hard) and ease through them in slow motion. Think "flow" and concentrate on your center. Another interesting drill is to climb on a familiar (indoor) route with your eyes closed, or to climb a route several times using as many different holds on each subsequent trip.

## Have a Heart

Cardiovascular (CV) fitness is a huge part of climbing. You might have great technique and sound strength, but if you flag halfway up the second pitch, all the technique in China won't do much good. Running, cycling (especially mountain biking), swimming, kayaking, and cross-country skiing are excellent ways to get your ticker running like the Energizer Bunny.

To prepare for my to climb on Cotopaxi (at 19,637 feet the tallest active volcano in the world), I cross-trained like mad: biking, running, swimming, kayaking, and rock climbing. It would have been great to live near some big mountains to get used to carrying a heavy backpack at altitude. I live in New York City, however, and the only altitude to be had is when I head up a skyscraper in an elevator.

### Hold On

Slowly build strength for carrying a heavy pack. Do not load your pack with 50 pounds of weight on your first outing. Start with a moderate weight and gradually increase the weight with each successive day of training.

What did I do? I loaded my pack with old textbooks and hiked the Rambles in Central Park, looking like a scholarly tourist. While I was a hurting cowgirl on Cotopaxi, I made it and managed to smile most of the way—especially as I headed down.

# Mind over Rock

Many of the world's best climbers say that the greatest challenges they face are between their ears. This is one of the things I love about climbing and mountaineering; while we deal with the weighty force of gravity and the capricious whims of Mother Nature, we are forced to confront ourselves in the process. The ability to roll with harsh weather, fatigue, and, most importantly, doubt and fear is what often separates a peaceful from a panicked climber. Noticing when you're negative is a good way to explore what makes you tick.

Dealing with internal and external obstacles is a big part of why we climb and why we endure the cold and dark and rain and snow. When we venture to high places, we're forced to play by a new set of rules. If we don't concentrate, we're likely to die. This focused effort has a healing effect on people who are often bombarded by the complexities of modern life.

Odds are that when you're scanning a rock face for that next best hold and your legs begin to quiver and your biceps buzz, you won't be thinking about your dry cleaning or paying that parking ticket that's been ticking you off. Climbing, more than any other sport, demands that you live in the moment. Climb once, and you might get hooked; climb a lot, and you'll never turn back.

**Finger Tips**

If you get tired and start to stray mentally while climbing, it's time to call it a day. Take a deep breath, review the skills critical to your safe descent, and go slow until you reach the ground.

## The Least You Need to Know

➤ Whether you're a fair-weather climber or a Mt. Everest-summiteer, improving your strength and fitness will make you a better and healthier athlete.

➤ Strength and endurance are severely compromised if you can't touch your toes.

➤ Climbing drills can target specific areas of fitness.

➤ Cross training will improve your cardiovascular fitness. And it's fun.

➤ A strong body without a strong mind is like a fine wine without the bottle—all over the place.

# Glossary

**adze**   The head of an ice axe opposite the pick. Typically made of steel, this wider sharp side of the axe is an all-purpose cutting and digging tool for snow and ice climbing.

**anchor**   The point of attachment at which the rope is fixed to the rock. Trees, rock spike, and flakes are examples of natural anchors. Nuts and bolts are examples of artificial anchors.

**antagonistic muscle**   A muscle that contracts with and limits the action of an agonist with which it is paired.

**arete**   A sharp, jutting corner of rock.

**belay**   The process of managing the rope for a climber. It is the system used to stop a climber in case of a fall by using a rope and a friction device. The climber is "on belay" when the belayer is ready to brake in the event of a fall.

**bend**   A knot that ties together two ends of rope, cord, or webbing.

**bolts**   Rods of metal secured into pre-drilled holes in the rock. Bolts are used for belays or running protection.

**bowline**   A knot—usually used to secure a loop—that will not slip or come undone by itself.

**brake hand**   The hand that the belayer uses to stop the movement of the rope while the climber is on belay, thus stopping the climber from falling.

**bridging**   A technique climbers use to push out to the side with their hands and/or feet to straddle a corner or chimney. Applying pressure to opposing walls keeps the climber from falling. It is also called *stemming*.

**buckets**   Large holds with positive lips.

**buttress**   A major rock outcropping, larger than an arete.

**calling back a rope**   When a climber doubles the rope through an anchor and uses both strands to rappel to the ground. After the climber reaches safety, he pulls one strand through the anchor to retrieve ("call back") the rope.

**calorie**   The unit equal to the amount of food necessary to raise the body temperature by one degree celsius.

**camming**   When a climber's elbow is in line with the crack while jamming.

**ceiling**   An overhanging horizontal section of rock or wall. Also called a *roof.*

**chimney**   A crack in the rock wide enough for a climber to push her entire body through.

**chimneying**   When a climber ascends a wide crack, or "chimney," by wedging his body through it and shimmying upward, pressing against the sides with the feet and back.

**chock pick**   Also known as a *nut tool*, this is a metal device with a pointy tip used to pry protection from the rock.

**cinch**   To pull tight.

**cleaning a route**   When the second climber removes and racks the gear as she follows the leader up a route.

**clove hitch**   A knot commonly used for tying the middle of the rope into an anchor point.

**cord**   Climber lingo for a rope. It usually refers to a rope thinner than nine millimeters in diameter.

**crack**   A natural fissure or space along the rock that climbers fill with body parts to aid in ascending.

**crag**   A small outcrop of rock, usually with routes of one or two pitches.

**crampons**   A set of metal spikes that clip on to mountaineering boots and are used for ice climbing or glacier trekking.

**crimpers**   Small yet positive edges of rock just big enough for the fingertips to grip.

**crimping**   Grasping small holds with fingers together and bent at the first knuckle.

**dihedral**   An inside corner of rock.

**dehydration**   Results when the body loses more water that it takes in. The symptoms of dehydration include nausea, headache, and eventual collapse. To avoid dehydration, drink enough water so that your urine remains clear or only slightly yellowish.

**double bowline**   A spin-off of one of the original sailing knots, the single bowline. A double bowline is commonly used to join rope to a harness and to tie the rope around a natural anchor. It is favored because of it's ability to hold heavy loads and untie easily.

**downclimbing**   A way to retreat from a difficult route, or to lower yourself off the rock.

**edges**   Small variously sized ledges of rock.

**edging**   A foot position on the rock in which a climber uses the side of his shoe's sole to adhere to a thin ledge.

**electrolyte**   A chemical compound (typically found in energy drinks) that helps the body conduct energy into muscles under load during activity.

**finger crack**   A thin crack in the rock that only fingers can fit into it.

**fist crack**   A crack the size of a fist.

**fist jam**   A space in the rock that climbers shove their fist into in order to create an anchor point.

**flakes**   Slabs of rock detached from the main face of a rock. They vary in size from the size of a finger nail to as big as 150 hunks of rock.

**friction climbing**   Typically done on low-angled rock, in friction climbing, the climber tries to get the optimal amount of shoe rubber on to the rock for adhesion.

**giardia**   A painful stomach virus caused by *Giardia lamblia*, protozoa which are found in the intestines of humans and animals—in other words, contaminated water. Giardia is curable with antibiotics.

**glycogen**   A polysaccharide, primarily converted from carbohydrates, that is stored in the body's tissues and fuels muscles.

**GORP**   Good Old Raisins and Peanuts—a sweet and salty treat for climbers.

**hand jam**   A space in the rock that climbers wedge their fingers and hands into for support and balance.

**hangboard**   A training apparatus with finger grooves that gets mounted overhead like a pull-up bar. It is used to improve upper-body strength.

**guide hand**   The hand that directs the rope while belaying a climber or helps retrieve excess rope during the climb and rappel.

**half-hitch**   A backup loop used to secure the end of a bomber (or secure) knot. Half-hitches are not a good backup for other knots.

**harness**   The device used to secure a climber to a rope and distribute the force of a fall. Harnesses are made of wide nylon webbing and fastened around the waist with a metal buckle.

**heel hook**   A maneuver used on steep, layered rock in which climbers "hook" their heels over a sharp hold above their head and imitate a chimpanzee, by using their feet as a third hand.

**hitches**   Distinguished by rock climbing purists as loops of single strands of rope wrapped around something.

**hypothermia**   A condition in which the body loses heat from its core. Hypothermia can be fatal if not treated early.

**jamming**   A crack-climbing technique in which the climber wedges her fingers, hands, or feet into a crack for support and balance.

287

**leading**   When a leader starts at the base of the route with no preset safety top-rope. He protects himself by placing or clipping anchors as he ascends.

**liebacking**   A technique for ascending aretes and cracks with off-set walls in which the climber uses her feet to push against one surface of the rock while pulling with her hands in the opposite direction. The climber then walks her feet up the rock, almost along-side her hands.

**mantle move**   An advanced down-pressure technique that allows feet to get onto the same hold as hands.

**nut tool**   A metal instrument used to pry the chocks from the rock and typically carried by the second climber on a lead climb.

**overhang**   Any piece of wall that juts outward.

**pick**   The head of an ice axe opposite the adze. Typically, the pick is curved, providing secure hooking action in snow or ice.

**pitons**   Steel wedges or blades hammered into cracks to protect or anchor climbers. Once the only form of protection available, pitons have been replaced by easily removable protection—such as nuts—because repeated placement and removal of pitons damage the rock. Today, pitons are used only when no other form of protection is available.

**positive lips**   Holds that protrude from the rock.

**pro**   An abbreviation for "protection." It is also used as a generic term for gear used to set up anchors.

**protection**   Bolts or pitons placed into the rock—usually by the first person to do a climb—to prevent the climber from falling too far and to anchor the climber or the rope to belay points.

**quick-draws**   Short slings that join two carabiners to set up protection.

**rack**   The set of protection carried on a climb.

**rappel device**   A metal gadget used to slow a climber's decent down the rope. It functions by applying friction to the rope.

**rappelling**   The act of sliding down a stationary rope and applying friction to the rope to control the speed of the descent.

**rating system**   A commonly agreed upon labeling of the difficulty of climbing routes.

**rise**   The distance between the waistband and the leg loops on a harness.

**Roof**   An overhanging horizontal section of rock or wall. Also called a *ceiling*.

**route**   A path up the rock. A route can follow a pre-mapped direction or cover new and unknown territory.

**shaft**   The handle of the ice axe, typically made of metal (such as aluminum or titanium) or a composite (such as fiberglass, Kevlar, or carbon filament.)

**slabs**   Large, smooth, inclined rock surfaces.

**slings**   Loops of nylon webbing. Capable of holding up to 4,000 pounds, slings typically come in 1-inch width and are available at most climbing shops.

**slingshot belay**   A rope tied to a climber that runs up to a secure anchor, through two carabiners (which serve as pulleys), and back down to the belayer. As the climber moves up, the belayer keeps the rope snug at all times to lock it off in the event the climber falls.

**smearing**   A foot position on the rock in which the climber uses the maximum surface of his shoe's sole to adhere to the rock's surface. It is mostly on low-angled rocks that don't have defined edges and knobs.

**spike**   The metal tip at the bottom of the shaft of an ice axe.

**sport climbing**   The climbing of routes that are protected with fixed protection, usually bolts.

**spotter**   A climber's bouldering partner who is on the ground following her along the route. The spotter is ready to assist the climber or control her landing in the event of a fall.

**stemming**   A technique climbers use to push out to the side with their hands and/or feet to straddle a corner or chimney. Applying pressure to opposing walls keeps the climber from falling. It is also called *bridging*.

**t-nuts**   The threaded inserts to which bolts are attached for securing artificial holds.

**thumb stack**   The method of holding on to the rock in which a climber wraps his thumb over the top two knuckles of his index and middle fingers.

**top-roping**   When the rope is above the climber as she ascends. She can be belayed from the top or if the rope passes through a top anchor, from the bottom.

**trad**   Climber lingo for *traditional climbing*.

**traditional climbing**   A type of climbing that requires climbers to place their own gear and protection, and attempt a route without first inspecting it.

**Yosemite Decimal System (YDS)**   The method of categorizing terrain according to the technique and equipment required to cross it.

# Books, Magazines, Videos, Maps, and CD-ROMs

## Books

Bensman, Bobby. 1999. *Bouldering with Bobbi Bensman*. Mechanicsburg, PA: Stackpoles Books.

Graydon, Don. 1992. *Mountaineering: The Freedom of the Hills*. Fifth Edition. Seattle, WA: The Mountaineers.

Greene, Ivan and Marc Russo. 1997. *Bouldering in the Shawungunks*. Jeffe Publications.

Hattingh, Garth. 1998. *The Climber's Handbook*. Stackpole Books.

Ilg, Steve. 1999. *The Winter Athlete*. Boulder, CO: Johnson Books.

Kraukeur, Jon. 1997. *Into The Wild*. New York City: Doubleday & Company.

Kraukeur, Jon. 1997. *Into Thin Air*. New York City: Doubleday & Company.

Luebben, Craig. 1993. *Knots for Climbers*. Evergreen, CO: Chockstone Press.

Long, John. 1998. *How To Rock Climb!* Evergreen, CO: Chockstone Press.

Long, John. 1992. *Climbing Anchors*. Evergreen, CO: Chockstone Press.

Mellor, Don. 1997. *Rock Climbing: A Trailside Guide*. New York City: W.W. Norton & Company.

Owens, Peter. 1993. *The Book of Outdoor Knots*. Lyons and Burford.

Padgett, Allen and Bruce Smith. 1987. *On Rope*. Huntsville, AL: National Speleological Society.

## *Books on Nutritional Grub*

Miller, Dorcas S. 1993. *Good Food for Camp and Trail*. Pruett Press.

*Gorp, Glop, and Glue Stew*. (The Mountaineers. 1982) by Yvone Prater and Ruth Dyar Medaengall

*NOLS Cookery*, (Stackpole Books, 1997) edited by Claudia Pearson

*Trail Food* (Ragged Mountain Press, 1998) by Alan S. Kesselheim

## Books for Performance

Prichard, Nancy. 1995. *The "I Hate to Train" Performance Guide for Rock Climbers.* Chockstone Press.

Goddard, Dale and Udo Neuman. 1993. *Performance Rock Climbing.* Stackpole Books

*Performance Rock Climbing,* by Dale Goddard and Ingo Neuman.

# Magazines

*Blue Magazine*
611 Broadway, Suite 405
New York, NY 10012
212-777-0024
www.bluemagazine.com

*Climbing Magazine*
1101 Village Road, Ste. LL-1-B
Carbondale, CO 81623 USA
970-963-9449
www.climbing.com

*Outside Magazine*
Box 54729
Boulder, CO 800322
http://outside.starwave.com

*Rock & Ice Magazine*
603A Broadway
Boulder, CO 80303-5926
303-499-8410
www.rockandice.com

# Videos

*Basic Rock Climbing*
Vertical Adventures Productions
3200 Wilshire Blvd, Suite 1207
Los Angeles, CA 90010

*The Art of Leading*
Chockstone Productions
526 Franklin Street
Denver, CO 80218

*Moving Over Stone*
*Moving Over Stone II*
Range of Light Productions
PO Box 2906
Mammoth Lakes, CA 93546

*Performance Rock Climbing—The Video*
1478 East Logan
Salt Lake City, UT 84105

*See also:*

*Anyplace Wild* (www.bpbasecamp.com)

*Basecamp* (www.bpbasecamp.com)

*Cool Works* (www.coolworks.com/natprk.htm)

*Escaping to Nature* (www.outdoorphoto.com)

*Great Outdoors Recreation Pages* (www.gorp.com)

*Outward Bound* TV Show on The Discovery Channel (www.discovery.com) (www.outwardbound.com)

*Rock Climbing Skills Basic and Beyond*

*Trailplace* (www.trailplace.com)

*Trailside TV shows*

# Cyber Book and Video Stores

www.AdventurousTraveler.com

www.amazon.com

www.barnesandnoble.com

www.mountainzone.com

# Map Resources

**US Forest Service**
202-205-1760
www.fs.fed.us

**Canadian Map Office**
800-465-6277

**DeLorme Mapping Company**
207 865-4171
www.delorme.com

**Earthvisions**
800-627-7236
www.earthvisions.com

**Europe Map Service**
914-221-0208

# CD-ROM Companies

**The Cordillera Group**
www.corgroup.com

**Mountain Images**
800-788-8958
www.mtnimage.com/~mtnimage

# Indoor Climbing Walls

## Organizations

**Climbing Wall Industry Group (CWIG)**
PO Box 1319
Boulder, CO 80306
303-44-3353 or 888-854-ORCA (6277)
info@orca.org or www.orca.org

**Outdoor Recreation Coalition of America**
PO Box 1634 Walnut Street, #303
Boulder, CO 80302
303-444-3353

## Climbing Walls Around the United States

**Boulder Rock Club:** Boulder, CO. 303-447-2804.

**Cats Gym:** Boulder, CO. 303-939-9699.

**Charlotte Climbing Center:** Charlotte, NC. 704-333-7625.

**City Climbing Club:** New York, NY. 212-408-0277.

**City Rock Gym:** Berkeley, CA. 510-564-2510.

**Classic Climbing Gym:** Franklin, TN. 615-661-9444.

**Cleveland Rock Gym:** Euclid, OH. 216-692-3300.

**Cliffhanger:** Vancouver, BC. 604-874-2400.

**Climb North:** Wildwood, PA. 412-487-2145.

**Climb On:** Allentown, PA. 215-435-4334.

**Climb Time:** Indianapolis, IN. 317-596-3330

**Climbnasium:** Harrisburg, PA. 717-795-9580.

**Clipper City Rock Gym:** Baltimore, MD. 410-467-9727.

**Crux Rock Gym:** Eugene, OR. 503-484-9535.

**Dyno Rock:** Arlington, VA. 817-461-3966.

**The Edge:** Vancouver, BC. 604-984-9080.

**Extra Vertical Climbing Center:** New York, NY 212-586-5718

**Footprints:** Minneapolis, MN. 612-884-7996.

**Higher Ground:** Grand Rapids, MI. 616-774-3100.

**Inner Wall:** New Paltz, NY. 914-255-7625.

**Joe Rock Heads:** Toronto, CN. 416-538-7670.

**Mission Cliffs:** San Francisco, CA. 415-550-0515.

**Pacific Edge:** Santa Cruz, CA. 408-454-9254.

**Prime Climb:** Wallingford, CT. 203-365-7880.

**Rockreation:** Los Angeles, CA. 310-207-7199.

**Rocks and Ropes:** Tuscon, AZ. 602-882-5924.

**Sport Rock:** Rockville, MD. 301-762-5111.

**Sports Center (Chelsea Piers):** New York, NY. 212-336-6083.

**Upper Limits:** Bloomington, IN. 309-829-2284.

**Vertical Hold:** San Diego, CA. 619-586-7572.

**Wild Walls:** Spokane, WA. 509-455-9596.

# Guide Services, Climbing Camps, and Organizations

**AAI, Alpine Ascents Int'l.**
206-378-1927
www.mountainzone.com/aai
E-mail: aaiclimb@accessone.com

**AAI, American Alpine Institute, Ltd.**
AAI 1515 12th M-19
Bellingham, WA 98225
360-671-1505
www.mtnguiide.com

**Adventure 16**
Corporate Office
4620 Alvarado Canyon Rd.,
San Diego, CA 92120
619-283-2362 ext. 100
Fax: 619-283-7956
E-mail address: info@adventure16.com

**American Mountain Guides
Association (AMGA)**
710 10th Street, Suite 101
Golden, CO 80401
303-271-0984
www.climbnet.com/amga

**Appalachian Mountain Club**
5 Joy Street
Boston, MA 02108
603-466-2727
www.outdoors.org

**Aventuras Patagonicas**
88-203-9354
www.climbnet.com/patagonia

**Beginner Rock Climbing in Central
Park, New York City**
212-348-4867

**CMH Classic Mountaineering**
Box 1660, Banff, Alberta
Canada T0L 0C0
1-800-661-0252
403-762-7100
Fax: 403-762-5879
www.cmhhike.com

**Chauvin Guides International**
North Conway, NH
603-356-8919
www.chauvinguides.com

**Colorado Mountain School**
P.O. Box 2062
Estes Park, CO 80517
970-586-5758
Fax: 970-586-5798
E-mail: cms-climb@sni.net

**Eastern Mountain Sports (EMS)
Climbing School, NH**
PO Box 514
North Conway, NH 03860
800-310-4504
www.emsonline.com

**Exum Mountain Guides**
Box 56
Moose, WY 83012
307-733-2297
www.exumguides.com

**Hi-Tec Adventure Racing Series**
29395 Agoura Raod, Suite 102
Agoura Hills, CA 91301
818-707-8867
www.mesp.com

**Jackson Hole Mountain Guides**
Box 7477
Jackson, WY 83002
800-239-7642 or 307-733-4979
www.serioussports.com/jacksonhole/
index.html

**Joshua Tree Rock Climbing School**
HCR Box 3034, Joshua Tree
CA 92252
760-366-4745 or 800-890-4745
Fax: 760-366-9315
E-mail: climb@telis.org

**Joshua Tree Rock Climbing &
Hiking (October to May). Yosemite
& High Sierra Rock Climbing,
Hiking, and Backpacking.**
800-231-4575
www.symg.com

**Mountain Travel—SOBEK**
6420 Fairmount Avenue
El Cerrito, California 94530
1-888-MTSOBEK (687-6235) or
510-527-8100
E-mail: info@mtsobek.com

European Sales Office:
44-1494-448901
Fax: 44-1494-465526
E-mail: sales@mtsobekeu.com

Australian Sales Office:
61-2-9264-5710
Fax: 61-2-9267-3047
E-mail: adventure@africatravel.com.au

**Outward Bound School**
100 Mystery Point Road
Garrison, NY 10524-9757
888-88-BOUND
www.outwardbound.com

**Raid Gauloises
Pub Events S.A.**
470 S. Wetherly Drive
Beverly Hills, CA 90211
310-271-8335
Fax: 310-271-8365
www.raid-gauloises.com

**Road Less Traveled**
2840 Wilderness Place, #F
Boulder, CO 80301
800-488-8483 or 303-413-0938
Fax: 303-413-0926
E-mail: fun@roadslesstraveled.com

**Sport Climbing Camp & Big Wall Camp**
California
510-647-1020

**Thomson Safaris**
347 Broadway
Cambridge, MA 02139
800-235-0289 or 617-876-7314
Fax: 617-497-3911
E-mail: Info@ThomsonSafaris.com

**Vertical Adventures, Inc.**
P.O. Box 7548
Newport Beach, CA 92658
800-514-8785 or 949-854-6250
Fax: 949-854-5249
E-mail: BGvertical@aol.com

**Wild Travel**
PO Box 65175
Burlington, VT 05406
888-277-7622

**Yosemite Mountaineering School**
Yosemite National Park
Yosemite, CA 95389
209-372-8344

# Climbing Organizations and Governing Bodies

**The Access Fund**—National, non-profit organization dedicated to keeping climbing areas open and conserving the climbing environment. 303-545-6772. Send your donation to the Access Fund, 2475 Broadway, Boulder, CO, 80308. www.outdoorlink.com/accessfund.

**American Alpine Club**—National mountaineering association dedicated to multitude of issues facing climbing today. 303-384-0110.

**American Mountain Guides Association**—Accreditation of mountain guide services. 303-271-0984.

**American Sport Climber Federation**—National organization of competitive climbers and sanctioning body for competition. 888-ASCF-Rox.

**Climbing Gym Association**—Promotes responsible growth and professionalism in the climbing gym industry.

**Climbing Sports Group**—Trade association of climbing industry. Promotes climber education through its Climb Smart! National risk awareness program.

**Climbing Wall Industry Group**—Provides education, testing, research and the establishment of standards for the artificial climbing wall industry.

**Leave No Trace, Inc.**—Non-profit organization that produces a nationally recognized educational program that promotes responsible use of public lands to individuals participating in non-motorized recreational activities. 303-442-8222.

**Outdoor Recreation Coalition of America (ORCA)**—Trade association that promotes and preserves the human powered outdoor recreation industry. Umbrella organization of the following industry subgroups. 303-444-3353.

**Access Committee**
**Alpine Club of Canada**
35 Front Street E.
Toronto, Ontario M5E 1B3
Canada

**Access Fund**
PO Box 17010
Boulder, CO 80308-0100
303-545-6772
www.accessfund.org

**Alpine Club of Canada**
PO Box 1026
Banff, Alberta TOL OC0
Canada

**American Alpine Club**
710 Tenth Street, Suite 100
Golden, CO 80401
303-384-0110
Fax: 303-384-0111

**American Mountain Foundation**
1520 Alamo Avenue
Colorado Springs, CO 80907
719-471-7736
www.clim-on.com

**American Sport Climbers Federation**
125 West 96th Street, Suite 1D
New York, NY 10025

**British Mountaineering Council**
177/9 Burton Road
West Didsbury
Manchester, M20 2BB
England
161-445-4747

**Climb Smart!** is a public information
program of the Climbing Sport Group
(ORCA).
303-444-3353.

**Climbing Wall Industry Group (CWIG)**
PO Box 1319
Boulder, CO 80306
303-44-3353 or 888-854-ORCA (6277)
info@orca.org or www.orca.org

**Club Alpino Italiano**
Via Ugo Foscolo 3
20121 Milano
Italy

**Federation Espanola de Montanismo**
Alberto Aguilera 3-4
Madrid 15
Spain

**Federation Francaise de la Montagne**
20 bis Rue La Boeti
75008 Paris
France

**National Centre for Mountaineering
Activities**
Plas y Brenin
Capel Curig
Gwynedd LL24 OET
North Wales

**Norsk Tindeklub**
PO Bods 1727
Vikas
Oslo 1
Norway

**Outdoor Recreation Coalition of
America**
PO Box 1634 Walnut Street, #303
Boulder, CO 80302
303-444-3353

# Mail-Order Companies and Manufacturers

The following companies are organized into:

➤ General Equipment

➤ Backpacks

➤ Shoes

➤ Water Purifiers and Filters

➤ Foodstuffs

## General Equipment

### Black Dome Mountain Sports
140 Tunnel Road, Asheville, NC 28805
800-678-2367
www.wnc.com/blkdome

### Black Diamond Equipment., Ltd.
801-278-5533
(Distributes Hexcentrics, Stoppers, Camalots, and other climbing equipment)
www.BlackDiamondEquipment.com

### Campmoor
PO Box 700-CLA
Saddle River, NJ 07458-0700
800-230-2151

### Climb Axe, Ltd.
301 West Holly, #D-1
Bellingham, WA 98225
360-734-8433
Fax: 360-734-8418

### Climb High
60 Northside Drive
Shelburne, VT 05382
802-985-5056
(Distributes HB and other climbing equipment)

### Climbers Choice International
1021 California Avenue
Klamath Falls, OR 97601
800-704-3891

### Hi-Tec Sports USA
4801 Stoddard Road
Modesto, CA 95356
800-558-8580
www.hi-tec.com

### Lowe Alpine Systems
303-465-0522
www.lowealpine.com

**Moonstone Mountain Equipment**
833 Indiana Street
San Francisco, CA 94107
800-390-3312
www.moonstone.com

**Mountain Gear**
2002 North Division
Spokane, WA 99207
800-829-2009
www.eznet.com/mgear.html

**Mountain High Ltd.**
123 Diamond Peak Avenue
Ridgecrest, CA 93555
800-255-3182
www.repnt.com/redpnt/rockrat/

**Mountain Tools**
140 Calle del Oaks
Monterey, CA 93940-5711
408-393-1000

**Pearlizumi**
620 Compton Street
Broomfield, CO 80020
800-877-7080
www.pearlizumi.com

**PMI-Petzl**
PO Box 803
LaFayette, GA 30728
800-282-7673
www.petzl.com

**Pika Mountaineering**
1387 South Roberts Street
Salt Lake City, UT 84115
801-485-1686
www.pikamtn.com

**Ragged Mountain Equipment**
PO Box 130 Route 16 & 302
Interval, NH 03845
603-356-3042

**REI**
Dept. N5014
Sumner, WA 98352
800-436-4840

**Salomon Sports**
877-Salomon
www.salomonsports.com

**Shoreline Mountain Products**
11 Navajo Lane
Madera, CA 94925
800-381-2733

**Sunrise Mountaineering**
490 Yenacio Valley Road
Walnut Creek, CA
800-910-ROCK

**Trango, USA**
800-860-3653
www.trango.com

**Wild Country, Ltd.**
230 East Conway Road
Center Conway, NH 03813
603-356-5590
http://members.aol.com/wctryltd/
wcusa.html
(Distributes Friends, Rocks, and other
climbing equipment)

# Backpacks

Arc'Teryx: 800-985-6681.

Brenthaven: 800-803-7225.

Camp 7, Inc.: 714-545-2204.

CampTrails: 888-245-4985. www.jwa.com.

Caribou Mountaineering: 800-824-4103. www.caribou.com.

Cirque Works: 503-294-0427.

Dana Design: 406-587-4188. www.ecotravel.com/dana.

Deuter Backpacks: 303-384-9148.

Diamond Brand: 800-258-9811.

Eagle Creek: 800-874-9925. www.eaglecreek.com.

Eastern Mountain Sports: 888-463-6367. www.emsonline.com.

Ecotrek: 800-858-1383.

EDKO Alpine Designs: 303-440-0446.

Esign Mountaineering: 800-560-7529.

Eureka: 888-245-4984. www.jwa.com.

Gregory: 800-477-3420.

JanSport: 800-346-8239. wwwjansport.com.

K2 Outdoor/Wilderness Exp.: 406-587-3522.

Kelty: 800-423-2320. www.kelty.com.

LL Bean: 800-341-4341.

Lowe Alpine: 303-465-0522. www.lowealpine.com.

McHale & Company: 206-281-7861. www.aa.net/mchalepeaks.

Mountainsmith: 800-426-4075. www.mountainsmith.com.

Osprey Packs: 970-882-2221.

The North Face: 805-379-3372. www.clubhousegolf.com/northface.com.

Treknology: 800 873-5725. Email: basecamp@eskimo.com.

# Shoes

Eastern Mountain Sports: 888-463-6367. www.emsonline.com.

Five-Ten Co.: 909-798-4222. www.fiveten.com

Hi-Tec Sports USA, Inc.: 800-521-1698. www.hi-tech.com.

La Sportiva USA: 303-443-8710. www.sportiva.com.

Sorel: 800-667-6735. www.kaufman.com.

Boreal: www.boreal.com. www.boreal-club.com

# Water Purifiers and Filters

American Camper: 913-492-3200.

Basic Design: 800-328-3208.

General Ecology, Inc./First Need: 800-441-8166. www.general-ecology.com.

Katadyn: 800-950-0808. www.sportsite.com/katadyn.

MRS: 800-877-9677. www.msrcorp.com.

Outbound: 800-433-6506.

PentaPure: 612-473-1625. www.pentapure.com.

Pur: 800-787-1066.

Relags USA: 303-440-8047.

SweetWater: 800-55-SWEET. www.sweet-h20.com.

Timberline Filters: 800-777-5996.

# Foodstuffs

## *Energy Food*

Balance Bar: 800-678-4246. www.balancebar.com.

Cliff Bar: www.cliffbar.com.

Designer Protein—Next Proteins: PO Box 2469, Carlsbad, CA 92018.

Gu: 800-400-1995. www.gusports.com.

PowerBar: 800-444-5154. www.powerbar.com.

Quic Disc: www.quicdisc.com.

## *Freeze-Dried Food*

**Adventure Foods:** 704-497-4113.

**AlpineAir:** 800-322-6325. www.alpineairfoods.com.

**Backpacker's Pantry:** 800-641-0500.

**Chamy:** 800-322-7010.

**Harvest Footworks:** 800-268-4268. www.harvest.on.ca.

**Uncle John's Foods:** 719-836-2710.

# Index

## Symbols

**313**